W9-CRT-515

THE CHINESE:

A

GENERAL DESCRIPTION

OF

THE EMPIRE OF CHINA

AND

ITS INHABITANTS.

BY

JOHN FRANCIS DAVIS, ESQ., F.R S., &c.

IN TWO VOLUMES.

VOL. I.

SCHOLARLY RESOURCES, INC.
1508 Pennsylvania Avenue
Wilmington, Delaware 19806

Reprint edition published in 1972
First published in 1836 by Harper & Brothers, New York

Library of Congress Catalog Card Number: 72-79817
ISBN: Two volumes 0-8420-1352-0

Manufactured in the United States of America

CONTENTS

OF

THE FIRST VOLUME.

CHAPTER I.

EARLY EUROPEAN INTERCOURSE.

CHAPTER II.

ENGLISH INTERCOURSE.

CHAPTER III.

ENGLISH INTERCOURSE—(CONTINUED).

CHAPTER IV.

GEOGRAPHICAL SKETCH OF CHINA.

CHAPTER V.

SUMMARY OF CHINESE HISTORY.

CHAPTER VI.

GOVERNMENT AND LEGISLATION.

CHAPTER VII.

CHARACTER AND MANNERS.

CHAPTER VIII.

MANNERS AND CUSTOMS.

ILLUSTRATIONS.

INTRODUCTION.

The following work owes its origin to a collection of notes which the author made while resident in China; and these notes were compiled for a reason not altogether dissimilar to the motive which a French writer alleges for an undertaking of the same kind—"le désir de tout connaître, en étant obligé de le décrire." A residence of more than twenty years (which terminated in the author succeeding, for some months previous to his final retirement, the late amiable and unfortunate Lord Napier as His Majesty's chief authority in China) has perhaps been calculated to mature and correct those opinions of the country and people which he had formed, as a very young man, in accompanying Lord Amherst on the embassy to Peking in 1816. If some acquaintance, besides, with the language and literature of the Chinese empire has not been of considerable assistance to him in increasing the extent and accuracy of his information, it must be his own fault entirely, and not any want of opportunities and means.

It is singular that no general and systematic work on China has ever yet been produced in this country, notwithstanding that our immediate interest in the subject has been vastly greater than that of any other European nation. At the head of *travels*, both as to date and excellence, stand the authentic account of Lord Macartney's Mission, by Staunton, and Barrow's China, to both of which works it will be seen that reference has been more than once made in the following pages. The above authorities have not been superseded by any thing that has since appeared in the course of thirty or forty years, though the works of Mr. Ellis and Doctor Abel, the results of Lord Amherst's embassy, are of a highly respectable class, and contain much valuable information on those points to which they confine themselves. Still no general account of the Chinese empire has ever issued from the English press; and Père du Halde's compilation has still remained the only methodized source of information on the subject. One century exactly has now elapsed since that voluminous, and in many respects highly valuable, work was first printed. A great deal has of necessity become antiquated, and it is not easy for any one who is personally unacquainted with China to separate the really sound and useful information it contains from the prejudice which distorts some portions, and the nonsense which encumbers others. Of the last, the endless pages on the "Doctrine of the Pulse" may be taken as one specimen.

It may be interesting to the general reader to see before him, in one view, and in chronological order, most of the miscellaneous works concerning China which have at different times appeared in various languages. To his original list the writer has added from the Catalogue* of the Oriental Library, presented by his venerable friend, Mr. Marsden, to King's College, where a spacious room has been expressly devoted to its reception.

The earliest in point of date are the Travels of Marco Polo, the Venetian, of which a Latin translation was made about the year 1320, and the first edition appeared soon after the invention of the art of printing, in the fifteenth century.†

* Bibliotheca Marsdeniana, p. 172.

† The best modern version of this work is in English, copiously illustrated with notes, by Mr. Marsden, 4to., 1818.

1585. Historia del gran Reyno de la China. By J. G. de Mendoça. 8vo.
1601. Historia de las Missiones en los Reynos de la China, &c. By L. de Guzman. Folio.
1617. Histoire de l'Expédition Chrétienne à la Chine. By N. Trigault. 4to.
1621. Epitome Historial del Reyno de la China. By Maldonado. 8vo.
1634. History of the Court of the King of China. From the French of M. Baudier. 4to.
1643. Relatione della Grande Monarchia della Cina. By Alvarez. *Lemedo.* 4to.
1653. Voyages du Père Alexandre de Rhodes en Chine, &c. 4to.
1655. Brevis Relatio de numero Christianorum apud Sinas. By Martini.
1659. Martini Martinii Sinica Historia. *Amst.* 8vo.
1660. Theoph. Spizelii de re Literariâ Sinensium. 12mo.
1667. Sinarum Scientia Politico-Moralis. By P. Intorcetta. Folio.
—— China Illustrata. Athanasius Kircher. Folio.
1673. Embassy from the East India Company of the United Provinces to the Grand Tartar *Cham*, Emperor of China. By Nieuhoff. (Englished by J. Ogilby.) Folio.
1679. History of the Tartars; their wars with and overthrow of the Chineses. From the Spanish of Mendoza. 8vo.
—— Basilicon Sinense. By Andrew Müller. 4to.
1686. Tabula Chronologica Monarchiæ Sinicæ. By P. Couplet. Folio.
1688. Nouvelle Relation de la Chine. G. de Magaillans. 4to.
1697. Nouveaux Mémoires sur l'Etat présent de la Chine. By Louis le Compte. 12mo.
1698. Journal of Russian Embassy overland to Peking. By Adam Brand, Secretary of the Embassy. 8vo.

1699. Histoire de l'Empereur de la Chine (*Kâng-hy*). By Joachim Bouvet. 12mo.

1700. Varia Scripta de cultibus Sinarum, inter Missionarios et Patres Societatis Jesu controversis. 8vo.

—— Relation du Voyage fait à la Chine, sur le Vaisseau l'Amphetrite. 12mo.

1711. *Libri Classici Sex* (namely, the Four Books, *Heaou-king*, and *Seaou-heo*). By Père Noël. 4to.

1714. Relation de la Nouvelle Persécution de la Chine. F. G. de S. Pierre. 12mo.

1718. Anciennes Relations de deux Voyageurs Mahometans. Par Eusebe Renaudot. 8vo.

1728. Nouveau Voyage autour du Monde, avec une Description de l'Empire de la Chine. By Le Gentil. 12mo.

1730. Museum Sinicum, opera Th. S. Bayer. 8vo.

1735. Description Géographique, Historique, Chronologique, Politique, et Physique de l'Empire de la Chine, &c. Par J. B. du Halde. Folio, 4tom.

1737. Meditationes Sinicæ, opera St. Fourmont. Folio.

1750. Authentic Memoirs of the Christian Church in China, with the Causes of the Declension of Christianity in that Empire. From the German of J. L. Mosheim. 8vo.

1760. Mémoire dans laquelle on prouve que les Chinois sont une Colonie Egyptienne. De Guignes. 8vo.

1763. Travels of John Bell, of Antermony. 4to. 2 vols.

1765. Voyage to China and the East Indies. By Peter Osbeck. 8vo.

1770. Le *Chou-king*, un des Livres Sacrés des Chinois. Par le Père Gaubil. 8vo.

1773. Lettre de Pekin, sur le Génie de la Langue Chinoise. Par le Père Amiot. 4to.

1773. Recherches Philosophiques sur les Egyptiens et les Chinois. Par M. de Pauw. 12mo.
1776. Mémoire de M. D'Anville sur la Chine. 8vo.
1785. Histoire Générale de la Chine, traduite du *Tongkien-kang-mou.* Par le Père Mailla. 12 tom. 4to.
—— Description Générale de la Chine. Par l'Abbé Grosier. 4to.
1797. Authentic Account of an Embassy from the King of Great Britain to the Emperor of China. By Sir Geo. L. Staunton, Bart. 2 vols. 4to.
—— Mémoires concernant les Chinois. 16 tom. 4to.
1798. Embassy of the Dutch East India Company to China. From the Journal of A. E. Van Braam. 2 vols. 8vo.
1804. Travels in China. By John Barrow. 4to.
1808. Voyages à Peking, &c., Par M. de Guignes. 3 tom. 8vo.
1810. *Ta-tsing-leu-lee;* the Penal Code of China. By Sir George T. Staunton, Bart. 4to.
1813. Dictionnaire Chinois, Français, et Latin. Par de Guignes. Folio.
1814. Mémoires concernant les Chinois, redigés par Silvestre de Sacy. 4to.
1815. Dictionary of the Chinese Language, in Three Parts. By R. Morrison. 6 vols. 4to. (Completed in 1823.)
1816. Dialogues and detached Sentences in the Chinese Language. By R. Morrison. 8vo.
1817. A Chinese Drama. Translated from the Original by J. F. Davis. 12mo.
—— Journal of Embassy to China. By Henry Ellis. 4to.
—— View of China. By R. Morrison. 4to.
—— Chinese Gleaner, Malacca. 8vo. (Concluded in 1821.)
—— Sacred Edict. Translated by W. Milne. 8vo.

1818. Narrative of a Journey in the Interior of China. By Clarke Abel. 4to.
1821. Chinese Embassy to the Khan of the Tourgouths. By Sir G. T. Staunton, Bart. 8vo.
1822. Miscellaneous Notices relating to China. By Ditto. 8vo.
—— Elémens de la Grammaire Chinoise. Par Abel Rémusat. 8vo.
1823. Chinese Moral Maxims. Compiled by J. F. Davis. 8vo.
1824. *Meng-tseu*, vel Mencium. Edidit S. Julien. 8vo.
1826. Les Deux Cousines; Roman Chinois. Par Abel Rémusat. 12mo.
1827. Voyage à Peking, à travers la Mongolie. Par M. G. Timkouski. 8vo.
1828. The Four Books, translated by D. Collie. 8vo.
1829. The Fortunate Union; a Chinese Romance. Translated from the Original by J. F. Davis. 8vo.
1831. Notitia Linguæ Sinicæ, auctore P. Premare. 4to.
1832. Cercle de Craie, Drame Chinois. Traduit par Stanislas Julien. 8vo.
—— Chinese Repository (commenced), Canton. 8vo.
1834. Miscellaneous Papers concerning China, in Three Volumes of Royal Asiatic Transactions, 4to. (Commenced 1823.)
—— China, an Outline, &c. By Peter Auber. 8vo.

The following pages being intended wholly for the use of the general reader, so much only of each subject has been touched upon as seemed calculated to convey a summary, though at the same time accurate, species of information in an easy and popular way. More detailed knowledge on each separate point must be sought for, by the few who are likely to require it, in one or other of the numerous works above named, and the catalogue here given may prove serviceable for that purpose.

The superiority which the Chinese possess over the other nations of Asia is so decided as scarcely to need the institution of an elaborate comparison. Those who have had opportunities of seeing both have readily admitted it, and none more so than the Right Honourable Henry Ellis, our ambassador to Persia, whose intimate personal acquaintance with China and India, as well as with Persia, renders him peculiarly calculated to form a just estimate. The moral causes of a difference so striking may perhaps occur to the reader of the subjoined work: the physical causes consist, it may reasonably be supposed, in the advantages which China possesses from its geographical situation; in the generally favourable climate, the average fertility of soil, and the great facility of internal intercourse which the country possesses from nature, and which has been still farther improved by art. The *early advancement* of China, in the general history of the globe, may likewise be accounted for, in some measure, by natural and physical causes, and by the position of the whole of that vast country (with a very trivial exception) within the *temperate* zone. On this point the author will repeat some observations which he long since made in another place; that "an attentive survey of the tropical regions of the earth, where food is produced in the greatest abundance, will seem to justify the conclusion that *extreme* fertility, or power of production, has been rather unfavourable to the progress of the human race; or, at least, that the industry and advancement of nations have appeared in some measure to depend on a certain *proportion* between their necessities and their natural resources. Man is by nature an indolent animal, and without the stimulant of necessity will, in the first instance, get on as well as he can with the provision that nature has made for him. In the warm and fertile regions of the tropics, or rather of the equinoctial, where lodging and clothing, the two necessary things after food, are rendered almost superfluous by the climate, and where food itself is produced with very little exertion,* we find how small a progress has in most instances been made; while, on the other hand, the whole of Europe, and by far the greater part of China, are situated beyond the northern tropic. If, again, we go *farther* north, to those arctic regions where man exists in a very miserable state, we shall find that *there* he has no materials to work upon. Nature is such a niggard in the returns which she makes to labour, that industry is discouraged and *frozen*, as it were, in the outset. In other words, the *proportion* is destroyed; the equinoctial regions are too spontaneously genial and fertile; the arctic too unkindly barren; and on this account it would seem that industry, wealth, and civilization have been principally confined to the temperate zone, where there are at once *necessity* to excite labour, and *production* to recompense it." There are, no doubt, other important circumstances, besides geographical situation, which influence the advancement of nations; but this at least is too considerable an ingredient to be left out of the calculation.

J. F. D.

* See the observations of Humboldt on the use of the banana in New Spain.

THE CHINESE.

CHAPTER I.

EARLY EUROPEAN INTERCOURSE.

China little known to the Ancients.—Embassy from Marcus Antoninus.—Nestorian Christians.—Arabian Travellers.—Ibn Batuta.—Jews in China.—First Catholic Missions to Tartary.—Travels of Marco Polo.—Portugese reach China.—Previous to arrival of Europeans, Chinese less disinclined to foreign intercourse.—Settlement of Macao.—Fruitless Embassies to Peking.—Catholic Missions.—Quarrels of the Jesuits with the other Orders.—Persecutions.—Spaniards.—Dutch settle on Formosa.—Expelled by Chinese.—Russian Embassies.

It is intended in the following pages to give such an account of the manners and customs, the social, political, and religious institutions, together with the natural productions, the arts, manufactures, and commerce of China, as may be deemed interesting to the general reader. The most fitting introduction to this sketch will be, a cursory view of the early acquaintance of the western world with the country of which we are about to treat, followed up by some notices of the more modern intercourse of Europeans, and particularly the English, with the Chinese.

Antiquity affords us but a few uncertain hints regarding an empire so far removed to the utmost limits of Eastern Asia as to have formed no part in the aspirations of Macedonian or of Roman dominion. Were a modern conqueror to stop on the banks of the Ganges, and sigh that he had no more nations to subdue, what has been admired in the pupil of Aristotle himself would be a mere absurdity in the most ignorant chieftain of these more enlightened times. We may reasonably hope that the science and civilization which have already so greatly enlarged the bounds of our knowledge of foreign countries, may, by diminishing the vulgar admiration for such pests and scourges of the human race as military conquerors have usually proved, advance and facilitate the peaceful intercourse of the most remote countries with each other, and thereby increase the general stock of knowledge and happiness among mankind.

It seems sufficiently clear that the *Seres*, mentioned by Horace and other Latin writers, were not the Chinese.* This name has, with greater probability, been interpreted as referring to another people of Asia, inhabiting a country to the westward of China; and the texture, termed by the Romans *serica*, in all likelihood meant a cotton rather than a silken manufacture, which latter was distinguished by the name *bombycina*. There appears sufficient evidence, however, of the fact, that some of the ancients were not altogether ignorant of the existence of such a people. Arrian speaks of the Sinæ, or Thinæ, in the remotest parts of Asia, by whom were exported the raw and manufactured silks which were brought by the way of Bactria (Bokhara) westward. It was under the race of Han, perhaps the most celebrated era of Chinese history, that an envoy is stated to have been sent in A. D. 94, by the seventeenth emperor of that dynasty, to seek some intercourse with the western world. This minister is said to have reached Arabia; and as it is certain that *Hoty*,

* It is noticed by Florus, that ambassadors came from the Seres to Augustus; but Horace notices the Seres in a way which makes it unlikely that they were the Chinese. "Nec *sollicitus times* quid *Seres*, et regnata Cyro Bactra parent."

the prince by whom he was deputed, was the first sovereign of China who introduced the use of eunuchs into the palace, it may be deemed probable that he borrowed them from thence. The contests of the Chinese with the Tartars, even at that early period, are stated to have been the occasion of a Chinese general reaching the borders of the Caspian, at the time when Trajan was Emperor of Rome. The growing consumption, among the luxurious Latins, of the valuable and beautiful silk stuffs with which they were supplied through the medium of India, seems to have tempted the Emperor Marcus Antoninus to despatch an embassy to the country which was reported to produce those manufactures. The numerous obstacles presented by a land journey induced him to send his mission by sea, A. D. 161. Like most attempts of the kind, this appears to have been an entire failure, and the ambassadors returned from China without having paved the way to a more frequent or intimate intercourse with that secluded country.

The Jesuits have informed us, that some of the Catholic missionaries discovered, in the year 1625, at one of the principal cities of the province Shensy, an inscription in Syriac letters, recording the first introduction of Christianity into China in the year 635, by certain Nestorian bishops, who had been driven eastward by persecutions in the Roman provinces. We are not indebted, however, to these refugees for any early account of the country. Their existence in the same province of Shensy, at the period when Marco Polo visited China, is clearly stated by that traveller, as may be seen in Marsden's edition, page 404. To those who travelled by land from Syria, and other countries bordering on the Mediterranean, it was the easiest of access, as being the most westerly point of the empire, towards Peking; and they were probably induced to settle there, from finding it one of the most populous and civilized portions of China at that early period.

Marco Polo besides states, that in a city in the neighbourhood of Nanking, on the banks of the Yang-tse-Keang, there were "two churches of Nestorian Christians, which were built in 1274, when his Majesty the Emperor appointed a Nestorian, named Mar Sachis, to the government of it (the city) for three years. By him those churches were established where there had not been any before, and they still subsist."* The editor justly observes, that the existence of these churches, of which no reasonable doubt can be entertained, is a curious fact in the history of the progress made by the Christian religion in the eastern or remoter parts of China. "It is remarkable," he adds, "that De Guignes, in describing a religious building not far from this city, mentions a tradition that gives strength to the belief of an early Christian establishment in that quarter: 'Les Chinois racontent qu'un Chrétien, nommé Kiang-tsy-tay, vivoit dans ce lieu il y a trois cents ans; on montre encore son appartement dans la partie de l'est.'"

It is to the Arabs that we owe the first distinct account of China, and of its peculiar institutions and customs. Their far-extended conquests brought them to the confines of that remote empire; and the enlightenment of science and literature, which they possessed in no small degree during the eighth and ninth centuries, led many individuals among them to explore unknown countries, and to record what they had seen. We possess an interesting specimen in Renaudot's translation from the itineraries of two Arabian travellers, in the years 850 and 877. These bear internal evidences of truth and accuracy no less indisputable than those which distinguish the relations of the Venetian traveller,

* Marsden's Marco Polo, p. 501.

Marco Polo; and as they have reference to a much earlier period than even his, must be considered to possess a very high degree of interest. We can perceive a remarkable identity between the Chinese, as they are therein described, and the same people as we know them at the present day, although a period of 1000 years, nearly, has since elapsed; nor can the occurrence of one or two very remarkable discrepances be considered as any impugnment of the general veracity of these travellers, where there is, upon the whole, so much of sound and correct information. They have, in fact, evidently proceeded from some confusion in the original manuscripts, by which observations that had reference to other countries lying in their route, and which are true of those countries at the present time, have become incorporated with the account of China itself. These Arabians describe a city called Canfu, which was probably Canton, at which place a very ancient mosque exists to this day. The frequency of fires, and the long detention of ships, from various causes, as stated by them, might be related of that emporium of foreign trade even at present. "This city," they observe, "stands on a great river, some days distant from the entrance, so that the water here is fresh." It seems at that time to have been the port allotted to the Arabian merchants who came by sea; and the travellers notice "many unjust dealings with the merchants who traded thither, which having gathered the force of a precedent, there was no grievance, no treatment so bad, but they exercised it upon the foreigners and the masters of ships." We learn that the port was at length forsaken, in consequence of the extortions of the *mandarins* of those days; and "the merchants returned in crowds to Siraf and Oman." It is remarkable that the travellers describe the entrance to the port of Canfu as the "gates of China," which may possibly be a translation of Hoo-mun,

"Tiger's gate," or *Boca Tigris*, as it is called from the Portuguese.

These Arabians mention in particular the relief afforded to the people from the public granaries during famine. The salt-tax, as it now exists, and the use of tea, are thus noticed:—"The emperor also reserves to himself the revenues that arise from salt, and from a certain herb, which they drink with hot water, and of which great quantities are sold in all the cities, to the amount of vast sums." The public imposts are stated to have consisted of duties on salt and tea, with a poll-tax, which last has since been commuted into a tax on lands: these Arabians likewise mention the *bamboo* as the universal panacea in matters of police; and they very correctly describe the Chinese copper money, as well as porcelain, wine made from rice, the maintenance of public teachers in the towns, the idolatry derived from India, and the ignorance of astronomy, in which the Arabians were their first instructers. It is, in fact, impossible to comprise within our limits all the pertinent remarks, or even a small proportion of the correct information, which may be found in this curious and antique relic of early Arabian enterprise. From the lights which it affords, as well as from other sources of information relating to the first intercourse of the Mahometans with China, it has with tolerable certainty been inferred, that, previous to the Mongol Tartar conquest, they resorted to that rich country by sea chiefly, and in the character of traders.

Subsequent to the establishment of the Mongol Tartar dynasty by Zenghis Khan, China was visited by the Arab, Ibn Batuta, whose travels have been translated by Professor Lee. He describes very truly the paper circulation instituted by the Mongols, a scheme which subsequently failed, in consequence of the paper being rendered utterly worthless by excessive issues, and the bad faith of the government, which derived a profit from the circulation. Even at that period, Batuta observes that "they did not buy or sell with the dirhem or dinar, for, should any one get these coins into his possession, he would melt them down immediately." If we may believe him, the Chinese junks in his time sailed as far as Calicut, and he himself embarked in one of them on his voyage to China.

The Mahometan creed seems to have been established and protected as the religion of a considerable part of the population soon after the Mongol conquest in the 13th century; and it meets with perfect toleration at the present day, its professors being freely admitted to government offices, from which Christians are rigidly excluded. There is a considerable mosque at Canton, of great antiquity, and forming, with its pagoda or minaret, a conspicuous object on the approach to the city by the river. Numbers of that persuasion occurred in every part of the route of the two British missions. Some gentlemen of the embassy were walking in 1816 with Dr. Morrison, at a village about fifty miles from Peking, when they observed, inscribed in Chinese on the lantern of a poor shopman, "an old Mahometan." Being asked whence his progenitors came, the old man answered, "from the western ocean;" but he could give no farther information, except that his family had resided there for five generations. Dr. Morrison met with another near Nanking, holding a government office, who said that his sect reached China during the Tang dynasty, or about the period of the visit of those two Arabians whom we have already noticed, in the ninth century. The same individual stated, that at Kae-foong-foo, in the province of Honan, there were some families of a persuasion denominated by the Chinese, "the sect that plucks out the sinew;" these, in all probability, must be the Jews mentioned by Grosier, who are said to have reached China as early as 200 years before Christ, in the time of the Han dynasty.

In the eighteenth volume of the *Lettres édifiantes et curieuses*, there is contained an account of the pains taken by the Jesuits in China to investigate the origin of this remarkable colony of Jews at Kae-foong-foo. The most successful in his researches was Père Gozani, who, in a letter dated 1704, thus wrote :—"As regards those who are here called *Tiao-kin-kiao* (the sect that extracts the sinew), two years ago I was going to visit them, under the expectation that they were Jews, and with the hope of finding among them the Old Testament; but as I have no knowledge of the Hebrew language, and met with great difficulties, I abandoned this scheme with the fear of not succeeding. Nevertheless, as you told me that I should oblige you by obtaining any information concerning this people, I have obeyed your directions, and executed them with all the care and exactness of which I was capable. I immediately made them protestations of friendship, to which they readily replied, and had the civility to come to see me. I returned their visit in the *le-pai-sou*, that is, in their synagogue, where they were all assembled, and where I held with them long conversations. I saw their inscriptions, some of which are in Chinese, and the rest in their own language. They showed me their religious books, and permitted me to enter even into the most secret place of their synagogue, whence they themselves (the commonalty) are excluded. There is a place reserved for the chief of the synagogue, who never enters there except with profound respect. They told me that their ancestors came from a kingdom of the west, called the kingdom of Juda, which Joshua conquered after having departed from Egypt, and passed the Red Sea and the Desert; that the number of Jews who migrated from Egypt was about 600,000 men. They assured me that their alphabet had twenty-seven letters, but that they commonly made use of only twenty-two; which accords with the declaration of St. Jerome, that the Hebrew has twenty-two letters, of which five are double. When they read the Bible in their synagogue, they cover the face with a transparent veil, in memory of Moses, who descended from the mountain with his face covered, and who thus published the Decalogue and the Law of God to his people: they read a section every Sabbath-day. Thus the Jews of China, like the Jews of Europe, read all the Law in the course of the year: he who reads places the *Ta-king* (great sacred book) on the chair of Moses; he has his face covered with a very thin cotton veil; at his side is a prompter, and some paces below a moula, to correct the prompter should he err. They spoke to me respecting Paradise and Hell in a very foolish way. There is every appearance of what they said being drawn from the Talmud. I spoke to them of the Messiah promised in Scripture, but they were very much surprised at what I said; and when I informed them that his name was Jesus, they replied, that mention was made in the Bible of a holy man named Jesus, who was the son of Sirach: but they knew not the Jesus of whom I spoke."*

The first pope who appears to have sent a mission for the conversion of the Tartars or Chinese to the Roman Catholic faith, was Innocent IV. He despatched Giovanni Carpini, a monk, through Russia, in the year 1246, to Baatu Khan, on the banks of the Volga, from whence they were conducted to the Mongol Tartar court, just as the Great Khan was about to be installed. Carpini was astonished by the display of immense treasures, and, having been kindly treated, was sent back with

* For farther particulars of the Jews in China, see Chinese Repository, vol. iii., p. 172.

a friendly letter; he was rather pleased than scandalized by the near resemblance of the rites of the Chinese Buddhists to the forms of Catholic worship, and inferred from thence that they either already were, or would very soon be, Christians. In 1253 Rubruquis was in like manner despatched by St. Louis, during his crusade to the Holy Land, with directions to procure the friendship of the Mongols. He reached at length the court of the Great Khan, where, like his predecessor, he observed the near resemblance of Lama worship to the forms of Roman Catholicism, and concluded that it must be derived from a spurious Christianity; perhaps that of the Nestorians.

It is needless in this place to enter into any detailed notice of the work of Marco Polo, which has been illustrated with so much erudition and industry by our countryman Marsden. The doubts which were once entertained of the veracity of Marco have long since given way to admiration of his simple and faithful narrative. Most of our readers will perhaps be aware, that in the reign of Coblai Khan, the Mongol conqueror of China, Nicholas and Matthew Paolo or Polo, two noble Venetians, reached his court: they were extremely well received, and invited to return to China on their departure for Europe. In 1274 they accordingly came back, bearing letters from Pope Gregory X., and accompanied by young Marco, son to one of them. The youth, by his talents and good conduct, became a favourite with the khan, and was employed by him for seventeen years, after which he with some difficulty obtained permission to return to his own country. The accounts which he gave at Venice of the vast wealth and resources of the Chinese empire, appeared so incredible to Europeans in those days, that his tale was most undeservedly discredited; and he obtained the nickname of "Messer Marco Millione." Another account of Cathay or China was some time after written by Hayton, an Armenian, and translated into Latin. According to him, the Chinese considered the rest of the world as blind, or seeing with only one eye; while themselves alone were blessed with a perfect vision.

John De Corvino, despatched to Asia in 1288 by Pope Nicholas IV., was the first successful promoter of the Roman Catholic faith in China: he arrived at Cambalu (as Peking was called by the Tartars), and met with a kind reception from the emperor, notwithstanding the hostility of the jealous Nestorians. He was allowed to build a church, furnished with a steeple and bells, and is said to have baptized some thousands of converts, as well as to have instructed numbers of children in the Latin language, and the tenets of Christianity. The news of his progress reached Clement V. on his accession to the popedom, and he was immediately appointed Bishop of Cambalu, with a numerous body of priests, who were despatched to join him in his labours. On the death of Corvino, however, it is probable that no successor, possessed of the same enterprise and industry, was ready to succeed him; for the establishment which he had founded appears to have ceased, or at least sunk into insignificance.

Abundant evidence is afforded by Chinese records, that a much more liberal as well as enterprising disposition once existed in respect to foreign intercourse than prevails at present. It was only on the conquest of the empire by the Manchows that the European trade was limited to Canton; and the jealous and watchful Tartar dominion, established by this handful of barbarians, has unquestionably occasioned many additional obstacles to an increased commerce with the rest of the world. We have already noticed the Chinese junks, which were seen by Ibn Batuta as far west as the coast of Malabar, about the end of the thirteenth century. Even before the seventh century, it appears from native records that missions were sent from China to the surrounding nations, with a view to inviting mutual intercourse. The benefits of industry and trade have always been extolled by the people of that country; the contempt, therefore, with which the present Tartar government affects to treat the European commerce, must be referred entirely to the fears which it entertains regarding the influence of increased knowledge on the stability of its dominion.

According to the Chinese books, commerce, on its first establishment at Canton, remained free from duties for many years, but its increasing importance soon led the officers of government to convert it into a source of gain. As in Siam and Cochin-china at present, the pre-emption of all imported goods seems at one time to have been claimed; but this did not last long, and the trade, after having continued to increase at Canton, was subsequently carried to other ports of the empire. The endeavour to prevent the exportation of silver appears to have been an error very early established; but the regulations on this subject, as might be expected, have always been as futile as they are at the present day.

It was not many years after the passage of the Cape by De Gama, that the Portuguese in 1516 made their first appearance at Canton. Their early conduct was not calculated to impress the Chinese with any favourable idea of Europeans; and when, in course of time, they came to be competitors with the Dutch and the English, the contests of mercantile avarice tended to place them all in a still worse point of view. To this day the character of Europeans is represented as that of a race of men intent alone on the gains of commercial traffic, and regardless altogether of the means of attainment. Struck by the perpetual hostilities which existed among these foreign adventurers, assimilated in other respects by a close resemblance in their costumes and manners, the government of the country became disposed to treat them with a degree of jealousy and exclusion which it had not deemed necessary to be exercised towards the more peaceable and well-ordered Arabs, their predecessors.

The first places of resort to the Portuguese were the islands at the mouth of the Canton river.* The vessel despatched by Alfonzo Albuquerque, the Captain-general of Malacca, reached one of these, under the command of Perestrello, and, as his voyage proved very successful, it had the effect of engaging others in similar enterprises. Being distinguished as the first person who ever conducted a ship to China under a European flag, he was followed in the ensuing year by a fleet of eight vessels, under the command of Perez de Andrade, who, on reaching the coast, was surrounded by junks of war, and his movements watched with suspicion. He was, however, permitted to proceed with two of his vessels to Canton; and, while successfully negotiating for a trade, received accounts that the remainder of his fleet had been attacked by pirates. Some of his vessels returned with cargoes to Malacca; the remainder sailed in company with some junks, belonging to the Loo-choo islands, for the province of Fokien on the east coast, and succeeded in establishing a colony at Ningpo. The Portuguese subsequently brought their families to that port, carrying on a gainful trade with other parts of China, as well as with Japan. But in the year 1545 the provincial government, provoked by their ill conduct, expelled them the place; and thus was for ever lost to them an establishment on the continent of China, in one of the provinces of the empire best adapted to the ends of European trade. The general behaviour of the Portuguese had, from the first, been

* We here quote, for convenience, from a small work printed at Macao in 1831, but never regularly published, called "The Canton Miscellany."

calculated to obliterate the favourable impression which the Chinese had received from the justice and moderation of Perez de Andrade. Only shortly after his visit, a squadron, under the orders of his brother Simon, was engaged in open hostilities, having established a colony at *San Shan*, near Macao (vulgarly called St. John's), and erected a fort there: they were finally defeated by a Chinese naval force, but continued to commit acts of piracy on the native trading-vessels. Subsequently to this career of violence, and during the more recent periods of their connexion with China at Macao, the Portuguese appear, on the other hand, to have entertained too extreme an apprehension of giving umbrage to the native government; and while they imagined they were securing favour to themselves, their conduct has often served to encourage Chinese encroachment.

Among the early and desperate adventurers from Portugal, the exploits of Ferdinand Mendes Pinto have, by the help of some exaggeration, handed his name down as one of the principal. Having arrived with a crew of other desperadoes at Ningpo, he learned from some Chinese that to the northeast there was an island containing the tombs of seventeen Chinese kings, full of treasure. Pinto and his companions succeeded in finding the place, and plundered the tombs, in which they found a quantity of silver: being attacked, they were obliged to retire with only part of the booty; and a gale having overtaken them upon their return, in the neighbourhood of Nanking, only fourteen Portuguese escaped with their lives: these were taken by the Chinese, and after some maltreatment were sent to Nanking, and condemned to be whipped, and to lose each man a thumb. They were next conducted to Peking, and on his way thither Pinto had occasion to admire the manners of the Chinese, their love of justice, and the good order and industry that prevailed among them.

Arrived at Peking, they were at length condemned to one year's hard labour; but, before the time expired, they were set at liberty by the Tartars, who were then invading the country. Pinto and his companions now joined their liberators, and, while in their service, saw one of the chief lamas, whom he called their pope. A curious description of this Tartar hierarchy has in later times been given by Père Gaubil. The Portuguese adventurers at length quitted the Tartars, found their way to the coast, and embarked again for Ningpo. Being treacherously abandoned on a desolate island, where they had almost died of hunger, Pinto and his companions were taken off by a pirate, and soon afterward driven by adverse winds on the coast of Japan. On his return to Ningpo, this adventurer gave his countrymen so favourable an account of what he had seen, that a large expedition was fitted out for Japan: several, however, of the vessels were lost, and Pinto himself driven on the Loo-choo islands, where he and his companions were taxed with the murder of some natives of Loo-choo, at the time when Malacca was taken by the Portuguese. The king being told that all his countrymen were pirates, gave orders that Pinto and the rest should be quartered, and their limbs exposed: they were saved, however, by the interposition of some native women, and Pinto at length returned to Malacca. He afterward engaged in a mission to Japan. It was about the same time, in 1552, that the famous apostle of the East, St. Francis Xavier, concerning whom so many miracles have been related, died at San-shan, or St. John's. The remains of his tomb are seen there at this day; and the Bishop of Macao used to make an annual visit there, for the purpose of celebrating mass, and bringing away a portion of the consecrated earth.

The first Portuguese embassy, and of course the first from any European power by sea, to Peking, took place as early as 1520, in the person of Thomas Pirez, the object being to establish a factory at Canton as well as at Macao. Advices, however, had preceded him of the ill conduct and violence of Simon de Andrade; and, after a course of humiliation, the unfortunate Pirez was sent back under custody to Canton, the provincial government of which place thus early showed its jealousy of any attempt on the part of strangers to communicate with the court. Pirez, on his arrival, was robbed of his property, thrown into prison, and ultimately, it is supposed, put to death. The various embassies which have since followed in three successive centuries to Peking, have met with different kinds of treatment; but, in whatever spirit conducted, they have been equally unsuccessful in the attainment of any important points of negotiation.

In the following year Alfonso de Melo arrived in China, ignorant of the events which had taken place, and having altogether six vessels under his command. "These," a Portuguese writer observes, "sent on shore for water, but returned with blood." They became immediately involved in conflicts with the Chinese, who put to death upwards of twenty prisoners that fell into their hands; and the squadron shortly afterward sailed away from China.

We have seen already that, previous to the arrival of Europeans on its shores, the government of the country had given every encouragement to foreign commerce, and that, at a very early period, Chinese junks had proceeded to the coasts of the peninsula of India. Statistical records exist to the present day, having reference to foreign intercourse, which display a perfect knowledge of the advantages of trade, and form a striking contrast to the indifference which the present Tartar government affects to feel towards it. Subsequent to a temporary prohibition of foreign trade, a certain Fooyuen of Canton thus addressed the emperor:—"A great part of the necessary expenses of both the government and the people of Canton is supplied by the customs levied on merchants; and if foreign ships do not come, both public and private concerns are thrown into much embarrassment and distress. It is entreated, therefore, that the Franks be permitted to trade. Three or four advantages result therefrom. In the first place, besides the regular tribute of the several foreign states, a small per centage has been taken from the remainder, adequate to the supply of the provincial expenditure. Secondly, the treasury appropriated for the annual supply of the army in Canton and Quong-sy is entirely drained, and our dependance is on trade to provide against exigencies. Thirdly, the contiguous province has looked to Canton for supplies, being unable to comply with any demands made on it; but when foreign ships have free intercourse, then high and low are all mutually supplied. Fourthly, the people live by commerce. A man holding a quantity of goods sells them, and procures what himself requires: thus things pass from hand to hand, and in their course supply men with food and raiment. The government is thereby assisted, the people enriched, and both have means afforded them on which they may depend." Admissions of a similar nature, of a very late date, contained in addresses from the provincial government to Peking, have proved that the Chinese authorities are by no means unmindful of the revenues derived from the European trade.

It was about the middle of the sixteenth century that the Portuguese established themselves at Macao, the only European colony that, with very limited success, has been planted on the coast of China; it seems that they had temporary shelter on shore as early as 1537. By bribery and solicitation, leave was obtained for erecting sheds to dry goods, which were introduced under the name of tribute. The foreigners were by degrees permitted to build substantial houses, and the petty mandarins connived at an increasing population, the establishment of an internal government, and the influx of priests, with their endeavours to convert the Chinese.* The story of important services rendered against pirates, and an imperial edict, transferring the dominion of Macao to the Portuguese, seems unfounded. Indeed, a bishop of Macao wrote, in 1777, that it was "by paying a ground-rent that the Portuguese acquired the temporary use and profit of Macao *ad nutum* of the emperor." This ground-rent, amounting to 500 taëls per annum, is regularly paid to the present day; and Chinese mandarins periodically inspect the Portuguese forts, as well as levy duties on the Macao shipping. Nothing, therefore, can be farther from the truth, than that the Portuguese possess the sovereignty of that place. In 1573 the Chinese erected a barrier-wall across the isthmus, which separates Macao from the Island of Heang-shan. A civil mandarin was very early appointed to reside within the town, and govern it in the name of the Emperor of China: this officer, called a Tso-tâng, keeps a watchful eye on the inhabitants, and communicates information to his superiors. The Portuguese are not allowed to build new churches or houses without a license. The only privilege they possess is that of governing themselves; while the Chinese population of the town is entirely under the control of the mandarins. The Spaniards, indiscriminately with the Portuguese, have the right of trading to Macao; but the number of shipping was, in 1725, by an order from the emperor, restricted to twenty-five, and it is actually not much more than half that number. The last emperor of the *last Chinese* dynasty sent to Macao for some

* A small compilation of ancient records concerning Macao was printed by a Swedish gentleman, long resident there, in 1832, and from him we derive our notes.

guns, and a small military force, against the Manchow Tartars; but in 1651 the inhabitants of that colony were enrolled as the subjects of the present Ta-tsing family. In 1809, when the ladrones, or native pirates, had become formidable to the Chinese government, Macao furnished by agreement six vessels to serve against them, at a charge of 80,000 taëls to the provincial government. The pirates were induced by other means than those of force to dissolve their confederation, and the Portuguese, although they claimed certain privileges for their services, were obliged to remain content with their former condition.

The advantages which Macao possesses over Canton, in respect to the Chinese duties, which are considerably less at the former place than at the latter, might perhaps be made available, to a certain extent, by British traders. The capital and enterprise of the Portuguese inhabitants are not sufficient to employ the few ships which they actually possess. Several of the vessels are freighted in part by the Chinese for the Malay peninsula and islands. Although the freight is much higher than in junks, the property on board is considered so much safer—and the Chinese do not practise ensurance. They frequently send adventures, too, on board English country ships, or those pertaining to the Indian trade, for there is a duty amounting to 10 per cent. additional charged on Portuguese ships at our Eastern presidencies. The trade of Macao is altogether in a very depressed state, and the whole income from customs, which amounted in 1830 to scarcely 70,000 taëls, is insufficient to meet the expenditure. The entire Portuguese population, including slaves, is not above 5000; while the Chinese of Macao are calculated to exceed 30,000.

It seems needless to notice the several fruitless embassies which the Portuguese, since their earlier resort to China, have sent to Peking, the last of which occurred in 1753: they exhibit the usual spectacle of arrogance on the one side, and profitless submission on the other. It will be more interesting to take a short view of the Catholic missions, which at first promised to make rapid and extensive progress, but were ultimately defeated by the dissensions among the several orders of priests, and the indiscreet zeal which some of them displayed against the ancient institutions of the Chinese. In 1579 Miguel Ruggiero, an Italian Jesuit, reached Canton, and in a few years was joined by Matthew Ricci, who may justly be considered as the founder of the Catholic mission. The literati of the country praised such of the precepts of Christianity as coincided with those of Confucius; but they found a stumbling-block in the doctrines of original sin, of eternal torments, of the incarnation, of the Trinity, and of not being allowed concubines as well as a wife. No difficulties, however, could dishearten Ricci, who, by his intimate knowledge of the mathematical and experimental sciences, had the means of making friends and converts. He soon abandoned the garb of a bonze, which he at first injudiciously assumed, and put on that of the literati. With great good sense he saw the folly of attempting at once to contend with those prejudices of the Chinese which were blended with such of their institutions as they considered most sacred, and which in fact formed the very foundations of their social system. Montesquieu has justly argued, from the peculiar character of the Chinese customs, against the facility of introducing material changes in them; and especially of substituting the Roman Catholic observances. The assembling of women in churches, their private communication with priests, the prohibition of offerings at the tombs of parents, were all abominations in their eyes which could never be endured. Ricci, for such reasons, made a distinction between *civil* and *sacred* rites, admitting the former in his converts, and particularly the ceremonies at tombs; and his success accordingly was considerable.

When he had passed about seventeen years in the country, Ricci proceeded to Peking, and by favour of one of the eunuchs of the palace became introduced to the emperor's notice, his presents being received, and a place appointed for his residence. Other Jesuits joined the mission, and established themselves at different points from Canton to Peking, proceeding quietly, and with great success, as long as they could remain unmolested by the hot and indiscreet zeal of the several orders of monks, who, in their haste to attack the Chinese prejudices, ensured their own discomfiture. The most distinguished of the Jesuits, for his talents and knowledge, was Father Adam Schaal, by birth a German: he reached Peking at the time when the last Chinese dynasty of Ming was about to be expelled by the Manchow Tartars. Through the influence of a Chinese Christian named *Paul Siu*, who was a co-lao, or principal minister, and by his own extensive knowledge of the physical sciences, Schaal became a great favourite at court, and even retained his place after the Tartars had possessed themselves of the empire. The first Manchow emperor, Shun-chy, to whom he easily proved the ignorance of the Arabian mathematicians, made him President of the Astronomical Board; and his own merits are a sufficient explanation of his success, without any need of the lying *miracle* with which Père Du Halde has not blushed to disfigure his work. According to him, Adam Schaal being condemned to death soon after the Tartar conquest, "this sentence was carried to the princes of the blood and to the regent for confirmation; but, as often as they attempted to read it, a dreadful earthquake dispersed the assembly. The consternation was so great, that they granted a general pardon; all the prisoners were released except Father Adam, and he did not get his liberty until a month afterward, when the royal palace was consumed by the flames."

Permission was given to the Jesuits to build two churches at Peking, and new labourers were allowed to enter the country: among these, Ferdinand Verbiest, another German Jesuit, and a man of distinguished science, became the coadjutor of Adam Schaal. On the accession of Kanghy, then a boy of eight or nine years of age, under the tutorship of four Tartars, the disputes which ensued with the intolerant Dominicans produced an unfavourable impression on the minds of the rulers of China. Accusations were preferred against the missionaries, and their zeal to make converts was condemned as dangerous. It is said that Schaal died of chagrin, and that Verbiest was compelled for some time to abscond. When Kanghy, however, a monarch of enlarged and liberal mind, came to exercise the government in his own person, Verbiest was made President of the Astronomers, and through his influence the expelled missionaries were allowed to return to their churches. By the aid of Verbiest, the emperor was enabled to cast guns, and to compose a mathematical work, with tables of logarithms. During this reign, although the emperor was never himself a convert, the state of Christianity in China was vastly more flourishing than it is at present, after the lapse of a century and a half: it was placed by Kanghy on the same footing of toleration with Mahometanism and Buddhism. In the itineraries of Le Compte and other Jesuits, churches with European priests are mentioned at almost every principal city. At Foshan, about four leagues above Canton, Père Bouvet speaks of a Milanese Jesuit as presiding over a church, with a flock of 10,000 persons: at this day there is probably not one single individual at that same place.

The decree of Kanghy in 1692, permitting the exercise of Christianity, was abrogated by his successor Yoong-ching, who expelled the missionaries from the provinces. These spiritual delegates, meanwhile, had been in constant collision with the native authorities throughout the empire, and perpetually at strife among themselves; and the jurisdiction of the field which they occupied became also a subject of discussion between the kings of Portugal and the popes. In consequence of the disputes which had arisen, from a very early period, among the Jesuits and the other orders concerning Chinese rites and ceremonies, Matthew Ricci had drawn up for the mission a number of rules, in which he considered the objectionable customs as merely civil and secular. Morales, however, a Spanish Dominican, declared them to be idolatrous, and as such they were condemned by Innocent X. Martinez, a Jesuit, subsequently proved that these rites were of a civil nature, in which light they came to be allowed by Alexander VII.: thus two opposite opinions were sanctioned by papal infallibility.

Notwithstanding every endeavour made by the more sensible and temperate of the missionaries to compromise the differences, a zealot named Carolus Maigrot, *soi-disant* bishop of some Chinese provinces, issued a mandate, in which, unmindful of the decree of Alexander VII., he decided that *Thien* signified only the visible and material *Heaven*, and that the Chinese rites were idolatrous. Kanghy himself, in 1700, declared in an edict, which was transmitted to the pope, that *Thien* means the true God, and that the customs enjoined by the ritual of China were of a political character. The decision of Maigrot, however, was supported and confirmed by a decree of Clement XI. To settle disputes which had disgraced the Christian cause for nearly a century, Tournon was despatched as apostolical vicar and legate to China; but this selection was not a wise one, for Mosheim describes him as a man "whose good disposition was under the influence of a narrow spirit and a weak understanding." Shortly after his arrival, in 1705, having received Pope Clement's decree, he issued a mandate, that no Chinese Christian should ever practise the customs which had been interdicted by the Bishop of Rome! The Emperor Kanghy, justly offended with this invasion of his sovereignty, promulged an edict, in which he tolerated the missionaries who preached the doctrine of Ricci, but declared his resolution to persecute those who followed the opinions of Maigrot. In 1720 the patriarch Mezzabarba was sent as legate from Rome, with the intention of carrying the points in dispute; but finding Kanghy determined never to allow the pope any kind of jurisdiction over his own subjects, he made certain temporary concessions, with a view to saving the Roman Catholic religion from the disgrace of being banished.

At length, by an imperial decree of Yoong-ching, in 1723, these disturbers of the public peace were formally denounced. A few monks were tolerated in Peking, a few remained concealed in the provinces, but the larger number were driven to Macao, with a positive injunction to leave the country by the first ship. The more enlightened and sensible Jesuits had acted with greater moderation, and the influence of their protectors reconciled them with the court. Ignatius Kœgler was appointed by the emperor President of the Astronomical Board, with a title of honour. On the accession of Kienloong, in 1736, his hatred of the mischievous priests, who were labouring in secret to subvert his authority over his own subjects, led him to seek them out with increased vigilance. Many of them were detected in disguise in almost every province; these were imprisoned, and their converts either fled or returned to their duty. To mitigate the severity of the persecutions, the Jesuits residing at Peking spared neither supplications nor bribes, but with little effect, until the decree of 1785, nearly fifty years after Kienloong first came to the throne, released the imprisoned monks, and allowed them either to join their brethren at Peking, or proceed to Europe. From that date to the present time the Roman Catholic mission has been in a declining state, and has occasionally had to suffer renewals of persecution. According to a return made by Père Marchini, procurator of the Propaganda mission at Macao, the actual number of European priests in China, in 1810, was twenty-nine, with about 200,000 native Christians. Since that date the last of the Europeans has been sent away from Peking, but a few still continue to lurk among the provinces.

The Spaniards, although they possess the privilege of trading at both Macao and Canton, as well as at Amoy, have derived less advantage from an intercourse with China than most other nations, notwithstanding the vast advantage which they possess in the locality of Manilla and the Philippine islands, within a few days' sail of China, and approached with equal facility in either monsoon. It has been suggested that, had bonded warehouses, with a system of drawbacks on re-exportation, been established at Manilla, one half of the trade to China might be centred there at present. The heavy charges and vexatious conduct of the Chinese government, together with the close monopoly of the Hong merchants, would have driven many a ship from Canton, could a neighbouring port have been found with a supply of goods in case of need. At present, American and English ships often find it convenient to touch at Manilla for a cargo of rice, by the importation of which to Canton they avoid the heavy port-charges; but, so ignorant is the Spanish government of the commonest principles of political economy, that rice is forbidden to be exported from Luconia when its price is above a certain limit.

The Dutch met with little success in their attempts to open a trade with China until 1624, when, by means of assistance from Batavia, they were enabled to form a settlement on the west side of Formosa, opposite to the Chinese coast. The vicinity of this to Manilla and Macao excited the jealousy of the Spaniards and Portuguese, as well as of the Chinese government. Liberty of trade with that empire was at first denied them; but the Dutch annoyed the coast with their ships, until it was agreed that, on their evacuating the Pescadores, some small islands between the mainland and Formosa, and confining themselves to the latter, liberty of commerce should be granted them. A fort was built at the principal harbour, on the southwest side of the island, named Fort Zealand, and measures were taken to civilize and reclaim the aboriginal inhabitants of the country. In the meanwhile Peking fell a prey to the Manchow Tartars, in 1644, and all the northern provinces, with most of the southern, acknowledged in a short time the foreign dominion. Many thousands of Chinese families emigrated from their country in the course of the struggle, and no less than 25,000 are said to have transported themselves to Formosa. This emigration tended greatly to the improvement of that new country, and was at first encouraged by the Dutch: but their fears were alarmed by the increasing numbers when they could no longer prevent them; and the influx of Chinese was a principal cause of the final expulsion of the Dutch from that settlement. This forms an episode in the history of European intercourse with China, deserving of some particular notice; and we shall give the account nearly as it stands abridged from Nieuhoff, in the second volume of the Chinese Repository.*

* Page 411.

A Chinese, for some time servant to the Portuguese at Macao, who had been baptized by the name of Nicholaus, grew by foreign trade to be the richest merchant in the country; and when the Manchows invaded the empire, he equipped at his own expense a small fleet against the Tartars. His success attracted a vast number of vessels, until he at length became commander of a very formidable fleet. After several battles, he was invited by the Tartar chief to Peking, with the offer of a high title, which he accepted, leaving the command of his fleet to his son *Kuo-shing*, called in Portuguese orthography Koshinga. The father was not permitted to return, but the son continued faithful to the Chinese cause, and opposed the enemies of his country. In the course of three or four years, however, the Tartars, by force or bribery, contrived to drive him from the coast to the numerous islands in the vicinity; and the large and fertile country of Formosa, now inhabited by numerous Chinese, became the object of his hopes. The Dutch were aware that the secret agents of Koshinga held a correspondence with the resident Chinese, and, foreseeing the danger, increased the garrison of Fort Zealand in 1650. They still remained unmolested for a time, until the exiled leader, being defeated before Nanking, had no refuge left for himself and his numerous followers except Formosa. On the application of Coyet, governor of the settlement, twelve ships were despatched from Batavia in 1660, with orders that, if the alarm at Formosa proved groundless, the fleet should proceed against Macao. The garrison now consisted of 1500 men, and the Dutch demanded of Koshinga whether he was for peace or war. In his reply, by letter, he affected the most friendly disposition towards the settlement; and, still farther to lull the Hollanders into security, sent several merchant vessels to Formosa. The governor's suspicions were not removed, as Koshinga still continued his preparations at Amoy; but the majority of the council being of opinion that there was no present danger, all the ships were ordered away to their respective destinations. The admiral, on his return to Batavia, accused the governor of unreasonable apprehensions; and the council, wearied with the expense, and with what they considered the groundless fears of the governor, suspended him from office, and ordered him to Batavia to defend himself. His successor, M. Clenk, sailed for Formosa in June, 1661.

Meanwhile, the events which were taking place on the island justified all the anticipations which had been thus contemned. Soon after the departure of the Dutch fleet from Fort Zealand, Koshinga and his forces were in motion: he embarked upwards of 20,000 of his best troops, and appeared before the settlement, where, assisted by thousands of his countrymen on shore, he soon began to land. Having occupied with his forces a point which would cut off the communication between Fort Zealand and another on the opposite side of the entrance, the governor ordered out 240 men to dislodge him. About 4000 Chinese had already occupied the place, but so confident were the Dutch that the enemy would not stand the fire, that they immediately attacked them. The Chinese, instead of giving ground, returned the fire with musketry and arrows, and sent a detachment to attack them in the flanks. The soldiers, seeing this, were alarmed and fled, leaving the captain and nineteen men in the hands of the enemy, while only half their company reached the fort alive. The defence by sea was no better; for, though the four ships in port attacked the junks, and sank some of them, one was burnt by the Chinese fire-vessels, and another sailed away with the news for Batavia. The Chinese now landed without opposition, and cut off all communication between the forts, as well as with the open country; and Koshinga summoned Fort Zealand, threatening to put all to the sword unless they surrendered at once.

Deputies were now sent to the Chinese camp, which consisted of about 12,000 men, armed in three different ways: the first with bows and arrows; the second with only swords and shields; and the third with back-swords and pikes, three or four feet long, with broad pointed heads of iron. The deputies were introduced into the tent, where Koshinga sat in an elbow-chair, behind a square table, surrounded by "the chief commanders, clad in long robes, without arms, and in great silence, and with a most awful countenance." Koshinga replied that "Formosa had always belonged to China; and now that the Chinese wanted it, the foreigners must quit the island immediately. If not, let them only hoist the red flag." On the following morning the red flag was seen over Fort Zealand, but the other fort was surrendered with its garrison and cannon. All the men able to fight were now taken within the citadel, and the town itself set on fire, in order to deprive the besiegers of shelter; but the Chinese saved many of the buildings, and brought up twenty-eight pieces of cannon to bear against the fort. They were, however, so galled by the fire of the Dutch, that the streets were strewed with the killed, and the besieged, making a sally, spiked their guns. Koshinga, finding all his attacks fruitless, began a close blockade, and turned his rage on the open country, making the Dutch residents, and especially the ministers, prisoners; one of these was sent to Fort Zealand to propose terms of surrender, on the refusal of which all the prisoners were to be put to death. This individual, by name Hambrocock, having left his wife and children with the enemy as hostages, like another Regulus, exhorted the Dutch to a good defence, and returned to Koshinga with the governor's refusal. As might have been expected, both himself and all the other prisoners were put to death, including many of the women and children.

Only two days after the council at Batavia had censured Coyet for his fears, and despatched his successor Clenk to Formosa, the ship which had sailed away arrived with the news of the attack on that place. They immediately revoked the censure, and fitted out ten ships, with 700 soldiers, for the island; but Clenk arrived first off Fort Zealand, where he saw the red flag flying, and hundreds of Chinese vessels lying in the north roads. He came to anchor, and sent his despatches on shore; but, instead of landing himself, sailed away for Japan. The succours from Batavia soon afterward arrived, and the besieged began to act on the offensive; but they were unsuccessful in the attempt to dislodge the enemy from the town. The garrison was now increased to the utmost; and the women and children, with the other useless persons, sent to Batavia. These preparations checked the approaches of Koshinga; but the inconceivable imprudence of the Dutch lost them their advantage. The governor received letters from the Tartar viceroy of Fokien (the opposite province), requesting his assistance in expelling the remains of Koshinga's forces from the coast, and promising his aid afterward to the Dutch at Formosa. Five ships were accordingly sent away for this purpose; but three were lost in a storm, and the remainder returned to Batavia. The wish of Koshinga was complete. A deserter from the Dutch encouraged the besiegers, and showed them the weakest points. They now assailed the fort from three batteries, and succeeded in making a breach, which they soon prepared to assault. The Hollanders upon this began to deliberate, and the majority of the council decided that the fort was untenable. Accordingly, after a siege of nine months, with the loss of about 1600 men,

Formosa was given up, and the Dutch returned to Java, in 1662. Koshinga now became independent sovereign of the island; but in 1683 it was surrendered by his grandson to the Manchow Tartar dynasty.

The intercourse of the Russians with China through Siberia not being of a maritime character, and confined altogether to the northern extremity of the empire, has differed altogether from that of other European nations, and we have not space to enter into the details of its history. One attempt was made by them in 1806 to communicate with Canton by sea in two ships under the command of Captain Krusenstern; but an edict was then issued forbidding to Russia any trade except by land, at the frontier station (established by mutual treaties) at Kiacta in Tartary. The most celebrated early embassies from Russia overland were those of Isbrand Ides, in 1693, and of Ismaloff, sent by Peter the Great, in 1719, an account of whose mission is well given by Mr. Bell, of Antermony. The ambassador in both instances was treated with a degree of respect unusual at Peking, and demonstrative of the estimation in which the power of Russia was held there. Catharine I., in 1727, despatched Count Vladislavitch to China as ambassador extraordinary, and by him a treaty was concluded, by which the Russians were to have a church at Peking, with an establishment of priests; and four young Russians were to remain at the residence of the embassy, for the purpose of studying the language, and serving as interpreters between the two nations. The Russian mission now consists of six ecclesiastical and four lay members, who study the Manchow and Chinese languages. Their abode at Peking extends to a period of about ten years, at the end of which they are relieved by others from St. Petersburg.

CHAPTER II.

ENGLISH INTERCOURSE.

First Trade between England and China.—Forts battered.—Leave to Trade.—Treaty of Commerce at Formosa.—Troubles at Canton.—Heavy charges on Trade.—Amoy and Ningpo.—Ten European ships at Canton in 1736.—Commodore Anson in China.—Intrigues of Hong Merchants.—Mr. Flint.—Quarrels of English and French.—Trade forbidden at Ningpo.—Seizure of Mr. Flint.—His Majesty's ship *Argo*.—The Portuguese give up an innocent Man.—Chinese Maxim for ruling Barbarians.—Violent conduct of a Ship-master.—Debts to the English recovered from the Chinese.—Shocking case of the Gunner in 1784.—Mission and Death of Colonel Cathcart.—Mission of Earl Macartney.

We now proceed to give a sketch of the early intercourse between Great Britain and China, the first attempt to establish which seems to have been as far back as 1596, when three ships were fitted out in charge of Benjamin Wood, bearing letters from Queen Elizabeth to the emperor; but the ships were lost on their way out, and no renewal of the project appears to have taken place. The oldest record of the company at Canton is dated April 6th, 1637, and commences thus:—"In the latitude of 6½ degrees we took leave of the ship *Planter*, whom God, we hope, hath conducted in safety. Upon her was laden as per invoice appeareth," &c. This was one of a fleet of five ships, of which the remaining four, the *Dragon*, *Sun*, *Catharine*, and *Ann*, proceeded on their way to China, under the command of Captain Weddel. They first arrived at Acheen in Sumatra. "At our reaching this (it is said) we found no Christians in the whole town, but there were three Dutchmen. Their capital was small, as likewise their wit and manners, being fellows of former slender employment, and sent hither rather to oppose any of our nation that should arrive in outfacing, outvying, and outlying them, than for any real intent or desire of trade."* The fleet proceeded on its way to China, and arrived off Macao on the 28th May. Here the Portuguese did all in their power to misrepresent them to the Chinese, and prevent the chance of a trade. After several fruitless attempts to establish a peaceful arrangement, and some vain endeavours to depute persons from the fleet to open a negotiation at Canton, it was resolved that all the ships should sail up the river. They arrived in a few days at the river's mouth, at present called the Bogue, in the neighbourhood of the forts; "and being now furnished with some slender interpreters, they soon had speech with divers mandarines in the king's jounkes, to whom the cause of their arrival was declared, viz., to entertain peace and amity with them, to traffic freely as the Portugalls did, and to be forthwith supplied, for their monies, with provisions for their ships: all which those mandarines promised to solicit with the prime men resident at Canton; and in the meantime desired an expectation of six days, which were granted; and the English ships rode with white ensigns on the poop; but their perfidious friends the Portugalls had in all that time, since the return of the pinnace, so beslandered them to the Chinese, reporting them to be rogues, thieves, beggars, and what not, that they became very jealous of the good meaning of the English; insomuch

* This rancour against the Dutch was the consequence of the mutual jealousies which existed between the rival traders of the two countries at that time in the East. A treaty concluded with Holland, called the *treaty of defence*, in 1615, had no effect ultimately in producing harmony; and the dreadful massacre of Amboyna, in 1623, at length became the crowning act of cruelty and perfidy on the part of the Hollanders.

that, in the night-time, they put forty-six of iron cast ordnance into the fort lying close to the brink of the river, each piece between six and seven hundred weight, and well proportioned; and after the end of four days, having, as they thought, sufficiently fortified themselves, they discharged divers shot, though without hurt, upon one of the barges passing by them to find a convenient watering-place. Herewith the whole fleet, being instantly incensed, did, on the sudden, display their bloody ensigns; and, weighing their anchors, fell up with the flood, and berthed themselves before the castle, from whence came many shot, yet not any that touched so much as hull or rope; whereupon, not being able to endure their bravadoes any longer, each ship began to play furiously upon them with their broadsides; and, after two or three hours, perceiving their cowardly fainting, the boats were landed with about one hundred men; which sight occasioned them, with great distractions, instantly to abandon the castle and fly; the boats' crews, in the meantime, without let, entering the same, and displaying his majesty's colours of Great Britain upon the walls, having the same night put aboard all their ordnance, fired the council-house, and demolished what they could. The boats of the fleet also seized a jounke, laden with boards and timber, and another with salt. Another vessel of small moment was surprised, by whose boat a letter was sent to the chief mandarines at Canton, expostulating their breach of truce, excusing the assailing of the castle, and withal in fair terms requiring the liberty of trade. This letter it seems was delivered; for, the next day, a mandarine of no great note, some time a Portugal Christian, called Paulo Noretty, came towards the ships in a small boat with a white flag, to whom the English, having laid open the injuries received, and the sincere intent they had to establish fair trade and commerce, and were no way willing (but in their own defence) to oppose the China nation, presented certain gifts, and dismissed him to his masters, who were some of the chief mandarines, riding about a point of land not far from the ships, who, being by him duly informed thereof, returned him again the same night with a small jounke, and full authority to carry up such as should be appointed to Canton, there to tender a petition, and to conclude farther upon the manner of their future proceedings." The result was, that the blame of the late skirmish was laid by the mandarins on the slanders of the Portuguese, and the captured guns being restored, the ships were supplied with cargoes.

No farther trade, however, ensued for many years. Soon after this period the interior of China was distracted by the contests between the Manchow Tartars and Chinese, while the coasts were overrun by large fleets of pirates, under the leaders whom we have already had occasion to notice. Another attempt was made by the English in 1664 to establish a commercial intercourse with Canton. The company's agents landed at Macao, and obtained a lodging there, with the view of prosecuting a negotiation with the Chinese: these, however, demanded 2000 taëls on each ship as a port-charge, and when 1000 were offered, they rejected the proposal. At length a guard of Chinese was placed over the English, and they were obliged to abandon the attempt and return to Bantam; there being every reason to suppose that the Portuguese, as usual, were instrumental to their failure. In 1668 peace with the Dutch encouraged the company to look towards China, and accordingly application was made to Sir Robert Southwell, ambassador in Portugal, to obtain good treatment for our ships, should they be obliged to touch at Goa or Macao. In the same year the company's servants at Bantam observed, in a despatch to the court, "Hockchue* will be a place of great resort, affording all China commodities, as tutanag, silk, raw and wrought, gold, China-root, tea, &c., for which must be carried broadcloth, lead, amber, pepper, coral, sandal-wood, red-wood, incense, cacha (cassia), putchuk," &c. These, all of them, form articles of trade at present with either England or India.

The records then show that, in 1670, a trade was established at Taywan, or Formosa, with the chief Koshinga, who, as we have before seen, had expelled the Dutch from that island in 1662. It is possible that, knowing the rivalry and animosity which existed between the Dutch and English, he encouraged the latter to come, as a counterpoise in his own favour, should the Dutch attempt to repossess themselves of Formosa. A treaty was entered into, called "The contract made with the King of Taywan for the settling of a factory," in which the company stipulate "that we may sell or truck our goods with whom we please, and likewise all persons may have the same free trade with us; that, for all injuries or wrongs that shall be done us by the people here, the king shall right us; and, on the other hand, that what injuries or wrongs the English shall do, application being made to the chief, satisfaction shall be made by them; that upon all occasions we may have access to the king's person; that we may have the choosing of our own interpreters and escrivans, and no soldiers to be put upon us, and also to be free to walk without Chinamen along with us; that what goods the king buys shall pay no custom; that rice imported pay no custom; that all goods imported pay 3 per cent. after sale, and all goods exported be custom free." It was provided, however, that all ships should deliver

* The provincial pronunciation for Fokchow Foo (which possesses great advantages for European trade) in Fokien province.

up their guns and ammunition while in port. It seems that this trade at length proved so unprofitable and vexatious, that the company, in 1681, ordered their establishments at Formosa and Amoy to be withdrawn, and a trade, if possible, established at Canton and Hockchue, or Fokchow. In 1683, Formosa, as already noticed, was surrendered to the Tartars, and in a curious despatch to the company, dated the 20th December in that year, it is observed, that "the inhabitants were ordered, in the name of the Great Cham of Tartary, to shave all their hairs off, save enough to make a monkey's tale, pendent from the very noddle of their heads, and betake themselves to his country's habit." The Tartars, from the very first conquest of China, have shown a great disinclination to foreign trade, which may have arisen partly from their having a less esteem for it than the native rulers of the country, and partly from a fear of some collusion taking place between Europeans and their Chinese subjects. It is, in fact, since the Tartar conquest that the English have been excluded from Ningpo and Amoy, having traded at the latter place while it remained independent of the Manchows, and some time after the rest of China had submitted to them.

The ship *Delight* was sent in 1685 to attempt the re-establishment of a trade at Amoy; and, about the same time, active exertions were made by the company towards securing a regular commerce at Canton. In the progress of all these trials one of the most striking circumstances is the stupid pertinacity with which the Portuguese of Macao excluded English ships from that port; and the perfidy with which they misrepresented their supposed rivals to the Chinese, with a view to prevent their getting a footing at Canton. In the course of time they have been unable to exclude us altogether even from Macao; but their systematic policy has been to attribute motives to the English which should injure them with the provincial government; and this was strikingly exemplified during the expedition under Admiral Drury, in 1808.

Soon after the Tartar conquest we find it stated by the mandarins, in reply to certain inquiries on the subject, that "a present to the emperor of *strange fowls and beasts* would be more acceptable than a ship's lading of gold." There can be no doubt that gifts of this kind are extremely well suited to Peking; and on the occasion of any future mission, it would be well to keep the advice in view, instead of confining the selection of presents *entirely* to works of art; as they were, in our past embassies, most of them unintelligible and useless to the emperor and his court. The troubles of the trade at Canton appear to have commenced very early. The hoppo, or chief commissioner of customs, in 1689, demanded 2484 taëls for the measurage (or port-charge) of the ship *Defence*; but, on finding that it would not be paid, he took 1500 taëls. In the meanwhile, one of the crew of the *Defence* had killed a Chinese, and a tumult ensued, in which several of the seamen, and the surgeon of the ship, lost their lives. Not satisfied with this, the mandarins declared, that unless 5000 taëls were paid, the *Defence* would not be allowed to sail; but, when they had refused 2000, the captain quitted Canton, and took his vessel out of the river. The present charges on a ship of about 800 tons in the port of Whampoa are very little short of 5000 dollars, or above £1000.

It appears from a letter of the court of directors to the factory in China, dated 23d November, 1699, that a consul's commission was sent out to the chief of the company's council; nor does any notice appear on the records of this having been subsequently recalled. They say, "We have obtained a commission from his majesty to constitute you, and those who shall be hereafter appointed by us, as our president in China, to be the king's minister or consul for the English nation, with all powers requisite thereunto." The court of directors appear to have been unaware of this when, in 1832, they denied that their president was any other than a company's representative; indeed, it was very correctly observed in Parliament, with reference to this proceeding of the court, that the complete powers with which the legislature had vested the chief in China over all British subjects, seemed alone to give him a national character.

From the beginning of the century until 1727, many very severe grievances were suffered at Canton, and, although the trade continued to proceed, it was with frequent interruptions. In that year we find that an exemption was required by the English from various extortions; among others, a total charge of 16 per cent. on the trade; heavy taxes on the compradors, or purveyors, for supplying the ships; and what was called the *present* of 1950 taëls, in addition to the measurage, or port-fee. For some time the local government had attempted to invest a single individual, called "the emperor's merchant," with the exclusive right of conducting the European commerce. This "monster in trade," however (as he is very properly termed on the records), was soon obliged to allow others to participate. The Hong merchants then endeavoured to establish a *hong*, or united firm, among themselves The supercargoes upon this declined trading until the combination was dissolved, and a representation to the viceroy was at length successful in removing it. On their declaring, moreover, that they should be obliged to proceed to Amoy, or some other port, unless the heavy charges on their trade were remitted, the hoppo promised them redress. Notwithstanding this, in the following year of 1728, an additional duty of 10 per cent. was laid on all exports to Europe, and the remonstrances of the English merchants proved unavailing.

From what appears to have transpired relative to this 10 per cent. duty, it seems clear that raw produce has, from the very first, found a better market at Canton than manufactures. It is observed on the records, "a duty of 10 per cent. hath really been paid by the merchants to the hoppo on all goods sold to the *Europe* ships for some years past, though, at the same time, the *country** ships remain free. At length one of the merchants gave this reason, which they hold as a very just one, that the hoppo, for several years past, observing that a considerable duty arose to the emperor upon goods imported by the country ships (the raw produce of India and the straits), and that the Europe ships brought few or none, he fixed that rate upon the merchants for all goods sold by them to the Europe ships." The great industry and ingenuity of the Chinese cause them to turn nearly all raw produce to good account; while the peculiarities of their national customs and tastes, added to the obstacles of both law and prejudice against European productions of art, render these far less acceptable in general.

In 1734 only one ship, the *Harrison*, was sent to Canton, simply on account of the high duties and extortions. An attempt, however, was made at Amoy, in the ship *Grafton*. The history of the negotiations at that place affords a notable specimen of Chinese rapacity and faithlessness. After spending months in the fruitless endeavour to obtain reasonable terms from the mandarins, they were compelled at length to take their departure for Canton, principally because they could not get liberty to trade with any persons but those who were leagued with the mandarins, one of whom was always stationed over them in the house they had rented on

* Those from India.

shore. In addition to the regular duties, which were very high, there was an extra charge of 20 per cent. for the hoppo. "The ignorance of the Amoy merchants (it is observed), and the little encouragement they gave us, make us almost despair of doing any business at that place." In 1736 the ship *Normanton* proceeded to Ningpo, and strenuous efforts were made to open a trade there, unfettered by the oppressions they had suffered formerly in the neighbouring Island of Chusan; but they found the mandarins very imperious and obstinate, insisting, as a necessary preliminary, on the surrender of their arms and ammunition. There moreover appeared few inducements to trade; for the record observes, "it seems rather to have been, than to be, a place of great commerce." It is probable that this, with other parts of China, had suffered by the Tartar invasion. After wasting nearly two months in fruitless attempts to procure a fair trade, the *Normanton* sailed for Canton: on arriving there it was found that the Emperor Kien-loong, who had just succeeded to the throne, had remitted the duty of 10 per cent., as well as the *present* of 1550 taëls, leaving that portion of the port-charges only which is called the *measurage*.* When the edict ordering this remission was to be read in the Imperial Hall of Audience, the Hong merchants informed the different European traders "that they must prostrate themselves, kneeling on both their knees."—"Suspecting that the merchants endeavoured to make us believe this, in order that by our compliance we might be brought down to the same servile level with themselves; considering, also, that the posture insisted on is such a mark of abject submission as we never pay to our own sovereigns in Europe, we

* Notwithstanding this, the provincial government contrived to exact the *present* to its full amount until 1829, when a trifling reduction was made in it.

unanimously agreed that we should dishonour ourselves and our countries in complying with it. Being apprehensive that they (the Hong merchants) might succeed in their design of weakening us, by creating in us mutual suspicions and jealousies, we met in a body, and, by unanimous agreement, gave our solemn words of honour that none of us would submit to the slavish posture required, nor make any concession or proposal of accommodation separately, without first acquainting all the rest." It was fortunate for them that they never prostrated themselves, for more substantial concessions would very soon have been demanded, had they gone through this form of allegiance and fealty. It seems that in that year (just a century since) the total number of European ships at Canton was ten, viz., four English, two French, two Dutch, one Dane, and one Swede.

At the close of 1741 his majesty's ship *Centurion*, under the command of Commodore Anson, arrived off Macao, in the prosecution of her voyage round the world, being the first British man-of-war that visited China. The interesting details of that ship's stay are well given in the popular history of the voyage, and familiar to most readers. After being hove down and repaired, the *Centurion* put to sea, and succeeded in capturing the *Acapulco* ship, with its valuable freight of treasure, with which she proceeded again to the Canton river, being in want of provisions. The commodore, on his arrival, was subjected, as usual, to numberless vexatious delays; and the following passages occur on the manuscript proceedings: "A new difficulty was now started, that Mr. Anson, being lodged at Mr. Townsend's, must first go to Macao; for, if he remained in the house after Mr. Townsend left it, the Hong merchants said they should of course become security for him to the mandarins; and should Mr. Anson take a Spanish ship near Macao, on the coast, they would then be made answerable for the damages, and perhaps lose their heads. Mr. Anson declared he did not want any person to be security for him, but told them that unless he got some provisions he would not stir out of Canton, for he had not five days' bread on board his ship. We assembled the merchants the third time, to persuade them, if possible, to prevail with the mandarins to grant Mr. Anson a general chop for all the necessaries he wants. They informed us, the mandarins had such a strange notion of a ship which went about the world *seeking other ships in order to take them*, that they could not be brought to hear reason on that head." At length the merchants became so uneasy at the commodore's stay in Canton, that they suffered a purveyor to ship the provisions without the inspection of the custom-house.

The loss of the *Acapulco* ship led the Spaniards, in 1744, to fit out several vessels for the annoyance of our China trade; and when the *Hardwicke* East Indiaman arrived off the coast, a note was delivered, by means of a Chinese boat, to say that three Spanish ships were lying off Macao to intercept her; the *Hardwicke* accordingly sailed away for Amoy. There, however, the mandarins insisted on the ship's proceeding into the inner harbour without any previous conditions, as well as delivering up all arms and ammunition. The merchants showed no disposition to trade, and, in fact, there seemed little to trade with. Accordingly, after fifteen days of ineffectual trial, the ship was compelled to proceed to India against the monsoon, without a single article of cargo! Nor was the condition of the trade much better at Canton. The extortions increased in spite of all attempts at representation on the part of the supercargoes. The Hong merchants used every endeavour, and at length succeeded, in preventing the access of Europeans to the officers of government, finding that by that means they could exercise their impositions on *both* with the greater success and impunity. To the foreigners they alleged, that the mandarins were the authors of all the exactions on the trade; to the mandarins, that the foreigners were of so barbarous and fierce a temper, as to be incapable of listening to reason. The records observe, that, "ever since they carried their point of preventing all intercourse between the Europeans and mandarins, they have imposed upon both in their turns, and put the trade of this place upon such a footing as without redress will render it impracticable to Europeans." In these difficult times it was that Mr. Flint, a person of uncommon talents and merit, contrived to master the difficulties of the Chinese language; but the ungrateful return which his energy and exertions in their service met with from his employers was such as tended, in all probability, more than any other cause, to discourage his successors from undertaking so laborious, unprofitable, and even hazardous a work of supererogation. We find Mr. Flint acting as interpreter in 1747, and he soon had to perform a very prominent part in China, as will appear hereafter.

The grievances suffered by our trade led to a remonstrance, in which the principal points were, the delay in unloading the ships; the plunder of goods on the river; the injurious *affiches* annually put up by the government, accusing the foreigners of horrible crimes, and intended to expose them to the contempt of the populace; the extortions, under false pretexts, of the inferior officers; and the difficulty of access to the mandarins. The ships were detained outside in 1754, until the viceroy had promised to attend to these various complaints; but little was ultimately gained. It is to be apprehended that the want of union among the Europeans had, as usual, the effect of frustrating their attempts at redress. "Some gentlemen," it is observed, "were of opinion that we ought to make a stand;

and as, by arguing the case, we seemed to be the farther from a determination, we parted without any resolve, except that every man would do as he liked best." This certainly was not the way to succeed with the Chinese. The animosities which prevailed between the English and French were productive of much trouble to both; and to such a height did the disorders arrive at Whampoa, between the crews of the different nations on shore, that an English sailor was at length shot by some of the French officers, and another taken prisoner; which was immediately followed by a letter addressed to the English supercargoes from "Le Conseil de direction de Canton, representant la nation Française à la Chine." The Chinese magistrate held an inquest at Whampoa, and desired the French, in the first place, to give up their prisoner, which they did, alleging, however, that the English had commenced the disturbance, by attacking their people. As the Frenchman fired a musket, of which he had deliberately gone in quest, it was plainly nothing better than a murder; and the English sailors were so exasperated, that there seemed to be no way of preventing their doing *themselves* justice, but to demand justice from the Chinese government. The viceroy stopped the trade until they should give up the criminal; and somebody was at length seized by the Chinese and taken into the city, confessing himself the guilty person. He was liberated the following year by order of the emperor, on occasion of a general act of grace; and, as a means of preventing farther disturbances at Whampoa, Dane's Island was allotted to the English, and French Island to the French sailors, for their recreation.

In 1755, Messrs. Harrison and Flint were despatched to Ningpo, with the view of re-establishing a trade there if possible. On their arrival they were well received, and the charges and customs appeared considerably lower than at Canton. The fooyuen, or deputy-governor, was so desirous of giving them encouragement, that he conceded almost all the articles in their memorial: in so doing, however, he appeared to have exceeded his power; for when the ship *Holdernesse* subsequently proceeded to Ningpo, to take advantage of this apparent opening, the viceroy, who was then in the province, sent an order for all the great guns, small arms, and ammunition to be taken out of the ship, and the same duties to be paid as at Canton. Though the fooyuen could not act directly against this order, he did not comply with it, but sent it straight up to Peking, with an account of what he had done, thereby putting it out of the viceroy's power, as well as his own, to make an absolute decision in the interim. As it would be the end of September before an answer could possibly arrive from Peking, the mandarins agreed to begin business, provided that half the guns and ammunition were delivered. Twelve great guns were accordingly given up, and the ships unloaded: the *Holdernesse*, however, paid to the mandarins 2000 taëls, and the other charges and duties proved double those at Canton, while no residence was allowed on shore. The objection made by the government to a trade at Ningpo was "the loss of revenue to the emperor, accruing from overland carriage of tea and other goods to Canton;" the very circumstance, of course, which enhanced the prices of those goods to the European purchaser. On their departure from Ningpo, the supercargoes were formally acquainted by the mandarins of all future trade being forbidden them at that port; and, on reaching Macao, the officers of the local government in like manner informed them of a public edict, confining the commerce to Canton.

At length, in 1759, the factory once occupied by the English at Ningpo was destroyed, the merchants with whom they had dealt were ordered to quit the place, and the war-junks directed to prevent any English ship from being supplied with provisions at Chusan. Mr. Flint, notwithstanding this, proceeded to Ningpo, upon which the Canton government forbade his return, desiring that he should be sent home to England whenever he reappeared. On arriving at Ningpo he was refused all communication: upon this he proceeded to the neighbourhood of Peking, and succeeded in making his complaints known to the emperor. A mandarin of rank was appointed to proceed with him by land to Canton, and there, in concert with others, to sit in judgment on the hoppo. Mr. Flint, on reaching Canton, remained ten days in the city, and then proceeded to the factory. Two days after, the foreigners of all nations were received by the Chinese commissioners, and informed that the hoppo had been degraded, his place being supplied by another. All impositions, moreover, were remitted, except 6 per cent. on goods, and the *present* of 1950 taëls from each ship.

It proved, however, that these fair appearances were destined only to be the prelude to a storm. Some days afterward, the viceroy desired to see Mr. Flint, for the purpose of communicating the emperor's orders; the council wished to accompany him, and their request was granted. When the party had reached the viceroy's palace, the Hong merchants proposed their going in one at a time, but they insisted on proceeding together; and on Mr. Flint being called for, they were received by a mandarin at the first gate, proceeding onward through two courts with seeming complaisance from the officers in waiting; but, on arriving at the gate of the inner court, they were hurried, and even forced, into the viceroy's presence, and (under pretence of doing homage after the Chinese fashion) a struggle ensued with their barbarian conductors, in which they were at length, by dint of numbers, thrown down. The viceroy, seeing their determined resolution not to submit to these base humiliations, ordered the people to desist; and then telling Mr. Flint to advance, he pointed to an order, which he called the emperor's edict, for his banishment to Macao, and subsequent departure for England. This he declared was on account of his endeavouring to open a trade at Ningpo, contrary to orders from Peking; he added, that the man who had written the Chinese petition was to be beheaded that day, for traitorously encouraging foreigners, "which execution," the record observes, "was performed on a man quite innocent of what these absolute and villanous mandarins were pleased to call a crime." At the same time, the complaints against the hoppo were admitted to be just. Mr. Flint was detained in the city, and conveyed to a place called Tsien-shān, or Casa Bianca, near Macao, where he was imprisoned, but pretty well treated, though all correspondence was cut off.

Some days after the above occurrence, the French, Danes, Swedes, and Dutch met in a body at the English factory, and jointly entered a protest against the act of the viceroy: but Mr. Flint remained in prison from March, 1760, to November, 1762, when he was carried by the Chinese to Whampoa, and put on board the ship *Horsendon*, to be conveyed to England.

The success and impunity of the Canton government on this occasion seem to have encouraged it in its assumptions for some time after. When, in March, 1765, his majesty's ship *Argo* arrived, convoying the *Cuddalore* schooner, with a supply of half a million of dollars for the company's treasury, the Chinese insisted on searching the schooner, on the plea that a woman was on board: but when this was declined, as contrary to all precedent, they said it would be sufficient if a mandarin were admitted "to walk two or three times up and down the deck." They were told that when a license had been granted for taking out the silver, they might send whom they pleased to walk up and down the deck. Provisions were denied to the *Argo* in consequence of this dispute, and it was at length arranged that a mandarin should go on board when the money was unladen. The Chinese next demanded to measure his majesty's ship *Argo*, but this was refused by Captain Affleck, more especially as there was a precedent against so strange a requisition from a king's ship, in the case of the *Centurion*, Commodore Anson, in 1742. The trade was again stopped in consequence, and the council at Canton offered to pay the amount of measurage of the company's largest ship in lieu of the *Argo;* but the mandarins would not consent, and Captain Affleck at length allowed the *Argo* to be measured. Had he sailed away at the commencement of the dispute, it is probable that this might have been avoided.

The ill-will generated on both sides by the insolence of the Chinese, and the consequences resulting from it, had the effect of constantly embroiling the English and natives for several years after, during a period in which a greater number of affrays and homicides occurred than have ever been known of late years. In 1772 the *Lord Camden* was detained from 17th December to 5th January following, in consequence of a tumult, in which several Chinese and Europeans were badly hurt; the wounded men were all conveyed into the factory, where two mandarins examined them. The ship was at first detained, but permission at length given for her sailing, on condition that the person who originated the mischief was detained in confinement; but the recovery of all the wounded soon after put an end to the affair. In the following year a most atrocious act of sanguinary injustice occurred at Macao, stamping indelible disgrace on the Portuguese of that place. A Chinese had lost his life, and some ungrounded accusation having implicated an Englishman, named Francis Scott, the local authority caused him to be apprehended and confined. The case was tried in the Portuguese court, the accused examined, and depositions of witnesses taken; but the slightest trace of guilt could not be attached to the prisoner. The mandarins, however, obstinately claimed him, and threatened the town in case he was not delivered. To bring this perplexity to a close, a general meeting or council was convened, and a member of the Macao senate argued, "it is unjustifiable to consent to the sacrifice of an innocent man; and, as the most accurate inquiry sufficiently proves that the Englishman is not guilty, our reasons for not surrendering him should be submitted to the mandarins, and persevered in until we shall have succeeded in saving him from an ignominious death." The vicar-general, however, named Francisco Vaz, argued in the following singular manner:—"Moralists decide that when a tyrant demands even an innocent person, with menaces of ruin to the community if refused, the whole number may call on any individual to deliver himself up for the public good, which is of more worth than the life of an individual. Should he refuse to obey, he is not innocent, he is criminal." Another Portuguese observed, with still less ceremony, "The mandarins are forcing away the Chinese dealers, determined to starve us; therefore we had better surrender the Englishman." The plurality of votes decided that Scott should be handed over, and the Chinese put him to death.*

The following case occurs on the proceedings of 1780:—"14th December. Some days ago, a French

* Taken from a "Contribution to an Historical Sketch of Macao," 1834.

seaman from the *Success* galley, country ship, killed a Portuguese sailor belonging to the *Stormont*, in one of the merchants' houses. The man took refuge at the French consul's, where he remained many days, but at last was given up to the Chinese, and was this morning publicly strangled by order of the fooyuen. This is the first instance of one European being executed for the murder of another in this country, and appears to be a very dangerous precedent, as it may involve us in inextricable difficulties, if even by *accident* one man should kill another. The man executed to-day could not have had any trial of common justice: the affair happened between him and the deceased in Seunqua's hong at night, nobody knowing of the quarrel until the *Stormont's* man was killed; and we do not understand that the Chinese government took any means to find out the truth. Foreigners are not here allowed the benefit of the Chinese laws, nor have they any privileges in common with the natives. They are governed merely by such rules as the mandarins for the time being declare to be their will; and the reason why more inconveniences do not occur is this :—the officers of government on such occasions rather choose to exact money from the security merchants, compradores, &c., than use harsh measures by which they gain nothing. Their corruption, therefore, is so far the foreigner's security."

The fundamental maxim of Chinese intercourse with foreigners has been accurately translated by Père Premare as follows, and it is quite sufficient to explain their conduct. "Barbari haud secus ac pecora non eodem modo regendi sunt ut reguntur Sinæ. Si quis vellet eos magnis sapientiæ legibus instruere, nihil aliud quam summam perturbationem induceret. Antiqui reges istud optimè callebant, et ideo barbaros *non regendo* regebant. Sic autem eos *non regendo* regere, præclara eos optimè regendi ars est." That is, "*The barbarians are like beasts, and not to be ruled on the same principles as citizens. Were any one to attempt controlling them by the great maxims of reason, it would tend to nothing but confusion. The ancient kings well understood this, and accordingly ruled barbarians by misrule. Therefore, to rule barbarians by misrule is the true and best way of ruling them.*" It is on this principle that all the benefits of Chinese law are denied to strangers, and that, in the case of even *accidental* homicide, they are required to be delivered up, not for trial, but execution. The mischiefs of such a system are obvious, and it is in consequence of this that acts of atrocious violence, on the part of foreigners, committed by them under the plea of doing themselves right, have been attempted to be justified, though coming strictly under the definitions of piracy, murder, or arson, which, under a more vigorous government, would render them the property of the public executioner. The following is a singular instance of successful daring. In the year 1781, a Captain M'Clary, master of a country ship from Bengal, had stopped a sloop on her way from Macao to Manilla. Being on shore at Macao, he told the Portuguese governor that he had ordered his mate to bring her into the harbour for examination, having reason to suspect that she was Spanish property. The Portuguese on this had him seized and imprisoned until he had sent an order for the sloop being released without examination. This order being taken to the mate, he bore down to the sloop in order to comply with it; but it blew such a gale of wind that the sloop got adrift, and was wrecked on the rocks. M'Clary upon this was detained in prison for two months, until, by ill treatment, and threats of being delivered to the Chinese, the Portuguese had extorted from him a payment of 70,000 dollars, under the pretence of its being the value of the sloop. Some time after his liberation, while M'Clary's ship was lying at Whampoa, in company with another vessel under Dutch colours, news arrived of war between England and Holland, upon which he seized upon the Dutchman as a prize. The Canton government immediately demanded restitution; but M'Clary told them that if they would not interfere, the duties should all be paid regularly; whereas, if they molested him, he would take her out of the river. On the Chinese insisting that he should restore the ship, he rigged her and began to drop down from his anchorage. There was immediately a great bustle among the Chinese, and all the troops available, about 200, were rendezvoused at Tiger Island to intercept his passage. The ship in the meanwhile was surrounded by mandarins and merchants, and when threats and civilities had all failed, the Chinese being very anxious for a compromise, the genius of Ponkhequa, chief Hong merchant, devised the following expedient. The prize being close to the river's mouth, the Chinese were allowed to board her in a shouting triumphant manner; and in return for his condescension, M'Clary was permitted to hold an iron chest, containing pearls and gold, freighted by certain Armenians.

Meanwhile the company's council were in a very unpleasant situation, being held responsible by the government for the acts of M'Clary, who certainly was little better than a pirate. They replied to the Chinese, that they could not control his proceedings otherwise than by protests, and very properly refused the demand of the mandarins, that they should accompany the Chinese officers to the river to give weight to their measures. "The more," it is observed, "they perceived their own want of power over the real offender, the more they appeared resolved to exert it over us, whom they had been accustomed to see observant of all their regulations." An application was made by the

Chinese to the Portuguese governor of Macao, to deliver them up, which he declined, and a conclusion was at length put to these difficulties only by the circumstances already stated.

Towards the year 1782, the large sums lent by the merchants of various nations to Chinese, at a high rate of interest, had occasioned an accumulation of debts on the part of the latter, amounting, it is said, to the enormous extent of a million sterling. Among the creditors were numerous individuals connected with the trade of the Indian presidencies; and these, after a course of fruitless measures for the recovery of the property at Canton, applied, through the Indian government, to the admiral on the station, Sir Edward Vernon, for his assistance. A frigate was accordingly despatched to China, bearing a remonstrance to the viceroy; and after a reference of the subject to Peking, an edict was received from the emperor, ordering the liquidation of the debts by the whole body of Hong merchants, as well as interdicting any one of them from borrowing money for the future from strangers. The debts were at length recovered, but so little effectual was the interdict that repeated failures of Hong merchants, for very large sums due to Europeans, occurred up to the year 1829.

Among the unhappy cases which have arisen from the sanguinary practice of the Canton government in the instances of homicides, whether accidental or otherwise, when committed by Europeans, the most remarkable, perhaps, is that frequently alluded to under the name of the *gunner's case*, in 1784. On the 24th November in that year, information reached Canton that a chop boat, alongside the *Lady Hughes*, country ship, being in the way of a gun fired in saluting, three Chinese had been badly injured. On the following day it was learned that one had died; and the gunner, though entirely innocent of any bad intent, and acting as he did in obedience to orders, absconded from fear of the indiscriminating cruelty of the Chinese. A *weiyuen*, or deputed mandarin, soon waited on the chief of the factory, Mr. Pigou, and, with the interpretation of the Hong merchants, required that the man should be submitted to examination, admitting, at the same time, that his act had apparently proceeded from mere accident. The mandarin was informed that there appeared no objection to the man's examination, provided that it took place in the factory; a stipulation which was founded on the recollection of what had occurred in the Frenchman's case in 1780. Two days after the weiyuen repeated his visit, accompanied by Ponkhequa, Hong merchant, with the same demands: he was informed that the *Lady Hughes*, being a private ship, was not to the same degree under the control of the chief as a company's vessel; but that, if they would be satisfied with an examination in the factory, every persuasion should be used to induce the supercargo of the ship, Mr. Smith, to produce the man. The Chinese declared that the trial must be before the fooyuen in the city, and at length retired, requesting that Mr. Smith might not leave Canton for three or four days, to which he assented. At eleven the same night they returned to say that the man should be examined in one of the factories; but the event soon proved that this was merely to lull their suspicions, for early the next morning it was found that Mr. Smith had been decoyed from his factory by a pretended message from Ponkhequa, and conveyed into the city by force. Meanwhile the avenues leading to the river had been barricaded, the merchants and linguists had fled, and the communication with Whampoa was suspended.

The heads of all the foreign factories justly considering this as a very threatening proceeding to the whole European community, united in a resolution to order up the boats of the several ships, manned and armed, both as a security, and to manifest in the strongest manner the light in which they viewed the acts of the government. Two English boats were despatched to Whampoa to carry this into effect. The watchful Chinese now endeavoured to quiet them by a message from the fooyuen, to the purport that they should not be alarmed by the seizure of the *Lady Hughes's* supercargo, as the intention was merely to ask him a few questions and send him back again. The greater number of ships' boats reached Canton, although attempts were made to prevent them, by firing from the junks and forts in the river, and notwithstanding their having been absurdly ordered to use no arms in their own defence. A very bombastic document was received from the fooyuen, threatening destruction if any opposition were made, and a show of force at the same time assembled in the river before the factories. On the 28th the foreigners all joined in an address in behalf of Mr. Smith, and in the evening the fooyuen desired to see a deputation from the factory of the several nations. These reported that "his behaviour was much agitated, and it was evident he would be glad to get handsomely out of the business." The Chinese were, in fact, frightened at their own boldness, and a little resolution on the other side might have saved the man's life.

A linguist soon arrived at the factory, bringing a letter from Mr. Smith to the captain of his ship, desiring he would send up the gunner, or some other person, to be tried by the mandarins; and this was forwarded on the 29th to Whampoa, backed by a letter from the council. On the 30th the unfortunate gunner, an old man, was brought to Canton and sent into the city, with an address, "signed by the English council, and the representatives of the foreign nations," in his favour. He was received by a mandarin of superior rank, who *verbally* stated that no apprehensions need be entertained as to his life, and that, when the emperor's answer had been obtained, he should be restored. In about an hour after Mr. Smith returned to his factory, stating that he had been very civilly treated. On the 8th January following the unhappy gunner was strangled!

This was the last instance of the kind to which the English had to submit in China, although not the last which has occurred at Canton; for the case of the poor innocent Italian, Terranova, given up by the Americans in 1821, was very similar. Our own countrymen, warned of what they had to expect from Chinese justice and good faith, have on all subsequent occasions been ready to undergo any extremities rather than be parties to the death of an innocent man; and their exertions have in several instances been crowned with signal success. Soon after the above unfortunate occurrence, in 1784, the attention of the British government was naturally drawn to the growing magnitude and importance of the trade at Canton; and it cannot be denied that, since the mission of Lord Macartney to Peking, the general condition of the English at that place has been considerably bettered. It was in fact only four years after the death of the gunner that Colonel Cathcart was sent from England (in 1788), in the *Vestal* frigate, as ambassador to China. His death on the passage out, in the Straits of Sunda, put an entire stop to the mission for the time, and the frigate returned to England;* nor was it until 1792 that the project was renewed on a larger scale. In the month of January of that year. Mr. Dundas set on foot the proposal of a Chinese embassy, grounded on the consideration of our trade having gradually increased until its ac-

* The tomb of Colonel Cathcart is still marked by a handsome monument, visible from the anchorage of ships at Anjier Point.

tual amount exceeded that of all other nations; to which it was added, that the intercourse of almost every other country with that empire had been attended with special missions to Peking. It was hoped that such a measure might relax the various trammels by which the commerce with China was shackled, relieve it from some of its exactions, and place our countrymen at Canton on a footing of greater respectability, as well as security, in relation to the local government. Lord Macartney accordingly proceeded from England in the *Lion*, a sixty-four gun ship, in September, 1792, accompanied by Sir George Leonard Staunton as secretary of legation. The occurrences and result of that embassy are so well known from the celebrated work of the last-named individual, as well as from the relation of Mr. Barrow, that it would be superfluous to dwell upon them here. One of the principal effects of the mission was to draw a much greater share of the public attention towards China, and to lead gradually to the study of the language, literature, institutions, and manners of that vast and singular empire—a field which had hitherto been occupied almost exclusively by the French.

CHAPTER III.

ENGLISH INTERCOURSE—(CONTINUED).

Objects and Results of the Embassy of 1793.—Affair of the Providence Schooner.—American Flag hoisted in 1802, hauled down in 1832.—First Expedition to Macao.—Mission to Cochin-China.—Admiral Linois repulsed by China Fleet.—Ladrones, or Chinese Pirates.—A Chinese killed by a Sailor, who is not delivered up.—Second Expedition to Macao.—Ill Success of Admiral Drury.—Interdict against Mr. Roberts at Canton.—A Linguist seized.—His Majesty's ship *Doris.*—Trade stopped by the Committee, who succeed in their objects.—Mission of Lord Amherst.—Question of the Ko-tow.—Forts silenced by the *Alceste* Frigate.—Cases of Homicide in 1820 and 1821.—His Majesty's ship *Topaz.*—Trade reopened.—Fire of Canton.—Failure of Hong Merchants.—Dissensions with Chinese.—Factory invaded by Fooyuen.—Letter from Governor-general to Viceroy.—Voyage of the *Amherst.*—Fighting between Smuggling Ships and Chinese.—Termination of the Company's Charter.

One of the principal objects of Earl Macartney's mission to Peking was to obtain, if possible, the permission of the emperor to trade at Ningpo, Chusan, Tien-tsin, and other places besides Canton. All discussions upon these points, and indeed every matter of business, were studiously avoided by the Chinese ministers and mandarins during the residence of the embassy at Peking; but, in his letter to the King of England, the emperor did not omit to state distinctly that the British commerce must be strictly limited to the port of Canton. "You will not be able to complain," adds he, "that I had not clearly forewarned you. Let us therefore live in peace and friendship, and do not make light of my words."

Were a judgment to be formed from the experiment which took place, in that same year, to trade at Chusan with the specific leave of the emperor, the privilege would not seem to be a very valuable one. Captain Mackintosh, of the company's ship *Hindostan*, who attended his majesty's ship *Lion* to the Yellow Sea, had free license to trade at Chusan if he pleased (on that particular occasion), and the ship was freed from all duties and port-charges, as pertaining to the embassy. He accordingly went there,* and "found the mandarins and people perfectly well disposed to comply with the emperor's orders in respect to the privileges to be granted to the captain and his officers in the purchase of a cargo there; and tea and silk were much cheaper than elsewhere: but the Chusan traders were not prepared for so extensive a concern as a cargo of goods fitted for the European market to fill a ship of the size of the *Hindostan*, full 1200 tons, nor for the purchase of the European goods on board her, better calculated for a larger city. They would therefore expect *specie* for most of the articles they could furnish for the *Hindostan*, which had not been provided by her commander. He found it therefore expedient to proceed to Canton."

As it was hoped that the embassy had not been without its effect in conciliating the good-will of the Chinese government to the British trade, it was resolved, shortly afterward, to follow it up by a letter from his majesty to the emperor, accompanied by presents. These accordingly reached Canton in January, 1795, with letters and presents from the ministers, and the chairman of the East India Company, to the viceroy; and the whole were conveyed into the city by the chief of the British factory. The viceroy received the address to the emperor with much satisfaction, and forwarded it, together with the presents, to Peking, from whence a reply,

* Staunton's Embassy, vol. ii., p. 523.

The Emperor Kien-loong.

with corresponding presents, was afterward returned. Objections, however, were made to accepting the letters and gifts intended for the heads of the Canton government, on the ground of its not being allowable for Chinese ministers to entertain a correspondence with the officers of a foreign government. It was recorded on this occasion, as well as on a subsequent one in 1805, that *tribute* had been sent by the King of England to the "Son of Heaven," and the record was quoted not long since by the Canton government in an official paper addressed to the writer of this, as president of the select committee in China, who stated, of course, in reply, that *presents* had been sent, but no tribute.

No untoward events occurred, for several years subsequent to the embassy, to interrupt the quiet progress of commercial affairs at Canton. The mandarins had improved in their conduct towards the merchants, and the highly objectionable measure of stopping the trade on the most trifling occasions had not been lately resorted to by the Chinese. At the same time, some of the heaviest burdens on the European trade still continued, being too profitable to both the local government and the Hong merchants to be readily abandoned by them. The most objectionable of these were, the *Consoo* fund, arising from a rate which the Hongs were permitted to levy upon the foreign commerce, in order to meet the heavy demands of the government on themselves; and the inordinate amount of the port-charges and fees.

An unfortunate occurrence, however, in 1800, threatened for some time to place British affairs at Canton in some jeopardy, although proceeding, as very usual on such occasions, from the fault of the natives. While his majesty's schooner *Providence* was lying at Whampoa, a party of Chinese in a small boat appeared one night to be attempting to cut the schooner's cable. As they returned no answer on being hailed, a shot was fired into the boat, by which one Chinese was wounded, and another, who jumped overboard in his fright, was drowned. The government, as usual, demanded that the person who fired the musket should be delivered up; but Captain Dilkes, who was then in China, commanding his majesty's ship *Madras*, required, on the other hand, that the Chinese in the boat should be punished for their delinquency; and refused to deliver up the seaman, or even to allow him to be tried, except in his own presence. The wounded Chinese at length recovered, and so the correspondence closed; but, some time afterward, an abstract of the Chinese law relating to homicide was handed to the select committee by the local government; although the shameful injustice and perfidy with which, on several occasions, the mandarins had treated foreigners accused of such offences, gave them no right to expect that their laws should be much attended to.

It was in the year 1802 that the American flag was first hoisted at Canton. The consular agent for the United States, who was, in all cases, appointed from among the American merchants resident in China, was simply a commercial officer, and called a *Tae-pan*, or factory chief, by the Chinese. He received no salary whatever from his government, but was permitted to levy fees in the transaction of business with his countrymen, besides trading on his own account. The American flag continued to fly at Canton until very lately, notwithstanding the interruption which the trade of the United States, for some time previous to 1815, experienced by the war with England; but in the year 1832 a dispute occurred between the consul for the time being and the captain of an American frigate then on a visit to China. The captain having failed to call upon the consul, the latter took offence on the occasion, and the two republicans were too tenacious of their respective ranks and dignities to come to an accommodation. The flag was struck, and the consul proceeded home.

An occurrence of some importance, in 1802, tended to establish, beyond all doubt, a point which had sometimes been questioned; and this was the nature of the tenure on which the Portuguese held *Macao* of the Chinese. It was in that year that Lord Wellesley, Governor-general of India, being apprehensive that the French republic had some designs against the Portuguese establishments in the East, considered it necessary to garrison the principal settlements of our "ancient ally" with British troops; and accordingly an expedition was sent from Bengal to take Macao under our protection. The Portuguese would have admitted the offered aid—indeed, they had not the power to refuse it—but the leave of the real masters had never been asked. The Viceroy of Canton indignantly repelled the idea of any portion of the Chinese empire needing aid from foreigners, and required the troops immediately to depart. In the meanwhile it fortunately happened that the brig *Telegraph*, despatched by the court of directors with news of the peace in Europe, arrived off Macao, and the whole of the troops accordingly returned at once to Bengal on the 3d of July. The Portuguese did not fail on this occasion to carry on their customary intrigues with the Chinese government, with whom they did their best to ingratiate themselves, by misrepresenting the views and designs of the English. An unfortunate priest, named Rodrigues, from whose knowledge of the Chinese language considerable assistance had been derived during the stay of the expedition, was in consequence so persecuted by his countrymen that he was compelled to quit the place. The Portuguese, however, have since had ample leisure to repent their short-sighted and narrow policy towards our countrymen, which had the effect of driving the whole of the Indian opium-trade from Macao to Lintin, and thereby depriving the former place of its most fertile, and indeed *only*, source of wealth.

The advantages of establishing, if possible, some commercial relations with the King of Cochin-china, on the part of the British, had been a subject of attention for some time, when the present Lord Strathallan, at that period Mr. Drummond, president of the select committee at Canton, appointed Mr. Roberts, a member of the factory, to proceed on that service in November, 1803. That gentleman was directed to attend to the instructions of the Governor-general of India, from whom he was the bearer of a letter to the Cochin-chinese king. Mr. Roberts was civilly received, and met with much liberal and friendly assistance from the French missionaries at Hue-foo, the capital. He had two audiences of the king, with an interchange of presents; but the council, with the usual cautious and exclusive spirit of the ultra-gangetic nations, would not consent to any written treaty of commerce; and the envoy returned to Canton, after some months' residence, without having been able to establish the ends contemplated: nor was the more recent expedition of Mr. John Crawfurd, to the same country, attended with any better success. It appeared, subsequently to Mr. Roberts's mission, that reports prejudicial to the English were raised by a Portuguese of Macao, named D'Abrio, stating that they meditated an attack on the country. Much alarm was excited, and, when the *Discovery* surveying vessel appeared on the coast, refreshments were denied to her.

The considerable naval force which had been maintained by France in the eastern seas for the annoyance of our India and China trade, had directed the particular attention of the company to the due arming of their ships, and an occasion occurred, in 1805, when the efficiency of those noble vessels was signally proved. The China fleet, consisting of sixteen sail, under the command of the senior officer, Captain Dance, was homeward bound on the 15th February, when it fell in with the French squadron, under Admiral Linois, who had been cruising for some time to the north of the straits, with the express view of cutting them off. The fleet, of which most of the ships mounted thirty guns and upwards, formed in order of battle, and advanced boldly to the engagement, the van being led by Captain Timins of the *Royal George*, who engaged the admiral's ship, a vessel of eighty guns, and received upwards of sixty shot in his hull and rigging. The fight concluded by the French squadron setting all sail, and leaving the English in quiet possession of the field, as well as of the immense amount of national property of which they were in charge. The commodore of the fleet was knighted in approbation of his gallant conduct, and the commanders of all the ships presented with swords, and other marks of distinction. This highly respectable service has been dissolved by the operation of the act which deprived the East India Company of their former privileges.

About this period, or shortly afterward, commenced the career of the Chinese pirates, called, after the Portuguese of Macao, *Ladrones*, who for some years spread terror along the coasts of the Canton province, and even up the river itself, as far as the city. The southern shores of China, from the innumerable islands with which they are studded, have always given employment and shelter to a hardy race of fishermen, whose poverty, joined to their independent habits, has at different periods led them to combine in large bodies for piratical purposes, in defiance of the weak and inefficient maritime force by which the coasts of the empire are guarded. The power of the celebrated leader Koshinga, and his successes against the Dutch settlers on Formosa during the seventeenth century, have been already noticed; and a squadron scarcely less formidable was destined to appear during the period which elapsed between 1806 and 1810. Very particular accounts have been obtained of these singular freebooters, not only from a Chinese work, but from the personal narratives of Messrs. Turner and Glasspoole, two Englishmen who had the misfortune to fall into their hands, and who were compelled under pain of death to attend the pirates in all their expeditions.

But however great their contempt for the imperial fleet of China, or any other native force to which they might be opposed, these Ladrones never willingly engaged a European vessel larger than a boat, and the following observations of the Emperor Kânghy seem to show that their predecessors in his time were equally cautious. "We have lately heard, from the pirate who surrendered and threw himself upon our mercy, that when his companions went to plunder vessels on the seas, it was their practice to avoid all European ships, being afraid of their fire-arms," &c. The force and number of the later squadron of freebooters have been pretty accurately ascertained from the accounts of Messrs. Glasspoole and Turner. Their junks or vessels amounted in 1810 to about 600 of various sizes, from 80 to 300 tons, of which the largest seldom mounted more than twelve guns, varying from six to eighteen pounders, which had been either purchased from European ships, or taken from the Chinese; but chiefly the latter. Their hand arms were pikes, with bamboo shafts, from fourteen to eighteen feet long, and they used, besides, the common Chinese pike, with a handle of solid wood, and an iron point, consisting of a slightly curved blade. They had also short stabbing-swords, not two feet in length. Their guns, as usual, were mounted on solid timber, without trucks, breechings, or tackles, and run out right abeam, so as to be fired only when they could be brought to bear upon the object, by wearing the vessel! The broadside being fired, they hauled off to reload, which is a difficult and tedious operation with the Chinese. The largest junks carried between 100 and 200 men, and were furnished each with an armed boat for committing depredations among the towns and villages on shore. Few narratives can be more interesting than that of Mr. Glasspoole, which was published in the United Service Journal, but which cannot be detailed in this place. Both that gentleman and Mr. Turner were ransomed for considerable sums by their friends at Canton, and escaped happily to relate their singular captivity and adventures.

Not the least remarkable feature about this formidable fleet of pirates was its being, subsequent to the death of its original chief, very ably governed by his wife, who appointed her lieutenants for active service. A very severe code of laws for the government of the squadron, or of its several divisions, was enforced, and a regular appropriation made of all captured property. Marriages were strictly observed, and all promiscuous intercourse and violence to women rigorously punished. Passes were granted to the Chinese junks or boats which submitted to the pirates; but all such as were captured in government vessels, and indeed all who opposed them, were treated with the most dreadful cruelty. At the height of their power they levied contributions on most of the towns along the coast, and spread terror up the river to the neighbourhood of Canton. It was at this time that the British factory could not venture to move in their boats between that place and Macao without protection; and to the Ladrones, therefore, may be partly attributed the origin of the valuable survey of the Chinese seas by Captain Ross; as the two cruisers which were sent from Bombay, at the select committee's requisition, to act against the pirates, were subsequently employed by them in that work of public utility, the benefits of which have been felt by the whole commercial world.

Finding that its power was utterly unavailing against the growing strength of the Ladrones, the Chinese government published a general amnesty to such as would submit and return to their allegiance; a stroke of policy which may be attributed to its acquaintance with the fact, that a serious dissension had broken out between the two principal commanders of the pirate forces. This proceeded even to the length of the black and red squadrons (which they respectively headed) engaging in a bloody combat, wherein the former was discomfited. The weaker of the two now submitted to accept the offers of the government, which promised free pardon, and kept its engagements; the leader was even raised to some rank in the emperor's service! Being thus weakened by the desertion of nearly half her forces, the female chieftain and her other lieutenant did not much longer hold out. The Ladrones who had submitted were employed by the crafty government against their former associates, who were harassed by the stoppage of their supplies, and other difficulties, and a few more months saw the whole remaining force accept the proffered amnesty. Thus easily was dissolved an association which at one time threatened the empire: but as the sources and circumstances, whence piracy has more than once sprung up, are still in existence, the success and impunity of their predecessors may encourage other bands of maritime robbers to unite in a similar confederacy at no distant period.

A considerable number of years had elapsed since the occurrence of one of those homicides, which, even when accidental, always proves so serious and embarrassing to the trade at Canton; but in the month of March, 1807, a case happened which showed in the strongest light the consequences which may at any time result from the riotous and unruly conduct of our seamen on shore, subject as they are in China to be supplied on the cheapest terms with ardent spirits, called samshoo, generally adulterated with ingredients of a stimulating and maddening quality. A portion of the crew of the ship *Neptune* had been drinking at a spirit-shop, and a skirmish soon took place with the Chinese, upon which the men were collected as soon as possible by their officers, and confined within their quarters. The idle Chinese, however, assembled in great numbers before the factory, and pelted the gates, as well as every European who passed, notwithstanding the presence of some Hong merchants, who had been summoned on the occasion. The confined sailors at length losing patience, broke through all restraint and sallied out on the mob, whom they scattered in an instant, and one Chinese was knocked so rudely on the head that he died.

The trade, as usual, was stopped by the Chinese, and the Hong merchant, who *secured* the *Neptune*, held answerable by the government for the delivery of the offender. Nothing could be elicited as to the identity of the individual, in a court of inquiry held on board the *Neptune*. The mandarins at first demanded that the men should be tried within the city, but the case of the poor gunner was retorted upon them, and the thing was declared to be impossible. It was at length arranged that an examination should take place within the factory, before Chinese judges, but in the presence of the select committee, and Captain Rolles, of his majesty's ship the *Lion*, who were provided with seats in court, while two marines with fixed bayonets stood sentries.

Eleven of the men, it was proved, had been more violent than the rest, but no individual could be marked as the actual homicide, though the Chinese still demanded that a man should be given up. It was at length settled that one of the eleven, named Edward Sheen, should remain in custody of the committee: the understanding at first was, that a fine to the relations of the deceased would be sufficient; but on the committee preparing to proceed to Macao, the government required his being left behind. Captain Rolles now interfered, and declared that, if Sheen was not permitted to be taken by the committee to Macao, he should take him on board the *Lion*, and the point was at length conceded. The local government being puzzled how to proceed, invented a tale, in which it was stated that Sheen, while opening an upper window, had dropped by misfortune a piece of wood, which struck the Chinese on the forehead, and caused his death. This was sent up to Peking as an official report, and an imperial reply was soon obtained, sanctioning the liberation of Sheen, on his paying a fine of about twelve taëls, or four pounds sterling, to the relations of the deceased. This singular transaction proves at once how easily the emperor may be deceived, and with what readiness the local government can get out of a difficulty. The firm and successful conduct of the committee and of Captain Rolles was much approved, and to the latter £1000 was voted by the court of directors.

Early in 1808, information reached India of the probability of ambitious views being entertained by France towards the East, and of the danger to which Macao might be exposed by the vicinity of Manilla, if the French should make that Spanish colony their own. In consideration of treaties, by which England was pledged to protect Portugal and its settlements against aggression, as well as of the interests which the English themselves had at stake in the neighbourhood of Canton, Lord Minto, having garrisoned the colony of Goa, by a convention with the governor of that place, deemed it fit to send an expedition for the protection of Macao, which he apprehended might be threatened by an enemy's fleet. It might reasonably be questioned how far such a measure was well advised, after the experience of the similar expedition just six years before, when it plainly appeared that the Chinese treated Macao as a portion of their empire, and the Portuguese as mere tenants at will: the result, at least, was an utter failure.

The Portuguese governor of Macao, with his 200 or 300 starved blacks, could of course pretend to offer no opposition; he in fact soon received an order from Goa to admit the troops; but, under a thin veil of compliance and affected friendship, it soon appeared that the Portuguese were doing every thing in secret to misrepresent the designs of the English to their Chinese masters, by whom they were forbidden to admit any force into Macao, without permission previously obtained. It being determined, however, by the president of the committee, and by Admiral Drury, who commanded the naval force, that the troops should land, a convention was signed on the 21st of September, and they were disembarked quietly on the same day. An order soon came from the viceroy for the troops to depart; and, when this was not complied with, the trade at Canton was stopped, and provisions denied both to the Indiamen and to the squadron of his majesty's ships. An edict of the Chinese observed, "Knowing, as you ought to know, that the Portuguese inhabit a territory belonging to the celestial empire, how could you suppose that the French would ever venture to molest them? if they dared, our warlike troops should attack, defeat, and chase them from the face of the country."

The admiral proposed to the viceroy by letter, that they should have an audience at Canton to accommodate matters, but no answer whatever was returned. All British subjects were soon after ordered to join their respective vessels, and his majesty's ships were moved higher up the river. As the viceroy still refused an audience to Admiral Drury, and declared that he knew no English authority but the company's chief, the admiral proceeded to Canton in person, and insisted on an interview, saying, he would be in the city in the course of half an hour. The viceroy persisted in declining the visit, and the admiral, instead of persevering in his intentions, returned to his ship.

Some time after this, the boats of all the men-of war and Indiamen were manned and armed for the purpose of proceeding on a second visit to Canton, and forcing a way through the line of Chinese vessels which were moored across the river, and filled with soldiers, in order to prevent the admiral's approach. On reaching the line, he pulled up in his own boat to address the principal mandarin, through the medium of a Portuguese priest, who acted as interpreter; no parley, however, was admitted, and after being fired at for some time, one of the admiral's men was wounded, when he ordered the signal to be made for attack. "The signal was not observed, and ordered not to be repeated. The admiral then declared his intention not to force the Chinese line, and returned with the boats to the fleet. Though a man of undisputed courage (as observed in the evidence before the Commons in 1830), Admiral Drury seems not to have possessed that cool and deliberate judgment which was essential to the success of the business he had been engaged in."* The attempt to proceed to Canton in the boats ought either never to have been made, or it should have been carried through. A pagoda was built by the Chinese near the spot, to commemorate their victory over the English.

The trade still continued at a stand, and the vice-

* Parliamentary Evidence, 1830.

roy issued an edict to repeat, that, while a single soldier remained at Macao, no commerce could be allowed. On the 8th of December, it was therefore determined to act on a document lately received from the emperor, which afforded a fair pretext for relinquishing the point in debate. A convention was concluded in a few days after at Macao, the troops were embarked, and Admiral Drury sailed away in the *Russell* for Bengal, on the 22d December. Thus, after a fruitless discussion of three months, the Chinese ended in gaining their point —the withdrawal of the troops; and their success was calculated to increase the arrogance by which they had always been sufficiently distinguished. The Viceroy of Canton, however, was disgraced and removed by the emperor.

The line of measures pursued by the president in China in concert with the admiral, on the occasion of the expedition, being disapproved in England, he was superseded by a fresh appointment from home. The Chinese, however, did not forget their grudge against Mr. Roberts, and they were encouraged by finding that he had been censured by the company; while the Portuguese, at the same time, with their usual servility, suggested complaints against him. Soon after he had again succeeded to a seat in the committee, and returned from a visit to England, the hoppo in 1813 issued an edict against that gentleman, expressly on account of his measures five years before, and it was declared that he was not permitted to proceed to Canton. Indisposition, it so happened, actually detained him at Macao on that occasion; but the committee were determined to deny the right of Chinese interference in the appointments of the English authorities; and, although the *Factory* reached Canton at the end of September, they would not permit the ships to unload until the interdict against Mr. Roberts should have been withdrawn. On the 22d November, the president addressed a strong remonstrance to the viceroy on the subject; but, before an answer could be returned, the gentleman who was the subject of discussion died at Macao of his illness. The president then declared that the principle on which the committee acted was in nowise altered by that circumstance; and as the hoppo issued a paper in which the local government disclaimed the right of interfering in the company's appointments, the trade was resumed.

The jealous and suspicious character of the Chinese government was eminently displayed in the year 1813, on the occasion of some presents from England being conveyed to a minister at Peking. Soong-tajin, a mandarin of high rank, who had acted as conductor to Lord Macartney's mission, and whose kind and conciliatory conduct to the English on that occasion, as well as when he afterward filled the office of viceroy at Canton, had made some of them his warm friends, became at length elevated to the rank of one of the emperor's council. It was therefore resolved in England that, both as an acknowledgment of past good offices, and an earnest of future ones, a letter and presents should be conveyed to the minister; the person selected for the performance of this service was a Chinese named Ayew, for some time linguist at Canton, and by him the gold box and letter were safely conveyed to their destination. He returned on the 25th August, with a card of acknowledgment from Soong-tajin; but not long after his arrival the linguist was seized by order of the government, and after a summary trial banished to Tartary, for the crime of illicit dealings with foreign barbarians! It was soon after learned that the unfortunate minister had been disgraced, and the present sent back; and it has been since remarked that the unguarded mandarin, whose amiable character distinguished him above the generality of his countrymen, never afterward regained his former power or favour with the emperor.

The foregoing circumstances came subsequently, in the year 1814, to be mixed up with discussions in which the select committee were involved with the local government, partly in consequence of the proceedings of his majesty's ship *Doris*, which was then exercising a very active blockade against the American merchantmen in the Canton river. In the month of April, the *Doris*, being on a cruise near Macao, captured the American ship *Hunter* off the Ladrone islands, and brought her in. The Chinese government immediately issued an edict, desiring the committee to *send the Doris away*, which they of course answered, by stating their inability to perform what was demanded. In May following, the *Doris's* boats chased an American schooner from the neighbourhood of Macao up to Whampoa, within ten miles of Canton, where they took her; but, before she could be carried out of the river, the Americans at Whampoa armed their boats and retook their schooner. This event, with the capture of the *Hunter* previously, commenced the troubles of 1814. The Chinese hereupon entered upon a course of aggressive measures, not against the frigate, but against the factory, which soon became intolerable. The local government first prohibited the employment of native servants: they then sent persons to enter the factory, and seize upon such Chinese as they found there. The boats of the Indiamen were molested while peaceably proceeding on their business on the river; and every attempt was made to prevent communication with our men-of-war.

The committee, seeing the hostile disposition of the government, determined on the bold measure of stopping the trade, as the only means of arriving at a remedy. The Chinese, somewhat startled at their old weapon being turned against themselves, began to display a more conciliatory temper, and, after some debate, a mandarin was appointed to meet Sir George Staunton, who was deputed to conduct the negotiation on the part of the committee. Accordingly, on the 20th of October, Sir George proceeded to Canton, accompanied by Sir Theophilus Metcalf and Mr. Davis. The first subject of complaint was the arrest of the linguist Ayew, for performing a service which was merely complimentary on the part of the English, and expressive of their respect for a dignified officer of government, who had conducted the first embassy through China, and been on friendly terms with its members. It was immediately replied, that his seizure was on account of a totally different affair, and that there was no intention of condemning the proceeding. Several meetings took place with the principal mandarins and one or two assessors, but little progress was made towards an adjustment; when the viceroy suddenly determined on breaking off the negotiation. The committee, upon this, resolved on issuing a notice to all British subjects to quit Canton: Sir George Staunton and the gentleman with him embarked in the *Wexford*, and the whole fleet proceeded down the river.

This step had the effect of completely curing the obstinacy of the viceroy. A deputation of Hong merchants was sent down to the ships, with authority to state that mandarins would be sent to discuss the remaining points in dispute if Sir George would return. On his reaching Canton, an attempt was made to retract the pledge, but this could not be persisted in; and, after several long and tedious audiences with the mandarins, the principal points in dispute were gained, and incorporated in an official paper from the viceroy, as the only security against a breach of faith on the part of the Chinese. The privilege of corresponding with the government under seal, and in the native character, was now for the first time established; an assurance was given that no Chinese officer should ever enter the British factory without leave previously obtained; and license was given to native servants to enter into the service of the English without molestation from the petty mandarins; together with some other points.

The measures above detailed were highly approved in England; but the conduct and disposition of the Chinese government for some time past had been such as to prove that the commercial interests of the nation in China were exposed to the utmost hazard from the chance of perpetual interruption at the will of a capricious and despotic set of delegates, who kept the court of Peking in profound ignorance of their own oppressive and arbitrary conduct towards the company's trade. To these circumstances is to be attributed the embassy of Lord Amherst in 1816, of which the object was to secure, if possible, the commerce of Great Britain upon a solid and equitable footing, under the cognizance of the emperor, and with the advantage of a ready appeal to him in case of need. The design of a mission to Peking had been for some time entertained by his majesty's ministers and the court of directors, when the arrival from China of the despatches of 1815 confirmed them in the resolution. It was hoped, as a collateral object, and one within the range of possibility, that an English resident might be admitted at the capital, or permission be obtained for trading to some of the ports on the northeast coast.

The embassy left England in the *Alceste* frigate on the 10th of February, attended by the *Lyra* brig, and the *General Hewett*, a company's ship, and arrived off Macao on the 12th of July, when it was joined by Sir George Staunton, the first commissioner, as well as by the Chinese secretaries, and the other gentlemen who were appointed from England to accompany it to Peking. The ships reached the Gulf of Pechelee on the 28th of July, but the ambassador did not land until the 9th of August. On the 12th the mission reached Tien-tsin, where a feast was conferred on the part of the emperor, and an attempt made to bring about the *practice* of the *ko-tow*, or prostration, before a yellow screen, preparatory to the grand performance of it before the emperor himself. This, however, was successfully avoided, on the plea that Earl Macartney had not been required to execute that act of fealty and vassalage.

As some uninformed persons have, without sufficient consideration or knowledge of the subject, ventured to argue that the non-performance of the *ko-tow* was too strict an adherence to punctilio on the part of both our ambassadors, it may be as well to show, that, putting (with them) all considerations of national honour and dignity entirely out of the question as mere vanities, and viewing the matter simply as one of commercial profit or loss, there is nothing to be *gained* by it, but the reverse. It was observed in the narrative of Lord Macartney's mission, " The Dutch, who in the last century submitted at once to every ceremony prescribed to them, in the hope of obtaining in return some lucrative advantages, complained of being treated with neglect, and of being dismissed without the smallest promise of any favour."* The fate of a later Dutch embassy was still worse; but it is fair to state their gains against their losses on the occasion. In return for beating their heads nine times against the ground before the throne, they certainly had some broken victuals sent them, as from the emperor. Of these, however, Van Braam observes, that they were principally sheep's trotters, "which appeared to have been already gnawed clean. This disgusting mess,"

* Vol. ii., p. 131.

he adds, "was upon a dirty plate, and appeared rather destined to feed a dog than to form the repast of a human creature." As this was the only advantage they gained by their painful corporeal exertions upon the ground, it may next be observed that the whole course of their treatment on the journey back was of the most mortifying and degrading character. This embassy occurred in 1795, during the era of small-clothes, and before liberal principles had been generally established in dress as in other matters; and these hapless Dutchmen were made, on the most trivial occasions of *ceremony*, to perform their evolutions, while the wicked mandarins stood by and laughed—and who would not?—at what has been diplomatically styled "the embarrassment of a Dutch-built stern in tight inexpressibles."

Sir John Malcolm, who understood, if any man ever did, the Asiatic character, has observed in one of his works:—"From the hour the first mission reached Persia, servants, merchants, governors of towns, chiefs, and high public officers, presuming upon our ignorance, made constant attempts to trespass upon our dignity; and, though repelled at all points, they continued their efforts, till a battle royal at Shiraz put the question to rest, by establishing our reputation, as to a just sense of our own pretensions, upon a basis which was never afterward shaken." Russia, whose ambassadors, like our own, have *refused* to perform the Chinese act of vassalage, has a residency at Peking, which may at least (as an advantage) be set against "les pattes d'un mouton," and "les ossemens rongés," which the Dutchmen gained by *performing* it. Admitting, however, that the balance was in favour of the latter, it may reasonably be questioned whether it is wise, on such occasions, to sink *all* considerations of national respectability. The Athenians were a politic as well as brave people; and when Timagoras, who was sent by them as ambassador to the King of Persia, had the imprudence to degrade his country by the act of prostration, he was condemned to die on his return.

But let us only do as the Chinese *themselves* have always done. Gerbillon tells us, that when an officer of the Emperor Kâng-hy was taken by the King of the Eluths, the latter insisted on his speaking on his knees; but the Chinese refused, saying he was *not his vassal*, but his own emperor's. A Chinese account of Japan expressly states, that an ambassador from Peking to that country refused the prostration, and, rather than compromise the honour of his nation, returned without communicating the orders of his court. But it has been mere ignorance to consider the *ko-tow* as nothing but a *ceremony*. The unthinking majority is led by names, and it is important to know that the prostration is the solemn rite by which the King of Cochin-china, and the rulers of the petty kingdoms of Corea and Loo-choo, do homage by their emissaries upon being confirmed by the Chinese emperor in the succession. The spirit and import of the *ko-tow* are those of the form by which the feudal tenant *in capite* did homage to his liege lord; and every country that, like Japan, has professed to be independent, has declined performing it.

However oddly it may sound to us, at the distance of more than 12,000 miles, the aspirations with which the court of Peking aims at universal supremacy are best expressed in the words of the old secular hymn:—

> "Alme sol, possis nihil urbe Româ
> Visere majus!"

All countries that send tribute, while their ambassadors go through the forms of allegiance, constitute a part of the empire, and their respective kings reign under the sanction of the "Son of heaven."

This of course signifies little enough at a distance, but the effect is felt in China; for any remonstrance against oppression, on the part of a subject of one of these states, must be stopped by such an unanswerable argument, which proves at once his relative inferiority and worthlessness; and what had been merely the rights of independence in another, become, in his case, rebellion. Mr. Barrow, who has really studied China, and understands it well, observes, that "a tame and passive obedience to the degrading demands of this haughty court serves only to feed its pride, and add to the absurd notions of its own vast importance." A Jesuit at Peking, quoted by Du Halde, observed, as long ago as 1687, that the princes of Europe should be cautious how they send letters and presents to China, lest "their kingdoms be registered among the tributaries."

As this is rather an important subject, and may become a question of expediency at some future time, it is as well to add Dr. Morrison's observations:—"There is a difference of submission and devotedness expressed by different postures of the body, and some nations feel an almost instinctive reluctance to the stronger expression of submission. As, for instance, standing and bending the head is less than kneeling on one knee; as that is less than kneeling on two knees; and that less, again, than kneeling on two knees, and putting the hands and forehead to the ground; and doing this once is, in the apprehension of the Chinese, less than doing it three times, or six times, or nine times. Waiving the question whether it be proper for one human being to use such strong expressions of submission to another or not, when any (even the strongest) of these forms are *reciprocal*, they do not interfere with the idea of equality or of mutual independence. If they are *not* reciprocally performed, the last of the forms expresses in the strongest manner the submission and homage of one person or state to another: and in this light the Tartar family now on the throne of China consider the *san-kwei kew-kow*, thrice kneeling and nine times beating the head against the ground. Those nations of Europe who consider themselves tributary and yielding homage to China, should perform the Tartar ceremony; those who do not consider themselves so should not perform the ceremony.

"The English ambassador, Lord Macartney, appears to have understood correctly the meaning of the ceremony, and proposed the only condition which could enable him to perform it, viz., a Chinese of equal rank performing it to the King of England's picture; or perhaps a promise from the Chinese court that, should an ambassador ever go from thence to England, he would perform it in the king's presence, might have enabled him to do it. These remarks will probably convince the reader that the English government acts as every civilized government ought to do, when she endeavours to cultivate a good understanding and liberal intercourse with China. But since, while using these endeavours, she never contemplates yielding homage to China, she still wisely refuses to perform by her ambassador that ceremony which is the expression of homage." This argument takes the question up on a higher ground than that sordid one of a mere commercial profit or loss; but, even according to *that*, we think it has been shown to be a losing speculation to kiss the dust before the Chinese emperor. The performance of the prostration by its ambassador places a country on a level with *Loo-choo*, and those tributary states whose kings reign by the sanction of the court of Peking. The non-performance of it (which has been the uniform course pursued by every *Chinese* ambassador sent to a foreign country) proves the independent sovereignty of a state and gains for its ambassador a far more respectful treatment than the contrary procedure, as experience has sufficiently proved.

In fact, the whole conduct of the persons deputed from Peking to negotiate the point of the ceremonial, joined to the information subsequently obtained, proved that the rejection of Lord Amherst's mission was not entirely on account of the *ko-tow;* and that, even had the embassy been received in the hurried and undignified manner which was very properly resisted, it would have been sent away again within a few days, contrary to the regulation by which forty days are assigned as the limit of stay. The provincial government of Canton well knew that a principal object of the embassy was to complain of the treatment which our commerce had there experienced, and its whole influence had in every way been exerted to frustrate the success of the mission. Lord Macartney, who declined submitting to the prostration, was more honourably received than almost any ambassador that ever entered China; and it was remarked that, if there was any difference in the treatment of Lord Amherst's embassy *before* and *after* its return towards Canton, it was in favour of the latter. But it was afterward clearly demonstrated that the emissaries of the provincial government had been busily at work: and even during the progress of the negotiations a rumour was heard that "one of the commissioners had *purchased* his situation, to which he had no proper title; that he had amassed an immense fortune by trade," &c., and other matters of the same kind, which, in conjunction with the treatment of the embassy, clearly proved the agency of the Canton viceroy and his colleagues.

Meanwhile, these same local authorities lost no opportunity of displaying their ill-will towards the *Alceste,* the *Lyra,* and the *Hewett* Indiaman, which had proceeded to Canton, and reached that place some time before the arrival of the embassy through the interior of China. The hoppo denied a cargo to the *Hewett*, on the plea of her being a "tribute-ship," looking, no doubt, for a handsome bribe from the Hong merchants for permission to load her. Leave was at the same time refused to the *Alceste* and *Lyra* to anchor at Whampoa, by which it was intended to degrade the British ambassador below the tribute-bearer from Siam, whose *junk* has free leave to enter the river! The *Alceste*, however, proceeded very leisurely on her way; and Captain Maxwell, on being fired at by the junks and the fort at the river's mouth, silenced the junks with a single shot; while one broadside sufficed to send the garrison of the fort scampering up the side of the hill, down which that defence is somewhat preposterously built. The effect of this decisive conduct was evinced in the short space of one day, by the arrival of all sorts of provisions to the *Alceste* at Whampoa, by a free consent to load the *Hewett*, and by a publication of a statement that the firing at the entrance of the river was an affair of saluting.

Those who composed the embassy were gratified to find, on their arrival at Canton on the 1st of January, that Captain Maxwell had not been deterred by any unnecessary apprehensions for their safety from duly maintaining the dignity of the British flag. The viceroy, it appeared, had a letter from the emperor for the prince regent, which he was bound to deliver in person to Lord Amherst. It was resolved by his excellency not to consent to any meeting with that functionary, unless the first place was yielded to himself and the commissioners, as Chinese of the rank of the viceroy were too much accustomed to arrogate to themselves the precedence on such occasions, even with their guests; and it was important at Canton, the seat of our connexions with the country, to take this public opportunity of maintaining his own rights. Accordingly, a yellow tent was erected, in which the viceroy, reverently lifting above his head with both hands the emperor's despatch, which was enclosed in a roll of yellow silk, delivered it with much solemnity into the ambassador's hands. The whole party then repaired to an adjoining tent, where his excellency, with Sir George Staunton (who had now resumed his former station at Canton) and the other commissioner, took their seats to the left; and the viceroy, his lieutenant, and the hoppo, on the other side. It was this same officer, by name Tseang Tajin, who had inflicted so many vexations on the English at Canton since 1814, of whom it was one of the principal objects of the mission to complain, and whose intrigues at court may be considered as a chief cause of its rejection. His looks on this occasion betrayed his unfriendly feelings; but an attempt which he made to say something uncivil met with such a reception as made him shrink within himself, and he was glad to hide his embarrassment in a hurried take-leave, which closed the business of the embassy in China. Mr. Barrow calculates* that Lord Macartney's mission cost the Chinese government a sum equal to £170,000 sterling. Lord Amherst's must have cost nearly the same during the five months it was on their hands; and it is hardly surprising if they are not anxious for many such expensive visits.

It has often been a subject of just remark, that this *unsuccessful* mission was followed by a longer interval of tranquillity, and of freedom from Chinese annoyance, than had ever been experienced before. From the year 1816 to 1829, not a single stoppage of the British trade took place, except in the affair of the *Topaze* frigate in 1822; and there the Canton government was glad to make the first advances to a resumption of the suspended intercourse, as we shall see. In 1820 an accidental occurrence took

* Travels in China, p. 605.

place, which gave rise to transactions of a very remarkable nature, proving in the strongest manner the anxiety of the government to avoid a discussion with the English. Some boats from one of the company's ships were watering in the river, when they were barbarously attacked by a party of Chinese with stones. The officer in charge of the boats fired over the heads of the assailants to make them desist, but the shot unfortunately took effect among some boys on a high bank opposite, and killed one of them. The Chinese, as usual, demanded that somebody should be given up; but the committee insisted on the urgent emergency which led to the discharge of the gun, as well as on the accidental nature of the case.

In the meanwhile, the butcher on board one of the ships committed suicide; and the Chinese, on hearing this, immediately took it up, thinking proper to assume that *he* must be the individual who had shot the boy! The utmost eagerness and haste were shown by them in appointing an inquest of mandarins, who proceeded to examine the body; and, as it was decided by them at once that the deceased butcher must be the homicide, the trade proceeded as usual. It must be observed, that the committee only granted permission for the ship to be boarded by the mandarins when they demanded it, and the whole proceeding showed the extreme anxiety of the local authorities to accommodate the affair, as soon as they despaired of getting possession of some victim to be strangled without a trial. But they carried the matter still further. A person of some rank, scandalized at this disgraceful proceeding on the part of the government, did his best to induce the father of the deceased boy to declare that he was not satisfied of the butcher being the slayer of his son. The mandarins immediately took all the parties into custody, and punished the instigator of the complaint, as one who conspired to promote litigation and trouble.

Two cases of homicide now remain to be briefly related, which occurred within a short period of each other, and which exhibit, in every point of view, a very remarkable contrast. The one which involved the Americans, proves the unhappy consequences of disunion among a number of private traders, each of them influenced by his individual interests and feelings; the other, which implicated the English, must ever remain an example of the benefits to be derived in China from a well-organized and steady union and perseverance against the barbarous conduct of the Chinese. On the 23d September, 1821, an Italian sailor, by name Francis Terranova, on board the American ship *Emily*, was the unfortunate cause of the death of a Chinese woman, whom he observed in a boat alongside selling spirits to the crew. He threw down a small earthen jar, which struck the woman on the forehead, and she immediately fell overboard and sunk, either in consequence of being stunned, or because the wooden pin, to which her oar was fastened, broke on her pulling away from the ship. The American trade was stopped until the man should be delivered up. They consented to his being tried by the mandarins on board the ship, and after this mockery of justice, in which not a single witness was examined for the prisoner, and the offer of Dr. Morrison to interpret was refused by the Chinese, the poor man was declared guilty, and put in irons by the Americans, at the desire of his judges. In a week after, complaints and discussions arose among those whose trading transactions were suffering from the delay, and, when it was required that the Italian should be delivered up for a second trial at Canton, the Hong merchants were told that they might take him. In the words of Dr. Morrison, he was "abandoned by those who should have protected him." All Europeans, as well as Americans, were excluded from his mock trial, and by daybreak next morning he was hurried to the place of execution, in opposition to all the delays and forms of Chinese law, and cruelly strangled. The Peking government was at the same time informed that he had been tried in open court, and that the American consul had witnessed his execution!

The success of the Chinese on this occasion was likely to inspirit them on the next, which happened shortly afterward, in the case of the English frigate *Topaze*. As that ship lay at anchor near the Island of Lintin, on the 15th December, 1821, an unarmed party of her men, who were watering on shore, suddenly found themselves set upon in a barbarous manner by the natives, armed with spears and long bamboos. The lieutenant in command on board the *Topaze*, seeing the desperate situation of his men from the deck, hurried a party of marines on shore, who by their fire covered the retreat of his sailors, at the same time that some guns were discharged on the neighbouring village to keep it in check. Fourteen seamen were carried on board wounded, some of them severely; while it proved afterward that two Chinese were killed and four wounded. Captain Richardson, on the 19th, wrote to the viceroy, complaining of the assault, and laying the blame of the transaction on the Chinese; but that officer would not communicate with him. Elated, no doubt, by his late success in the American case, he threatened to make the select committee responsible, and to stop the company's trade until two Englishmen were delivered up.

The committee, finding their remonstrances unavailing, perceived there was no better way of meeting the obstinacy of the Chinese than to embark in their ships, and quit the river until the affair should be settled. Accordingly, on the 11th January, the flag at Canton was hauled down, and the whole fleet proceeded to the second bar anchorage: this immediately produced an alteration in the viceroy's tone. On the 13th he issued a paper, declaring that, as the committee had taken such a step as to remove from Canton, he was convinced that they could not control Captain Richardson. They were therefore invited back, but at the same time informed that, unless the men were delivered up, the trade should be stopped: the committee, of course, declined to return on such conditions. In the meanwhile, as the frigate had removed to Macao, the Chinese hoped for an opportunity of saying that she had absconded; but her speedy return rendered this impossible. The discussions went on without any result (the country ships carrying on their business as usual) until the 25th January, when the Hong merchants brought down a paper from the viceroy, rejecting Captain Richardson's proposal to refer the matter to England, and reiterating the demand for the delivery of the men. The committee immediately ordered the fleet to get under weigh, and move below the river to Chuenpee. The Chinese pilots had been forbidden to assist them, but they moved down with perfect ease and safety, having their guns double-shotted, in case the Chinese forts ventured to fire.

Though it had been before declared that no farther intercourse could be maintained after the ships quitted the river, the merchants hurried down on the 29th to propose that the committee should address the viceroy, stating it to be Captain Richardson's declaration that two men had disappeared from the frigate; by which the local government would be enabled to show that these two men must be the homicides. On this ingenious proposal being indignantly rejected, it was next hinted that the frigate should go away, if only for a few days, to enable the viceroy to report that she had absconded. The committee reiterated their inability to return to

Canton, unless they were totally separated and absolved from the proceedings of his majesty's ships. Captain Richardson being present, took occasion to state formally that the time of his departure was approaching, in order to prevent their misrepresenting his motives hereafter.

On the 1st February a letter was received from the merchants, stating that an officer of government would be sent to Lintin to investigate the business; and on the 4th a mandarin proceeded, by leave of Captain Richardson, to a conference on board the *Topaze*, where he saw some of the wounded seamen. Visits of civility passed between the president, Captain Richardson, and the Chinese admiral, as well as the deputed officer from Canton; and on the 8th of the month, the frigate, having no farther occasion to remain in China, set sail. A number of attempts were subsequently made to induce the committee to make a false statement to the viceroy; but, when all these had failed, a paper was received from the Chinese authorities, fully and freely opening the trade, and absolving the committee from responsibility. They accordingly returned to Canton on the 23d February, the discussions having lasted just six weeks.

The local government was on this occasion for the first time brought to acknowledge that the committee had no control over, nor connexion with, his majesty's ships. The subject of the two men's death was subsequently renewed in 1823, but eventually dropped. The first lieutenant of the *Topaze* having been tried by a court-martial on his return home, was honourably acquitted; and the result was conveyed in a letter from the president of the board of control to the viceroy. It was, however, left to the discretion of the committee to present this letter or not, as they might deem most proper; and as an edict had in the meanwhile been received from the emperor, acquiescing in the conclusion of the discussions, the letter was withheld.

A calamity of fearful extent, affecting equally the Chinese and Europeans, which will not soon be forgotten at Canton, occurred towards the end of 1822; this was the great fire, which has been calculated to have equalled in its ravages that of London in 1666. At nine o'clock, on the night of the 1st November, a fire broke out at the distance of about a mile northeast of the factories, and, as the wind was then blowing with great fury from the north, it soon spread with such fearful rapidity that at midnight the European dwellings appeared to be threatened. Representations in writing were sent from the British factory to the viceroy, offering every assistance with engines and men, and recommending that the houses nearest the fire should be pulled down to prevent its spreading. This, however, was not attended to, and at eight o'clock on Saturday morning the factories were on fire. All efforts during that day to arrest the flames were rendered ineffectual by the violence of the wind, and on Sunday morning every thing was consumed, with the exception of a few sets of apartments. The company had goods to a very considerable amount burnt in their warehouses; but their treasury, which was arched with solid blocks of stone, and secured by treble doors, and which contained not much less than a million of dollars, remained safe and entire, though surrounded by the ruins of consumed buildings. It was said that full 50,000 Chinese were rendered houseless by this calamity, and the numbers who lost their lives were very considerable. A police and guard were appointed by the government to protect property near the river and about the factories; but this was greatly aided by a well-organized body of armed men and officers from the company's ships, who relieved each other by turns. Without these precautions, there was every reason to fear a general pillage from the multitudes of vagabond Chinese which had been brought together, and seemed ready to take advantage of the confusion. A considerable amount of property was saved by means of boats on the river, and these boats for some time served many of the Europeans as their only available lodging; but, through the assistance of a Hong merchant, who lent them his house, the company were able to recommence their business in a week after the fire. Such is the frequency of Chinese conflagrations near the foreign factories, that the recurrence of a similar catastrophe may at any time be viewed as a probable event.*

From this period a number of years elapsed during which affairs at Canton proceeded tranquilly, without accident or hinderance of any kind; but in the meanwhile the mismanagement or dishonesty of some of the Hong merchants was preparing embarrassments of another description. Their number had of late years consisted of ten or eleven, and of these one or two of the poorer individuals, who had never enjoyed much credit or confidence, failed for a small amount, without producing much effect on the general trade; but, about the beginning of 1828, the known difficulties of two of the principal Hongs began to display the evil effects of a system of credit, which had grown out of the regulations of the government in respect to the payment of the Hong debts.

It had been for many years enacted, by an order from the emperor, that the whole body of Hong merchants should be liable for the debts of their insolvent brethren to Europeans. It was at the same time ordered, that no money obligations should

* Another great fire took place in January, 1836, by which more than 1000 houses were destroyed; but the factories escaped.

be contracted by them to foreigners; but the prohibition proved utterly ineffectual. The solid guarantee of the Consoo, or general body, which afforded every certainty to the European or American capitalist that he should ultimately recover his loan, whatever might be the fate of the borrower, gave to the Chinese merchants such a facility in obtaining credit, as led some of the more prodigal or less honest ones to incur very large debts at the usual Chinese rate of 10 and 12 per cent. One of them failed in 1828 for the amount of more than a million of dollars. He was banished to Tartary, which, in Canton English, is called "going to the cold country;" but being a broken constitution, and withal a smoker of opium, he died on his journey. In the following year, 1829, another Hongist, who had borrowed very largely of Europeans and Americans, failed for a nearly equal sum. This last, however, was altogether a fraudulent transaction, for Chunqua (which was the man's name) made off to his native province with a large portion of the money: and such was the influence of his family, some of whom were persons of high official rank, that he contrived to keep his ill-gotten gains, and to make the Consoo pay his creditors.

These two failures, to the aggregate amount of about two millions of dollars, produced, as might be expected, a considerable sensation and loud clamours among the foreign merchants at Canton. Discussions subsequently arose with the Consoo, as to the period in which the debts were to be liquidated; the Hong merchants contending for ten annual instalments, while the creditors would not extend it beyond six. At length, by the powerful influence of the select committee, which was exerted on the side of the Europeans and Americans, it was settled that both the insolvents' debts should be finally liquidated by the end of 1833, which was about six years from the occurrence of the first failure. The eyes of the government were however opened to the mischievous consequences of the regulation, which obliged the corporation of Hong merchants to be answerable for the debts of any member of the Consoo, however improvident or dishonest; and it was enacted, that from henceforth the corporate responsibility should cease. The whole amount of the two millions was strictly paid up at the end of the limited period; and there was no real cause of regret to the foreign merchants in the rule which made every man answerable for his own debts; for, in the first place, the previous arbitrary system had generated a hollow species of credit, which was any thing but favourable to the trade at large; and, secondly, the debts, though they might seem to have been paid by the Hong merchants, were in reality paid by the foreigners; as a tax on imports was expressly levied for the purpose, and this had even been known to remain unremitted, after the object of its creation was answered.

The last two failures had reduced the number of Hong merchants to six, a body altogether inadequate to conduct the European trade; in fact, it was very little better than the *emperor's merchant*, or "monster in trade," noticed in the last chapter. The six themselves were, of course, in no way anxious that the number should be augmented; but the attention of the select committee became seriously directed to that object. It is a singular fact, that, notwithstanding the close monopoly enjoyed by the Consoo, and the opportunities of making money possessed by its members, the extortions and other annoyances to which a Hong merchant is at any time exposed, by being *security* for, or having any connexion with, foreigners, are such, that most persons of capital are disinclined to join the number. As the local government seemed disposed to show its usual indifference and contempt for the representations of strangers, the company's fleet of 1829 was detained outside the river on its arrival, with a view effectually to draw attention to the subject.*

On the 8th September an address was sent to the viceroy, in which the principal points urged were, the necessity for adding to the number of Hong merchants; the heavy port-charge on ships at Whampoa, amounting on a small vessel to about £800 sterling; and some check on the rapacity of the government officers connected with the customs. The reply and subsequent proceedings of the viceroy were in favour of making new Hong merchants, but unsatisfactory as to other points; and the committee, on the 16th November, renewed their remonstrances, and continued the detention of the ships at their present anchorage. The local authorities, however, showed no disposition to swerve from their last declaration, and the viceroy added, "As to commerce, let the said nation do as it pleases; as to regulations, those that the celestial empire fixes must be obeyed." The discussions continued without any alteration on either side until the 11th January, at which date the necessity was contemplated of sending the greater number of ships over to Manilla, until the Chinese government should be induced to concede the points in dispute.

The committee, at the same time, applied to the Governor-general of India to assist them by forwarding a representation to Peking, and suggested the expediency of some ships of war being sent to give weight to their representations: the supreme government, however, declined interfering without authority from home. There is reason to apprehend

* In 1832 a newly-made Hongist took for his establishment (according to custom) a particular designation, and the one selected by him signified "happiness, or prosperity, complete;" but this was rather premature, for, before he could begin trading, all his capital was expended in fees or bribes to the mandarins, and he failed.

that the Chinese authorities had been confirmed in their obstinacy by a knowledge of the fact that the committee were not unanimous, the majority being opposed to Mr. William Plowden, the chief supercargo, who at length, finding himself at variance with his colleagues, and of little weight in the factory, made up his mind to quit China, which he did about the end of January. The viceroy, on the 2d February, issued an edict, stating that an additional Hong merchant had been already appointed, and that others would follow; that the debts of the two bankrupt Hongs would be paid; and that the subject of the port-charges had been referred to the emperor. This appeared to the committee sufficiently satisfactory to warrant their ordering the fleet up to Whampoa, and on the 8th of the month the viceroy was apprized of their having done so. By the 1st of March three new Hongs were created.

Matters now proceeded in peace and quietness, and the ships were all laden and sent home as usual; but, in the following season, events occurred which threatened at one time to produce much confusion and mischief. The detail is instructive, as it shows from what small and contemptible beginnings the most serious results may ensue, in a place like Canton, where the Chinese and strangers live, in respect to each other, very much in what the lawyers call "a state of nature," that is, governed by no rule but their own passions or interests. A Swiss watchmaker, named Bovet, lodged in the same factory with some Parsees,* having a back entrance common to the premises. The watchmaker, being a violent fellow, took it upon himself to fasten up this gate, on the ground of the annoyance that

* Natives of Bombay, fire-worshippers, or disciples of Zoroaster, and the real representatives of those ancient Persians who fought with the Greeks. They left their country after its conquest by the Mahometans, and settled in the west of India, and are the most commercial of our Eastern subjects.

he experienced from the free passage. This, as might be expected, very soon led to a squabble: an unfortunate man, named Mackenzie, master of a trading vessel, being roused by a loud disturbance about nightfall, ran down with a stick, and struck one of the most active of the Parsees, upon which they all fell upon him, and inflicted such blows as occasioned his death.

The Parsees were immediately shipped off by the committee as prisoners to Bombay; but the Chinese presently applied for the delivery of the homicides for trial (or rather execution), quoting the case of the Frenchman who had killed a Portuguese in 1780.* At the same moment, an edict was issued by the viceroy, insisting on the removal from Canton, forthwith, of the president's lady, who had proceeded thither contrary to the custom by which females were restricted to Macao; and no unequivocal threats were held out, that force would be resorted to in the event of non-compliance. This, combined with the risk to which Mackenzie's murder seemed to expose the English, led the committee to order up from the fleet a guard of about a hundred seamen, and a couple of eighteen-pounders, informing the Hongists that, until the threats were withdrawn, these men should not be removed. This measure, having been adopted with celerity and vigour, was successful in intimidating the Chinese. An assurance was given that no violence was intended, upon which the guns and men were ordered down to the ships, after having been about a fortnight at Canton.

The court of directors had in the meanwhile disapproved of the detention of their ships in the preceding season, and superseded the committee, whose successors arrived in November, 1830, soon after the events above related. They found, as

* Page 66.

might be expected, much irritation prevailing on all sides, and were assailed by papers from the viceroy, insisting on the withdrawal from Canton of all the foreign ladies. Those actually on the spot were allowed to remain there until the conclusion of the winter season, but none came up in the following year, as it was not deemed a point of sufficient consequence to proceed to extremities upon; and indeed the very discussion itself rendered Canton an undesirable residence for females of any delicacy while it continued, the language and epithets used by the Chinese, in reference to them, being of a shocking description. But matters of a graver character were soon forced upon the consideration of the company's authorities.

A considerable encroachment had been made upon the river, subsequent to the rebuilding of the foreign factories after they were burnt down by the great fire of 1822, the new ground being principally composed of the rubbish and ruins of the former buildings. The space in front of the company's factory had been extended in common with the rest, and there remained only a corner to fill up in order to complete a small square, which it was intended to plant with shrubs, and convert into a garden for exercise and recreation. This seemed from the very commencement to excite the spleen of the Chinese, and the committee lately superseded had been repeatedly required to undo the work. As this appeared merely vexatious, the demand had been unheeded; and even when the Chinese, during the absence of the factory, had destroyed a portion of the work, it was subsequently restored by the aid of a party from the ships. The newly-appointed committee found things in this state on their arrival in China, and it was not long before an explosion took place.

Some time after the departure of the last ship of the season, and during the absence of the committee from Canton, the fooyuen, or viceroy's deputy, came suddenly, on the morning of the 12th May, to the factory, and, sending for the Hong merchants and linguists, demanded of them an explanation regarding the completion of the garden and quay in front of the company's factory, contrary to the orders of the viceroy. When these pleaded their innocence of any participation in the business, chains were sent for, and the linguists put in confinement, while the chief Hong merchant remained on his knees until the hoppo, who was present, had interceded for him. An order was given to remove the quay and restore it to its former condition, on pain of death to the wretched Howqua and linguist; and the fooyuen, ordering the late king's picture to be uncovered, seated himself down with his back to it. Soon after this occurrence an edict was published, containing eight regulations for the conduct of foreign intercourse, which tended to make the condition of Europeans in China even worse than it had been. No persons were to remain during the summer at Canton; the native servants were to be under stricter surveillance; all foreigners were to submit to the government and control of the Hong merchants, and not to quit the factories in which they lived; none might move up and down the river without a license; and restrictions were contemplated on the mode of addressing the government, contrary to the stipulations of 1814. In consequence of these threatening proceedings of the local government, notices in English and Chinese were issued by the committee, stating that, unless the apprehended evils were redressed or removed, the commercial intercourse would be suspended on the 1st of August following. A letter was at the same time despatched to the Governor-general of India, suggesting the expediency of an address from his lordship to the viceroy, to be conveyed by one of his majesty's ships. At the end of May the English merchants and agents at Canton published a set of resolutions, concurring in all that had been done by the committee, as the only safeguard against additional evils and encroachments.

On the 9th June an edict was received from the viceroy (who had, in the meantime, been absent on account of an insurrection in Hainân), sanctioning what the fooyuen had done, and forwarding the *emperor's confirmation* of the eight regulations which threatened the trade. The sanction of the emperor having been thus obtained to the noxious clauses, their abrogation no longer rested with the local government. It therefore became necessary for the committee to review their position, as the probability, or rather possibility, of any alteration in these threatened regulations previous to the 1st August could no longer be contemplated. They accordingly came to the resolution of postponing any measures as to stopping the trade, and any active steps towards obtaining a redress of grievances, until the result of their reference to India could be ascertained. This was accordingly made known by a second notice, and the Bengal government was apprized of the resolution. In the meanwhile, the stir made by the committee appeared not to have been without its effect upon the Chinese authorities, for no attempt was made to put the new regulations in force, and Europeans carried on their business unmolested at Canton.

In the month of November, his majesty's ship *Challenger* arrived from Bengal, conveying the letter of remonstrance from the governor-general to the viceroy. After some negotiation, this was delivered in a suitable manner to a deputation of mandarins; but the written replies, though they disavowed any intention of insult or outrage to the factory, were so far from satisfactory, and conveyed in so objectionable a mode, that the committee refused to accept them. Thus the matter rested, and subsequent instructions from England put a stop to all farther proceedings on this subject.

The smuggling trade in opium, which the exactions of the Portuguese at Macao drove from that place, in 1822, to Lintin, a small island between Macao and the entrance of the Canton river, increased with extraordinary rapidity from its first commencement, in consequence of the negligence or connivance of the Chinese government. This soon led to hopes (which were at length destined to be disappointed) that a surreptitious trade of the same kind might be extended along the whole coast of China to the eastward, not only for opium, but for *manufactured goods*. The local government of Canton had placed itself in so false a position, with respect to the emperor as well as to Europeans, by its long course of secret and corrupt practices in relation to the prohibited drug, that it was even disabled from interfering to protect its own subjects at Lintin, where the armed smugglers lay in open defiance of all law and control. Chinese were on several occasions shot from the smuggling ships with perfect impunity. The relations of the deceased, as usual, appealed to the mandarins, but the anomalous situation of these functionaries, in respect to the Lintin trade, always obliged them in the end to evade or relinquish the demand for satisfaction; and the company's authorities of course disclaimed all responsibility for proceedings out of the limits of the river, where the smuggling system being connived at by the mandarins themselves, they must take the consequences of their own iniquity.

The attempts to establish a surreptitious trade were soon extended from Lintin to the eastern coasts; but the success did not answer expectation. Beyond the limits of the Canton province, as *all* European trade was expressly prohibited by a long-established ordinance of the country, the mandarins had not the same shelter for corrupt practices; and, though opium might be introduced in small quantities, a smuggling trade in manufactures proved altogether visionary. The conductor of one of these experiments, in 1831, reported that he could obtain "no traffic besides opium; nor had any of the vessels which had gone to the eastward been ever able to deal in other articles, except occasionally a little saltpetre." It soon appeared, in short, that, without the consent of the supreme government of Peking, no prospect existed of an advantageous trade in manufactures, except at Canton.

So much, however, had been both imagined and asserted at home, regarding the facilities for trade at the prohibited ports of China, that it seemed desirable to the select committee, in 1832, to try a final experiment, in order to prove or disprove what had been given in evidence before Parliament. After ascertaining to what extent the disposition of the local authorities on the coast might favour such a smuggling trade, the next point of inquiry related to the ports or stations at which it might most conveniently be carried on. The *Lord Amherst*, a small country ship, was accordingly sent on this service, in charge of one of the company's servants, who was accompanied by Mr. Gutzlaff, well versed in the spoken language of China, and especially of the coast. Every possible advantage was thus afforded to the experiment, and the selection of the goods was as various, and as well adapted to the occasion, as a previous knowledge of the tastes or wants of the Chinese could suggest. The ship sailed on the 26th of February, and did not return until the 4th September. Among other points on the coast, she touched at Amoy and Foochowfoo in Fokien, at Ningpo in Chĕkeang, and at Shanghae in Keangnân. On the return, Corea and Loo-choo were visited. No device of ingenuity or enterprise was spared to dispose of the goods on board, and to establish a traffic with the natives. These showed a very hospitable disposition towards the strangers; but all commerce was effectually prevented by the mandarins, except in one or two trivial instances. Some of the officers of government were civil and forbearing, and even accepted of small presents; others, less condescending, were fairly bullied by the people in the *Amherst*, their junks boarded, or their doors knocked down, and their quarters invaded. Still the same vigilance was exercised to prevent trade, and trade was prevented.

On the conclusion of the voyage, it was stated in the report, that "much alarm and suspicion had invariably been manifested, on the part of the local governments, at their appearance; and to *fear* might be mainly attributed the civility which on some occasions they experienced." As a commercial speculation, it was observed, the voyage had failed, for they had "only succeeded in disposing of a portion of the goods shipped." These goods, being intended for experiment only, and not for profit, amounted only to about 200 bales in the aggregate, but comprised every variety of articles in demand at Canton. The larger portion were brought back exactly as they went, and, of the few things which were not returned, a considerable number had been *given away*. The loss on the expedition amounted to £5,647.

In proceeding to the northward, the *Amherst* found the authorities especially unfriendly, and hostile to commerce. "Our sudden appearance on the coast (says Gutzlaff's journal) spread general terror." The committee, in their report to the directors, admitted the unsatisfactory result of the experiment, and acknowledged that, though the Chinese natives were by no means averse to a more extended intercourse, the government had displayed the most effectual opposition. The expedition was upon the whole condemned by the court; and their animadversions were particularly directed against the fictitious characters and false names assumed by those who conducted the voyage. They commented on the inconsistency of the frequent complaints against the duplicity of the Chinese, while the English, at the same time, were presenting themselves in an assumed shape, and in direct violation of the laws of the country.

With some it may be a question how far the system of exclusion, practised by the Chinese government, justifies such means in order to defeat it; but there can be none whatever with regard to those deeds of violence on the part of individuals, who have themselves attempted no other justification than the extent of the provocation. Among these instances may be mentioned the shooting of Chinese from the smuggling ships near Lintin in 1831 and 1833, and the notorious case of an English subject, who, by his own confession in the papers, actually set fire to a mandarin's house. There can be no permanent peace or security for either natives or strangers as long as acts like these can be committed with impunity; and, under the circumstances of our anomalous relations with the country, it befits our government to place a very summary controlling power in the hands of whomsoever it appoints as its representative in China.

Towards the close of 1833, when the authority of the company was drawing to an end, and before it had been replaced by any other, the effects were seen in a series of violences that took place not far from Lintin, where some furious engagements occurred with the natives, and one of them was killed. In revenge for this, an unfortunate lascar, belonging to the smuggling ship principally concerned, who had been taken prisoner by the enraged Chinese, was put to death by them. An organized attack of armed boats from the opium-ships was now prepared against the town or village near which the occurrence took place; but the natives were prepared for them, and such a fire was opened from a small fort when the boats made their appearance, that it was thought better to return *quietly*, without attempting to land.

The relatives of the deceased Chinese, not yet satisfied, applied to their government for redress; but the transaction had occurred in connexion with the opium trade, and the provincial authorities found themselves hampered with the usual difficulties. A singular device was fallen upon by the Hong merchants :—One of these, by authority of the government, caused to be conveyed to Canton some individual out of a trading junk, in the harbour of Macao, who, for a bribe or reward, was to personate the culprit who had shot the Chinese. He was to be imprisoned for a certain time, and, previous to his trial, was to be furnished with a prepared story which was to acquit him of the murder, and convert the case into one of mere accident or misfortune. Information of this scheme reached the select committee at Canton, who, though they were pretty well assured of the safety of the individual, and quite certain that he was no British subject, still felt themselves bound to address the viceroy, and to protest against these strange proceedings, with which the English name was associated by report. After some trouble, and a renewed correspondence, a public edict was issued by the government, declaring that the affair in which the man was said to be involved was accidental, and "assuredly would not lead to the forfeiture of his life;" and it was subsequently understood that he was liberated.

On the 22d of April, 1834, the trade of the East India Company with China, after having lasted just two hundred years, terminated according to the provisions of the new act, and several private ships soon afterward quitted Canton with cargoes of tea for the British islands. One vessel had, previous to that date, sailed direct for England, under a special license from the authorities of the East India Company. A most important national experiment was now to be tried, the results of which alone could set at rest the grand question of the expediency of free trade against the *Chinese monopoly*. The success of it (whenever this shall have been established beyond dispute) will be universally hailed, not only as a vast national benefit, but as a signal corroboration of the leading principle in the comparatively new science of political economy. Years, however, must elapse before we can judge of its effects in counterworking the Hong monopoly, or, on the other hand, adding strength to that combination.

CHAPTER IV.

GEOGRAPHICAL SKETCH OF CHINA.

Eighteen Provinces of China.—Comprise about twenty degrees of latitude, by twenty of longitude.—Extremes of Heat and Cold.—Principal Chains of Mountains.—Two great Rivers. —The Grand Canal.—Crossing the Yellow River.—Great Wall.—Province of the Capital.—Other Provinces.—Independent Mountaineers.—Chain of volcanic symptoms in the west of China.—Manchow and Mongol Tartary.—Neighbouring and tributary countries.—Chinese account of Loo-choo—of Japan.

This chapter will be principally devoted to a succinct view of the chief geographical features of China Proper, under which may be included, on account of their unparalleled magnitude, and the important stations which they hold in the maps of the country, a particular description of the *Imperial Canal*, and of the *Great Wall*. The scientific skill of the Jesuit missionaries accomplished a survey of the whole of this fine country on trigonometrical principles, so admirably correct as to admit of little improvement; and, with the exception of the British possessions in India, there is no part of Asia so well laid down as China.

Since the time of the Jesuits' survey, however, an alteration has taken place in the divisions of the country. The provinces of China, which then consisted of *fifteen* in all, have been increased, by the subdivision of three of the largest, to *eighteen*. Keang-nân has been split into Keang-soo and Gân-hoey, Hoo-kuâng into Hoo-nân and Hoo-pe, and the western part of Shensy has been extended, and called Kân-so. These eighteen provinces constitute a compact area, extending (if we leave out the island of Haenân) from about 21° to 41° of north latitude, and measuring in extreme length from north to south about 1200 geographical miles, with an average breadth from east to west of nearly 20° of longitude, or something less than the extent north and south. Perhaps no country in the world of the same magnitude can be considered upon the whole as more favoured in point of climate. Being situated, however, on the eastern side of a great continent, China follows the general rule which observation has sanctioned in attributing to regions so placed an excess of both cold and heat at opposite seasons of the year, which its precise position in regard to latitude would not lead us to expect. In the month of September, near Peking, Lord Amherst's embassy found the thermometer occasionally above 90; while the huge solid blocks of ice which were at the same time carried about for use, and exposed on the stalls, proved the severity of the cold in winter. In the Yellow Sea, during the month of July, and at 35° north latitude, the temperature of the water at

40 fathoms proved to be 65°, while that of the air was between 80° and 90°. Even at Canton, the southern extremity of the empire, and nearly in the latitude of Calcutta, the mercury frequently falls below freezing-point during the nights of January, while in summer it sometimes, though not often, rises to 100°. Notwithstanding these apparent extremes of heat and cold, the climate must be generally characterized as highly salubrious—a circumstance no doubt arising in great measure from the extension of cultivation and drainage. As a confirmation of the observations of Humboldt, in his treatise of Isothermal Lines, it may be added, that the French missionaries were struck by the resemblance which the climate and products of northern China and Tartary bore to those of the east coast of North America; and that the wild plant *ginseng*, long a monopoly of the emperor in the Manchow country, has been imported in large quantities by the American ships to Canton, to the great surprise of the Chinese.

The whole surface of China is varied in elevation, rising generally in terraces from the sea towards the west, but there would seem at the same time to be no mountains of very remarkable height. The principal chains are two. One of these extends from Yun-nân along the borders of Kuei-chow and Kuâng-sy, passing to the north of Canton province, where a road is cut through the Mei-ling pass, which has been described in both our embassies: it then takes a northeast direction through Fokien, and terminates in Che-keang. The larger portion of the ridge to the northwest of Canton province forms the inaccessible country (at least to the native government) of the Meaou-tse, who have never entirely submitted to the Tartars. Even in Chinese maps their country is left a *blank*. The second principal chain of mountains extends from Sse chuen to Shensy, causing the Yellow river to make an abrupt bend northward through the great wall. There are, besides, mountains of considerable elevation westward of Peking, towards Shân-sy province, but the plains from which they rise are little raised above the sea.

The two principal rivers of China occupy a very high rank in the geographical history of the globe. Taking the Thames as unit, Major Rennell estimated the proportions of the Yangtse-keang and Yellow river at fifteen and a half and thirteen and a half respectively, and they are secondary only to the Amazon and the Mississippi. The Yangtse-keang, *the* river, or the "son of the sea," has been by some people styled the Blue river, but there is no such name for it in Chinese. It rises in Kokonor, the country between Thibet and China, not far from the sources of the Yellow river; turning suddenly south, it makes an abrupt bend through the provinces of Yun-nân and Sse-chuen, where it takes the name of the "Golden-sanded river;" and then flowing northeast and east, it subsequently makes a gentle bend southward, and receives the superfluous waters of the Tong-ting Hoo, the largest lake of China; thence, in its course towards the sea, it serves as a discharger to another large lake, the Poyang Hoo, in Keang-sy province; after which it runs nearly northeast, and flows past Nanking into the ocean, which it reaches exactly under the thirty-second parallel of latitude. This great stream runs with such a strong and prevailing ebb, that Lord Amherst's embassy found great difficulty in sailing up its course towards the Poyang lake, being unable to make any way at all, except with a strong northeasterly breeze. The flood tide was felt no higher than Kua-chow, below Nanking.

The Yellow river rises also in the country of Kokonor, but soon turning as abruptly north as the Keang does south, it passes across the great wall, and makes an elbow round the territory of the Ortous; passing back again across the wall, it flows due south, and forms the boundary of Shân-sy and Shensy; whence it turns sharply eastward and reaches the sea in latitude 34°. From the excessive rapidity of its stream, this river is nearly unnavigable through its greater length. In the old maps of China, the Yellow river has been represented as flowing into the Gulf of Pechele, *north* of the Shantung promontory. If, then, in the construction of the canal under Koblai Khan, its ancient course was turned, it is possible that this violence to nature has occasioned the constant recurrence of the dreadful accidents which attend the bursting of its artificial, but ill-constructed, banks and dikes. It is a source of perpetual anxiety and heavy expense to the government, and there is a tax on the Hong merchants at Canton expressly on this account. The enormous quantity of mud held in suspension by the waters of the Yellow river (whence its name) causes depositions at its mouth which tend rapidly to lessen the depth of water. It is remarkable that the two great rivers of China, which rise at a small distance from each other, after taking opposite courses to the north and south, and being separated by a distance of full fifteen degrees of latitude, reach the sea within two degrees of the same point.

The coast of China, south of the promontory of Shantung, is generally bold and rocky, except at the points where the Yellow river and Yangtse-keang empty themselves. The province of Peking is a sandy flat, and the gulf which skirts it extremely shallow, so that a large ship cannot approach the shore within many miles. The whole coast of the empire abounds in safe and commodious harbours, of which those on the south have been accurately surveyed under the East India Company. The east coast, however, though very correctly traced in the missionary maps, has still to be *nautically* surveyed for the purpose of shipping. Generally speaking, from the mouth of the Peking river to Chusan, the sea has been found to be as free from danger as in any part of the world.

For the internal commerce of the empire, however, the Chinese are rendered almost wholly independent of coast navigation by their Imperial canal, which, in point of extent and magnitude of undertaking, is, as well as the great wall, unrivalled by any other works of the kind in the whole world. The canal, as we have already had occasion to notice, was principally the work of Koblai Khan and his immediate successors of the *Yuen* race. In the MS. of a Mongol historian, named Rashid-uddeen, written in A. D. 1307, and made available to us by MM. Von Hammer and Klaproth, there is the following curious notice of it:—"The canal extends from Khanbalik (Peking) to Khinsai* and Zeytoon; ships can navigate it, and it is forty days' journey in length. When the ships arrive at the sluices, they are raised up, whatever be their size, by means of machines, and they are then let down on the other side into the water." This is an exact description of the practice at the present day, as may be seen by reference to the accounts of the two English embassies.

It must be observed, however, that although the canal has been generally considered to extend from Tien-tsin, near Peking, to Hangchow-foo in Chekeang, being about 600 geographical miles, the canal, *properly* so called, that is, the *Chă-ho*, or "river of floodgates," commences only at Lintsing-chow, in Shantung, and continues beyond the Yellow river. The principal river that feeds it is the *Wun-ho*, rising from the Taeshan in Shantung, and falling into the canal at its highest elevation, in a line perpendicular to its course. The waters of the river

* *Kingsze*, or capital, the present Hangchow-foo, the residence of the Soong dynasty.

striking with force against a strong bulwark of stone that supports the western bank, part of them flow to the northward, and part southward; at this point is the temple of the "dragon king," or genius of the watery element, who is supposed to have the canal in his special keeping.

One principal merit of this great work is its acting as a drain to the swampy country through which it flows, from Tien-tsin to the Yangtse-keang. Being carried through the lowest levels, and communicating with the neighbouring tracts by floodgates, it has rendered available much that would otherwise be an irreclaimable swamp. As it is, however, some individuals of the embassy, in passing through this desolate flat in 1816, were laid up with intermittents of rather malignant type. The large city of Hoae-gan-foo, near the Yellow river, extends for about three miles very much below the level of the canal. In passing along its dilapidated walls, upon which we looked down from our boats, it was impossible not to shudder at the idea of any accident occurring to the banks of the canal, as the total destruction of the town must be certain. Near this point resides the ho-tsoong, or surveyor-general of the river, who has charge of its banks.

Many readers will be aware that to the period of Yaou, something more than 2000 years before our era, the Chinese carry back their tradition of an extensive flood, which by some persons has been identified with the universal deluge recorded in the Old Testament. After a careful examination of their own written accounts, we feel persuaded that this deluge of the Chinese is described rather as interrupting the business of agriculture, than as involving a general destruction of the human race. It is observed, in the book of Mencius (Ch. V.), that the great Yu "opened nine channels; Yu was eight years abroad regulating the waters." This could hardly mean the universal deluge, and in fact seems

Passing a Sluice.

to have been some aggravation only of the natural condition of those low countries through which the Yellow river and canal now flow. Were they both of them to burst their banks at present, the deluge of Yaou would be repeated. It was for his merit in draining the country, or drawing off the waters of the inundation, that the great Yu was so celebrated.

To return to the canal. Many persons, and among the rest Dr. Abel, have not been disposed to estimate very highly the labour and ingenuity displayed in the construction of that artificial channel. He observes, "This famous monument of industry, considered simply as a channel of communication between different parts of the empire, appears to have been somewhat overrated as an example of the immense power of human labour and of human art. In every part of its course it passes through alluvial soil, readily penetrated by the tools of workmen, and is intersected by numerous streams. It would be difficult to find any part of it carried through twenty miles of country unaided by tributary rivers. The sluices which keep its necessary level are of the rudest construction: buttresses formed of blocks of stone, with grooves fitted with thick planks, are the only locks of the Imperial canal. It is neither carried through any mountain, nor over any valley." Much of this is certainly true, and confirmed by the observation of Du Halde, that "in all that space there were neither hills, quarries, nor rocks which gave the workmen any trouble either to level or penetrate." But if the canal is admitted to be a work of high national utility in more lights than one, the simplicity of the means by which the end was attained can scarcely be considered to derogate from its merit: it would seem, on the contrary, to be a proof of the sagacity with which the plan was formed.

The following account of the process of crossing

the Yellow river, at the point where it is intersected by the canal, is given from two unpublished journals of the last embassy. "On our left (proceeding south) was a stream called the 'New Salt river,' which, like the canal, opened into the Yellow river; and on our right we had for several days, very close to us, the Yellow river itself, which just before this point of junction with the canal suddenly turns northeastward, after having run in a south-easterly direction. When we had been a short time at anchor, during which interval some of the chief mandarins visited the ambassador, we all got under weigh, and prepared to cross the famous Hoâng-ho. All the boats, on entering the river, struck right across the stream without observing any order, and gained the opposite bank in less than an hour. The weather being fine and moderate, and the water perfectly smooth, our boatmen were not so particular in the observance of their ceremonies and libations on the passage of the river as those of the last embassy; but every boat, I believe, burnt a few pieces of gilt paper, and let off a volley of crackers in honour of the occasion. The breadth of the river in this part was about three quarters of a mile, the direction of the stream northeast by east, with a current of three or four miles per hour, but the water not much more muddy or yellow at this point than it has been observed in the Pei-ho and elsewhere.

"The stream was certainly violent, and carried us down a considerable way before we could reach the opposite bank, which was lined with a great number of boats, of various shapes and dimensions, some of them being constructed exactly in the form of oblong boxes. Many of these were stationary, and laden with the straw or stalk of the *holcus sorghum*, and with coarse reeds, ready to be transported to different parts of the river and canal for the repair of the banks. This assemblage of boats, though the greatest we have yet noticed in this part of China, bore no comparison to what may be daily seen in the river of Canton. When the current had carried us down some distance to the eastward, we had a mile or two to reascend the river, before we came to the opening through which we were to pursue our route to the south; and the passage in the vicinity of the bank, to which we kept on account of the current, was so obstructed with boats, that this was not effected under four hours from our first getting under weigh. The worst part was now to come in passing through a sluice, on the hither side of which the water, which had been confined in its passage through the abutments, raged with such fury as to suck down large floating substances in its eddies. This sluice upon a large scale was near one hundred yards across, and through it the waters rushed *into* the river at a rate of not less than seven or eight miles an hour. The projecting banks at the sides were not constructed of stone-work, but entirely of the straw or reeds already mentioned, with earth intermixed, and strongly bound with cordage.

"Through this opening or sluice, and in close contact with the bank on our left, our boats were successively dragged forward by ropes communicating with several large windlasses, which were worked upon the bank; by these means the object was slowly accomplished, without the least damage or accident. After thus effecting a passage through the sluice, we found ourselves nearly in still water; not yet, however, in the southern division of the great canal, as we had expected, but in the main stream of another large river, hardly inferior in breadth to that which we had quitted. We were told it communicated at no great distance with the great lake Hoong-tse Hoo, to the right of our course. The stream by which this lake discharges its waters into the Yellow river is marked in all the maps of China, but represented as totally distinct and unconnected with the grand canal. It seems evident, therefore, that the course of the navigation has been latterly altered here, either from the overflowing of the Yellow river, or some other cause. That a change has taken place seems indicated by the name 'New Salt river,' on the other side of the main stream of the Hoang-ho.

"Entered the southern division of the grand canal. A great deal of labour and contrivance has been employed here in constructing the embankments and regulating the course of the waters. In the first place, two or three artificial bays or basins have been hollowed out in the bank of the river, where the boats proceeding to the southward assemble in security and wait their turn to pass. There are then two other narrow passes, or imperfect sluices, subsequent to the first opening that leads from the river to the canal, having also broad basins between them, and embankments constructed as before, with the straw or reeds confined with cordage. The object of this repetition of sluices, with the basins between, seems in some degree similar to that of the locks on our own canals."

The important figure which the great wall makes in the maps of China entitles this vast artificial barrier to be considered in a geographical point of view. We have already stated that it was built by the first universal monarch of China, about 200 years before the commencement of the Christian era, or rather more than 2000 years from this time. It bounds the whole north of China, along the frontiers of three provinces, extending from the shore of the Gulf of Pechele, 3½° east of Peking, to Syning, 15° west of that capital. The emperors of the Ming dynasty built an additional inner wall, near to Peking on the west, which may be perceived on the map, enclosing a portion of the province between itself and the old wall. From the eastern extremity

Plan, elevation, and section of the Great Wall.

of the great wall there is an extensive stockade of wooden piles enclosing the country of Mougden, and this has, in some European maps, been erroneously represented as a continuation of the solid barrier.

The gentlemen of Lord Macartney's embassy had the good fortune to pass into Tartary by one of the most entire portions of the wall, and a very particular examination of the structure was made by Captain Parish. On the first distant approach, it is described as resembling a prominent vein or ridge of quartz, standing out from mountains of gneiss or granite. The continuance of this line over the mountain-tops arrested the attention, and the form of a wall with battlements was soon distinctly discerned. It was carried over the ridges of the highest hills, descended into the deepest valleys, crossed upon arches over rivers, and was doubled in important passes, being, moreover, supplied with massy towers or bastions at distances of about one hundred yards. One of the most elevated ridges crossed by the wall was 5000 feet above the level of the sea. It far surpasses, in short, the sum total of all other works of the kind, and proved a useful barrier until the power of Zenghis Khan overthrew the empire of the Chinese.

The body of the wall* consists of an earthen mound, retained on each side by walls of masonry and brick, and terraced by a platform of square bricks. The total height, including a parapet of five feet, is twenty feet, on a basis of stone projecting two feet under the brick-work, and varying in height from two feet to more, according to the level of the ground. The thickness of the wall at the base is twenty-five feet, diminishing to fifteen at the platform. The towers are forty feet square at the base, diminishing to thirty at the top, and

* See plan, section, and elevation, from folio plates to Embassy.

about thirty-seven feet in total height. At particular spots, however, the tower was of two stories, and forty-eight feet high. The bricks are, as usual in China, of a *bluish* colour, about fifteen inches long, half that in width, and nearly four inches thick; probably the whole, half, and quarter of the Chinese *Chĕ*, or covid. The blue colour of the bricks led to a doubt of their having been burnt; but some ancient kilns were observed near the wall, and, since then, the actual experiment of Dr. Abel in 1816 has proved that the brick-clay of the Chinese, being red at first, burns blue. The thinness of the parapet of the wall, about eighteen inches, justifies the conclusion that it was not intended to resist cannon: indeed, the Chinese themselves claim no such antiquity for the invention of fire-arms. The above description confirms upon the whole that of Gerbillon, about a century before. "It is generally," says he, "no more than eighteen, twenty, or twenty-five geometrical feet high, but the towers are seldom less than forty."

The same missionary, however, informs us, that beyond the Yellow river to its western extremity, or for full one half of its total length, the wall is chiefly a mound of earth or gravel, about fifteen feet in height, with only occasional towers of brick. Marco Polo's silence concerning it may therefore be accounted for by the supposition that, having seen only this imperfect portion, he did not deem it an object of sufficient curiosity to deserve particular notice; without the necessity of imagining that he entered China from the westward, to the south of the great barrier.

As a minute geographical description of each province of the empire would be out of place in this work, we will notice generally the points most deserving of attention in all, commencing with those which lay in the route of the British embassies. The flat, sandy, and steril province in which Peking is situated, offers little worthy of notice. The vast plain which surrounds the capital is entirely devoid of trees, but wood is procured from that long hilly promontory of Tartary which forms the eastern boundary of the Gulf of Leaoutung, and was named by Sir Murray Maxwell the "regent's sword." The most considerable town, next to Peking, is Tien-tsin, though it does not rank as a city: it forms the *trivium*, or point of junction between the canal, the capital, and the sea. Here are seen the immense piles or hills of salt described by Mr. Barrow, this being the depôt for the salt provided for the enormous consumption of Peking, and manufactured along the marshy borders of the sea. On entering the adjoining province of Shantung to the south, the attention is soon drawn to the commencement of the *canal;* and on the lakes, or rather extensive swamps through which it is carried, are seen the fishing corvorants, birds which will be more particularly described hereafter, exercising their profession for their masters in numerous boats. The surface in the north of this province and in Pechele is so flat and low, that the tide, which rises only nine or ten feet in the adjoining gulf, flows upwards of one hundred miles above the mouth of the Peiho. The country, therefore, consisting entirely of an argillaceous sand abounding in mica, is frequently laid under water, the general level not being more than two feet above the surface of the river at high tide. In this circumstance, joined to the vicinity of that constant source of inundations, the Yellow river, we may perceive, perhaps, an explanation of the great inundation or deluge, which the celebrated *Yu* is said to have carried off in the course of eight years by constructing "nine channels."

On entering Keangnân, which is divided into the subordinate provinces of Keangsoo and Ganhoey, the country soon improves, and inequality of the surface renders the locks, or floodgates, very frequent on the canal. This is certainly the richest province of China. It is famous for its silks and japanned goods, made principally at Soo-chow. Nanking, the ancient capital, became permanently abandoned for Peking by Yoonglo, in the fifteenth century. The area of the ancient walls, only a corner of which is occupied by the present city, measures seventeen miles in circumference, being rather more than the circuit of Peking. The reigning Tartar dynasty find it their interest to retain the modern capital, from its vicinity to Mougden, their birthplace, but the ancient one is greatly more central, with a finer climate, and altogether better calculated to promote the prosperity of the empire. Shanghae, a seaport near the mouth of the Keang, was visited by Mr. Gutzlaff in 1831, and described by him as the most considerable trading place of any on the coast: it is, in fact, close to Soo-chow and Hangchow. On the Keang, not far from the mouth, is that remarkably beautiful little island called the "Golden isle," surmounted by numerous temples, inhabited by the votaries of Buddha, or Fo, and very correctly described so many centuries since by Marco Polo. At no great distance from this are the gardens of Kien-loong, erected for him when he visited his southern provinces, and viewed by us in the embassy of 1816: they were laid out in the usual style of Chinese gardening, with artificial rocks and ruins, and wooden bridges over a piece of water. The embassy saw the room in which the emperor dined, and a stone tablet, having engraven on it some sentences composed by himself. The whole, however, was in a sad state of dilapidation and ruin, like almost every thing else of the kind that we see in the country.

In the district of Hoey-chow-foo, the most southern city of the province, is grown the best green tea. The soil in which it is reared is a decomposition of granite, abounding in feldspar, as is proved by its being used for porcelain. Thus the same soil produces the tea, and the cups from which it is drunk. In this province, too, is Foong-yang-foo, the birthplace of the founder of the Ming dynasty, who served, at first, as a menial in a monastery of bonzes. He then joined a body of insurgents against the Mongol dynasty, and became their chief. From beating the Tartars in every battle, and at length chasing them from the country, he was styled *Hoong-woo*, "the great warrior."

The adjoining province of Keang-sy is, perhaps, in point of natural scenery and climate, the most delightful part of China. The Poyang lake, in size approaching the character of an inland sea, is bordered on its west side by strikingly beautiful mountain scenery. It was only hereabout that the two British embassies varied in their respective routes. That of Lord Amherst proceeded along the Yang-tse-keang after leaving the canal, until it reached the lake; while Lord Macartney crossed the Keang below Nanking, visited Soochow and Hâng-chow, and, proceeding south and west, approached the lake at its southern extremity. The following account of the west side of the Poyang is from a MS. journal:—"Arrived early in the day at Nan-kang-foo. A long mole was built on the southeast side of the town, making a small harbour for boats to lie in, secure from the tempestuous waters of the lake in bad weather. While we were here, sufficient swell existed to make it resemble an arm of the sea, and the shore was covered with shingles in the manner of a sea-beach." A description of the mountains in the neighbourhood will appear in another place, as well as of *King-te-ching*, the most noted manufactory for porcelain, to the eastward of the Poyang.

From Keang-sy to the adjoining province of Kuâng-tung, or Canton, the passage is cut through the precipitous ridge of mountains which separates them. It was formed by an individual during the dynasty of Tâng, more than a thousand years since; and an arched gateway in the centre, of later construction, marks the boundary between the two provinces. The name of the pass, Meiling, is derived from the flower of a species of *prunus* which grows wild in profusion near the summit. After reaching the foot of the steep acclivity on the north side, the embassy were obliged to dismount from their horses, or quit their chairs, in order to walk up. On reaching the summit, where the rock is cut to the depth of above twenty feet, the view on the Canton side breaks upon the eye in full grandeur, consisting of ranges of wild mountains, well wooded. The rocks at the pass have been erroneously stated to consist of gneiss and quartz: they are, in fact, limestone, in common with the whole north of Canton province, and supply the gray marble which is so plentifully brought down the river. Immense square blocks of the stone which compose the mountain are piled up in pyramidal shapes on each side of the road down the southern declivity; the separate masses, however, preserving the remains of a horizontal stratification.

The only two provinces to the east, or left of the route pursued by Lord Amherst's mission, are Chĕkeang and Fokien, both of them bordering the sea. The first of these competes with Keang-nân in the production of silk, and the country is thickly planted with young mulberry-trees, which are constantly renewed, as the most certain way of improving the quality of the silk which is spun by the worms. The principal city of the province is the celebrated Hâng-chow, at the end of an estuary of the sea, where the tide, according to Barrow, rises six or seven feet. Close to this opulent town, on the west, is the famous lake Sy-hoo, about six miles in circumference, the water quite limpid, and overspread with the nelumbium. This extensive sheet of water is covered with barges, which appear to be the perpetual abodes of gayety and dissipation. On the coast, in the 30th parallel of latitude, is the well-known port of Ningpo, the former seat of European trade. The entrance is said to be difficult, as there are scarcely twenty feet of water on the bar at the highest tides. Fifty or sixty miles from it, among the islands on the coast, is Chowsân or Chusan, with a good harbour, but inconvenient for trade in comparison with Ningpo itself.

The contiguous province of Fokien preserved its independence against the Manchow Tartars longer than any portion of the empire, being supported by the squadron of the famous pirate (as he is sometimes called, though he deserves a better name) whose son expelled the Dutch from the adjoining island Formosa, when the Tartars had dispossessed him of the main. The people of Fokien retain an hereditary aptitude for the sea, and chiefly supply the emperor's war-junks with both sailors and commanders. A large proportion, too, of the trading-junks that proceed to sea pertain to Fokien. Two circumstances probably tend to maintain the maritime propensities of the inhabitants:—first, this province is so far removed from the grand canal as to afford fewer inducements to inland navigation and trade, always preferable, if practicable, to a Chinese; secondly, the proximity of the opposite coast of Formosa keeps up a constant intercourse by sea. The language or dialect of Fokien is so peculiar as hardly to be intelligible elsewhere, and this may chiefly be attributed to its long independence of the rest of the empire. *Ch* is always pronounced *T*, and hence the difference between *cha* and *tea* for the great staple production of China: the first name for tea being adopted by the Portuguese from Macao, and the second by the English from Amoy. This port, the name of which is a corruption of the native word Heamun, is well known to have been formerly the seat of the English trade, being placed on an island near the coast in latitude 24° 25′. Fo-kien is the great country of the black teas, and Bohea is a corruption of *Vu-ee* Shan, the hills where they are principally grown.

We have now taken a cursory view of the finest and most opulent parts of the empire. All the remainder are inland provinces, less known to Europeans, and probably much less suited to the purposes of commerce. Of these, one of the largest is Hoo-kuâng, divided by the vast lake Tongting Hoo,* with its tributaries, into two subordinate provinces, Hoo-pĕ, and Hoo-nân; that is, "*north and south of the lake*;" the last is to be distinguished from Ho-nân, a province to the north. Immediately adjoining, to the southwest, is the province of Kuâng-sy, under the same viceroyalty with Canton, but greatly inferior in wealth. North of Kuâng-sy lies Kuei-chow, a small mountainous province, of which the south boundary has always been independent. It is peopled by a race of mountaineers called Meaou-tse, who thus defy the Chinese in the midst of their empire. They gave the government much trouble in 1832, and are said to have been "soothed" rather than "controlled," to use favourite Chinese expressions.

The fact that an independent race of people exists in the heart of a country so jealous of its dominion as China, is certainly a singular one. The principal seats of these mountaineers are between the provinces of *Kuei-chow* and *Kuâng-sy*, though some of them exist in other parts of the same ridge, and in the Chinese maps their borders or limits are marked off like those of a foreign country, and the space left vacant. L'Amiot has given an account

* The English translation of Du Halde, we observe, states that the lake is very *venomous*, being thus absurdly rendered from the original, *poissonneux* (abounding with fish).

of Kien-loong's expeditions against them; but, as his narrative is taken from the official papers sent to the emperor, which are in general not more correct or veracious than Napoleon's bulletins, it must be received with some allowances. According to him, the viceroy of a neighbouring province had sent an army against the Meaou-tse, who enticed the Chinese into their mountains, and entirely cut them off with their general. To revenge this, Kien-loong despatched a leader named *Akuei* at the head of his best Tartar troops to subdue them. This person is said to have entered their country, and, in spite of all opposition, to have taken their king prisoner, and nearly exterminated the race. Still, however, they remain as independent as ever, and the Chinese are contented to keep them within their own limits by small fortresses erected on the borders.

The mountainous ridges occupied by this people extend full six degrees, or about 360 geographical miles, from west to east, comprising the southern borders of Kueichow, with the northern of Kuâng-sy, and the northwest limits of the Canton province; but the Chinese contrive to weaken their force by separating their different tribes. The men do not shave their hair like the Tartars and Chinese, but wear it tied up, in the ancient fashion of the latter people before they were conquered. The Chinese, in affected contempt, give them the names of *Yaou-jin* and *Lâng-jin*, dog-men and wolf-men. They are said to inhabit houses of one story raised on piles, occupying the upper part, and placing their domestic animals below. The Chinese, without entering their mountains, purchase the woods of their forests by agreement, and these, being thrown into the rivers which intersect the hilly country, are floated down into the plains. They make their linen from a species of hemp, probably the material of what is called *grass-cloth* at Canton; and likewise manufacture a kind of carpet for their own use. As soon as the children can walk, the Chinese say that the soles of their feet are seared with a hot iron, to enable them to tread on thorns and stones without pain; but this perhaps deserves little more credit than the grave assertion at Canton that the people have *tails*,—a piece of information which would have been duly appreciated by Lord Monboddo, in his speculations on the possible elongation of the vertebral chain in the human race.

In the month of February, 1832, a great rising took place among the Meaou-tse, extending to the neighbourhood of *Lien-chow*, on the northwest of Canton. The leader took the name of the "Golden Dragon," and assumed a *yellow* dress: this gave great offence and alarm at Peking, and it was apprehended that some of the "Triad Society," whose object is the overthrow of the Manchow Tartars, had got among them. They made their way into the plains, and defeated several bodies of Chinese troops with considerable slaughter, and the loss of their arms and stores. The commander-in-chief of a neighbouring province was among the killed. The mountaineers possessed themselves of several towns, but issued notices to the Chinese people that they made war only against the government. Of a thousand men, sent from Canton to recruit the emperor's forces, two hundred were ordered back again as entirely useless, from the baneful effects of opium.

The Viceroy of Canton (called by the English "Governor Le") proceeded against the insurgents, and, though they at first retired, it was only to return to the amount, it is said, of 30,000, who engaged the Chinese army, and slew 2000 of them, with a considerable number of mandarins. One officer of rank, who understood their language and customs, was sent to treat with them; but, on his entering their territory, they seized him and cut off his head, saying that the spirit of *Chang-ke-urh* (Jehanghir), the Mahometan prince who was perfidiously murdered at Peking, had appeared and advised them to make no terms with the faithless. While "Governor Le" was unsuccessful in the south, the Viceroy of Hoonân attacked the insurgents on the north, and retook one of the towns of which they had possessed themselves, killing a great number, and taking some of the chief men prisoners. At length, two imperial commissioners were sent from Peking, and they performed by policy much more than had been likely to be done by arms. Reports were spread of the innumerable forces that were coming to exterminate the mountaineers, and they were at the same time invited to come to terms. At length it was agreed that they should confine themselves to their hills, and that the Chinese should not invade their territories; and the emperor's troops were withdrawn. "Governor Le," however, was, in consequence of his ill success, deprived of his station at Canton, and ordered to proceed to Peking to be put upon his trial and degraded. The Viceroy of Hoonân, on the other hand, was honoured with the peacock's feather, a distinction of a military character, pendent from the back of the cap, and a multitude of rewards were conferred on others, significant of the important advantages which had been gained over the enemy. These, however, continue as independent as ever, and must be a source of some anxiety to the Manchow dynasty.

The province of Yun-nân, the most western part of China, which borders on the Burmese territory, and is not very far from Umerapura, the capital, is extremely mountainous, and abounds in metals and other valuable minerals. Gold is found in the sands of the river, and the Keâng, in this part of its course, is named *Kin-shâ*, or golden-sanded. There is a salt-water well near Yaou-gân-foo. Towards the northwest of this province, on the borders of the Thibet country, is found the *Yak*, or cow of

Thibet, the tail-hairs of which are used in various manufactures, particularly carpets. The large province of Szechuen, lying northeast of Yun-nân, is traversed by a portion of the great Keâng. From the name of "snowy mountains," applied by the Chinese to some of those which extend along the northwest of this province, bordering on the Thibet country, they must be of considerable elevation, and from their situation are probably higher than any in China. Salt springs are found here as in Yun-nân, towards the southwest. The province of Shensy, bordering on Thibet, has been enlarged and divided into two, of which the westernmost is called Kân-sŏ. Both this country and the adjoining province of Shansy, towards Peking, abound in symptoms of volcanic action, as the connexion of salt-water lakes and springs, with jets of inflammable gas and hot wells. These may be traced towards the southwest, through Szechuen and Yun-nân, to the Burmese country, where they also occur in abundance, and are seemingly a continuation of those volcanic traces which extend up through the Malay peninsula from Sumatra and Java, both which islands contain numerous volcanoes in full action. In Shensy, near the city of Yen-gân-foo, there distils from some rocks an inflammable substance, which the Chinese burn in lamps, and call Shĕ-yew, or *stone oil*, being probably, what its name imports, a kind of *petroleum*.

Although not precisely included in our plan, which is confined to China proper, it may not be amiss to take some notice of the countries immediately contiguous. The region of Manchow Tartary, formerly the territory of the *Kin*, whence the present rulers of China proceeded, has been generally described as consisting of three provinces. Mougden, or Shing-king, the birthplace of the reigning family, commences just at the eastern extremity of the great wall, and is bounded on the south by the Gulf of Pechele. Here it is that the emperors are buried, and their family mausoleum is established. The country is surrounded on the northwest and northeast by a stockade of timber, about eight feet in height, which has been incorrectly inserted in some European maps as a continuation of the great wall. At Mougden is erected a sort of epitome of the imperial government of Peking, with various tribunals for the regulation of all parts of Tartary immediately dependant on the emperor, whose subjects in this part are called Bogdois by the Russians. To the eastward of Mougden, and bordering Corea on the north, is the second province of Manchow Tartary, called Kirin: it is here that the famous wild plant ginseng, to which the Chinese attribute wonderful properties, is gathered as an exclusive monopoly of the emperor. Not long since, however, the same plant was brought to Canton by the Americans, having been discovered in their northern states, in a climate and situation very similar to that of Eastern Tartary. The missionaries, who constructed the map for the emperor, were at a loss to explain the extremes of heat and cold prevailing in these regions; "why countries which lie near the 40th degree of latitude should differ so much from ours (in Europe), in respect to the seasons, and the productions of nature, as not to bear comparison even with our most northern provinces. The cold begins much sooner in these parts than at Paris, notwithstanding the latitude of that city is almost 50°." A small English vessel, which went up to the Gulf of Pechele in the winter of 1832, was nearly frozen up there; and yet, during the month of August, in 1816, we observed that the fishermen on the coast went stark naked on account of the excessive heat, and their skins were burnt almost black by the sun. Nothing can prove more strongly that the climates of places are not influenced by their latitude merely. The third province of Manchow Tartary, of which the inhabitants are the Tagours, bordering on the Russian territory, is that of Hĕloonkeang, or "the river of the Black Dragon," otherwise called the Saghalien, or river Amûr.

The Western, or Mongol Tartars, commencing from the great wall, extend as a distinct race even to the borders of the Caspian. They are distinguished by their nomadic habits, dwelling in tents, driving their flocks to pasture from place to place, and accoutred with the bow for sport or war. Of those dependant on China, but governed through the medium of their own princes, or khans, the most considerable are the Kalkas, lying to the north of the Shamo, or sandy desert called Cobi.* They are all Buddhists, and the wandering priests of that persuasion are styled shamans, in Chinese written *sha-mun*. The Ortous are confined between a bend of the Yellow river and the great wall, which in this part is a mere earthen mound, about fifteen feet high. The principal seat of Chinese rule in Mongol Tartary is at Ee-ly, a place to which criminals from China (sometimes Hong merchants from Canton) are occasionally exiled: they are generally condemned to military service, and in some cases become slaves to Tartars. It is likely, however, that money serves to mitigate their treatment, for a former linguist of Canton, banished thither for conveying presents to Peking from the chief of the English factory to a minister of state, returned after a banishment of fifteen years, in very good case, and by no means dissatisfied with his residence.

Gerbillon, in the account of his expedition in 1688, gives a miserable history of the Mongol and Kalka Tartars. Entirely devoted to their lamas, whom

* In the *Shamo* desert, no water is to be had except in pits dug in the sand, and that of the worst quality. The surface is strewed with the bodies of animals, victims to thirst.

even the Emperor of China honours, on account of their influence over the various tribes, the Mongols live in tents of coarse felt, eat nothing but flesh half raw, and exchange their sheep and cattle for a few of the necessaries of life, having no value for money. Timkowski states that the usual medium of exchange is *tea*, made up into the shape of bricks. As late as the reign of Kâng-hy, the chief of the Kalka Tartars styled himself emperor; but, becoming tributary to China, in return for protection against the Eleuths, he submitted to the rank of wâng, or king. At the time, however, when Gerbillon visited Tartary, the brother of the Kalka Khan told Kâng-hy's envoys that he expected to be treated as the son of an emperor, and was so treated accordingly. The most westerly of the Mongol Tartars are the Calmucs, or Eleuths, stretching towards the Caspian. They waged war with Kâng-hy in 1696, but were defeated; and these victories of the emperor's army were, as we have before stated, painted by the Jesuits, and engraved in France.

On the western side of China, bordering principally on Szehuen province, are the Sy-fân, or Toofân, who, according to the Chinese, call their country *Too-pĕ-tĕ* (Thibet), and, like the other Tartar races, are worshippers of Buddha, or Fo, and under the dominion of Lama priests. Their inaccessible mountainous retreats make them pretty independent of Chinese control, though they are counted among the subjects of the emperor. They appear to have made some show in Chinese history previous to the dynasty of Yuen, or that of the Mongol Tartars, and their princes even compelled the sovereigns of China to yield them their daughters in marriage; but the arms of Zenghis Khan involved them in the common subjugation, and they have since remained very quiet within their hilly country, contented with the exercise of their superstitions. There is a Chinese resident at Lassa, the capital of Thibet, the high road to which from Peking lies through Sy-ning, in Kân-sŏ province.

To the south, bordering on the western part of Yunnân province, are the Lolos, the original inhabitants of a portion of Yunnân, and very similar in habits, religious observances, and language, to the Burmese, or people of Ava. The Chinese exercise but a doubtful control over them; for, though the emperor is said to confer titles on their principal rulers, they appear to be entirely subject to their native chiefs in all matters of consequence. On the outskirts of the empire towards the west are a number of towns or stations called *Too-sse*, or "native jurisdictions," where the aborigines are more or less independent, and where there is, in fact, a kind of divided authority, each party being immediately subject to its own chiefs. This is particularly true of the Lolos.

The two large islands of Formosa and Haenân being external to the main body of the empire, and therefore exposed to the power of any maritime and commercial nation that might wish to try the experiment of an insular settlement near the coast of China, are both of them deserving of some attention. Of these two, Formosa is by far the most favoured and the most desirable region. It lies principally between the 25th and 22d parallels of north latitude, just opposite the coast of Fokien, from which it is distant, at the nearest point, little more than twenty leagues. The length is nearly two hundred geographical miles, with an average breadth of about fifty; and the climate, as might be expected from an insular situation in that latitude, very favourable. The island is divided longitudinally by a ridge of high mountains; and the western portion, having been colonized by the Chinese since the Manchow Tartar conquest, is now held by them as a portion of the opposite province of Fokien. The side that lies eastward of the hills is still inhabited by the aborigines, who have always been described as a primitive and savage race, bearing some common resemblance to the Malays and to the inhabitants of the islands in the Pacific ; since they blacken their teeth like the former, and tattoo their skins, as a distinctive mark of rank, after the manner of the latter. The expulsion of the Dutch by the Chinese, nearly two hundred years since, from their settlement on the west coast of Formosa, has already been described in the first chapter. The island continued for some years to be held by the Chinese, independently of the Tartar conquerors of the empire ; but in 1683 it submitted to the Manchow emperor, Kâng-hy, and became annexed to the empire as a part of the province of Fokien. The position of Formosa, opposite to the central coasts of China, would render it a most advantageous situation for the promotion of European trade.

Haenân is rather smaller than Formosa, its greatest length being under one hundred and fifty miles, with an average breadth of about a degree. It is divided from the province of Kuâng-tung (to which it is subject) by a very narrow, as well as shallow strait, on the shore of which the principal city of the island, Keung-chow-foo, is situated. The climate of the island, from its situation south of the 20th parallel of latitude, is naturally hot, but the worst feature of the country consists in the dreadful hurricanes by which it is devastated during the southerly monsoon, and from which Formosa seems to be nearly, if not entirely, free. During the months of August, September, and October, the interior of Haenân, as well as its coasts, is peculiarly liable to the destructive typhoons for which the Chinese Sea is so notorious, and which have, at different times, wrecked many European vessels on the island, besides the numbers that have foundered at sea. Haenân has its aborigines as well as Formosa : they are said to inhabit the mountains towards the middle of the island, and occasionally to give trouble to the Chinese government.

The Chinese affect to consider all countries tributary that have once sent an ambassador; but those which have really been so, and whose tribute is periodically forwarded to Peking, are Corea, Cochin-china, Lewkew (or Loo-choo), and Siam. Corea (called Chaou-sien by the Chinese), is said to have become a kingdom about 100 years before our era: it is entirely ruled by its own sovereigns, but the investiture of a new king is obtained from the Emperor of China, who, whenever there is a vacancy, deputes two officers to confer on the next in succession the title of kuŏ-wâng. To prevent contests after death, the reigning king sometimes names his heir, and applies to the emperor to confirm him. The Coreans use the Chinese character, but have a syllabic alphabet of their own. The coasts of Corea are very far from being correctly laid down in the maps, nor is it surprising that the ships of the embassy in 1816 found them so erroneously represented; for P. Regis states that no European had ever entered the country, and that the only authority for the missionaries' map of Corea was a *native* map, brought back to Peking by a Chinese envoy, and adopted for want of a better. He expressly says, "There should be some farther observations on the south and east sides, which would complete the account of Corea as a part of the general geography of Asia." The chief productions of Corea are sable-skins, ginseng, and a strong paper used by the Chinese for windows, in lieu of glass.

Cochin-china, including Tonkin, bordering on Kuangsy province, had its limits fixed as a separate state about A. D. 250, by a brass pillar, which remains to this day, and of which the situation is marked in the Jesuits' map. The tribute of Cochin-china, as well as of Siam, is sent periodically to Canton, whence it is forwarded in charge of the ambassadors to Peking, and the vessels claim exemption from port-charges and duties. The late war, however, between Siam and Cochin-china has interfered with the regular transmission of tribute from both countries.

Lewkew, or Loo-choo, has been made in some degree familiar to us by the relations of Captain Basil Hall and Mr. M'Leod, since when it has been visited by Captain Beechey. There is every reason to suppose that the people of those islands are a jealous and suspicious race, and that their anxiety to exclude Europeans from their country was veiled, on the occasion of the *Alceste* and *Lyra's* visit, under a cunning and plausible semblance of courtesy and good-will,—for hospitality it could hardly be called. The King of Loo-choo derives his investiture from the Emperor of China, and sends an embassy with tribute about once in two years. Those islands seem to have had but little or no intercourse with China before the *Yuen*, or Mongol dynasty; and there is reason to suppose that the unsuccessful expedition sent by Koblai Khan against Japan may have had some communication with them, and originated the relations which have since existed.

According to the Chinese account of Loo-choo (printed at Peking with moveable types), the island was formerly divided into three nations or tribes, which were subsequently united into one. It is stated that they have a written character of their own (identical with that of Japan), in which is recorded the ancient history of the country, but that they also use the Chinese character. So far from the people of Loo-choo having no weapons, the same account relates that the foundation of the kingdom was laid by military force, and that, in the temple dedicated to the conqueror, there is to this day an arrow placed before the tablet where his name is inscribed, in conformity with his will, to show that his kingdom was established by arms.

They have also a copper coin of their own; but, as the metal is scarce on the island, it exists in no large quantity; and this may perhaps account for the first English visiters having seen none. The Chinese say they sometimes use *their* copper coin, and sometimes that of Japan, both of which are introduced in trade. Loo-choo, in fact, lies equidistant from both countries, and is tributary to both.

According to the same authority there is a nominal king of Loo-choo, but the real power is exercised by a minister, who is absolute. They have borrowed from China the gradation of nine ranks, and compiled a system of law from the penal code of their great neighbour. They likewise borrowed from China its best institution—a national education, with district schools, and public examinations for promotion. They venerate the memory of Confucius, and study his works, with the notes of his great commentator Choofootse. Their religion is that of Fo, or Buddha, and they have all the subordinate idols attached to that persuasion. Among other articles of food, the Chinese say that the Loo-chooans make a sort of *pemmican*, composed of meat and pulse pounded and pressed together, which is dried in the wind, and keeps a long time. Their dislike of foreign visiters no doubt arises in some measure from fear of giving offence to the Chinese, on whom they are dependant; a consideration which likewise influences the people of Corea in their exclusion of strangers.

The intercourse of China with *Japan* from the earliest ages seems to have been little better than an infliction of mutual injuries, the latter country being too independent and proud to yield the homage which was demanded by the former. The Mongol conquerors of China, urged by the spirit of universal dominion, made the most frequent and determined attempts, first to persuade the Japanese to send tribute, and then to subdue them; but all without success. The missions appear to have been principally on the part of China, the Japanese sometimes receiving them and sometimes refusing to communicate; but making few or no returns, and not only denying the homage which was so much coveted, but demanding it from the other party. At length an armament of 15,000 men was sent by the way of Corea, but they only plundered the coast and returned. Six years afterward an envoy was again despatched, who, with his whole retinue, was murdered by the Japanese. This led to an armament of no less than 100,000 men being despatched from China by Koblai Khan for the conquest of the country. On their arrival upon the northern coast a storm arose, which destroyed the greater number of the vessels; and the Japanese, attacking them on shore in several engagements, either killed or made captives of nearly the whole force, of which it is said that only three individuals ever returned to their own country. This agrees in the main with the account given by Marco Polo.

The Chinese dynasty of *Ming*, which drove out and succeeded the Mongols, suffered severely from the predatory attacks of the Japanese on the coast, in return for the hostilities which the latter had experienced from the family of Koblai Khan. Envoys were sent to remonstrate on the subject, and to invite the Japanese to friendly intercourse, in which a hint at homage seems not to have been forgotten. They were permitted to land, as they were not sent by the hateful Mongols; but no better success appears to have attended their efforts to obtain tribute, although some of the persons employed as envoys were priests of Buddha, for whom the Japanese have a respect, on account of their connexion with their own national religion. Th piracies along the eastern coasts of China were frequently repeated, but they seem to have led to no renewed attempts on the part of the celestial empire to punish or subdue Japan. Some commercial intercourse at present subsists between the two countries, principally carried on in junks from Ningpo and Amoy. The Chinese justly value the real Japan-ware above their own inferior manufacture in lacker, and this ware, with copper, seems to be the chief article of import.

CHAPTER V.

SUMMARY OF CHINESE HISTORY.

Early History of China mythological.—Three Emperors.—Five Sovereigns.—Periods of Hea and Shang—of Chow.—Confucius.—Period of Tsin.—First universal Sovereign.—Erection of Great Wall.—Period of Han—of three States—of Tâng.—Power of the Eunuchs.—Invention of Printing.—Period of Soong.—Mongol Tartars.—Koblai Khan.—Degeneracy of his Successors—who are driven out by Chinese.—Race of Ming.—Arrival of Catholic Priests.—Manchow Tartars take China—opposed by Sea.—Emperor Kâng-hy.—Kienloong.—First British Embassy.—Keaking's last Will.—Present Emperor.—Catholic Missionaries finally discarded.

Although a laboured history in detail of the Chinese empire is not suited to the character and objects of this work, still a rapid sketch of such revolutions as that country has undergone, more especially in the last Tartar conquest, seems requisite, in order rightly to understand some peculiarities in the customs of the people, and even some *changes* that have taken place among a race, generally remarkable for the unvarying sameness of its manners and institutions.

Without attempting to deny to China a very high degree of antiquity, it is now pretty universally admitted, on the testimony of the most respectable native historians, that this is a point which has been very much exaggerated. In reference to the earliest traditions of their history, a famous commentator named Choofootse observes, "It is impossible to give entire credit to the accounts of these remote ages." China has, in fact, her *mythology* in common with all other nations, and under this head we must range the persons styled Fohy, Shin-noong, Hoang-ty, and their immediate successors, who, like the demigods and heroes of Grecian fable, rescued mankind by their ability or enterprise from the most primitive barbarism, and have since been invested with superhuman attributes. The most extravagant prodigies are related of these persons, and the most incongruous qualities attributed to them;—according to Swift's receipt for making a hero, who, if his virtues are not reducible to consistency, is to have them laid in a heap upon him. "National vanity, and a love of the marvellous, have influenced in a similar manner the early history of most other countries, and furnished materials for nursery tales, as soon as the spirit of sober investigation has supplanted that appetite for wonders which marks the infancy of nations as well as of individuals."*

The fabulous part of Chinese history commences with *Puon-koo*, who is represented in a dress of leaves, and concerning whom every thing is wild and obscure. He is said to have been followed by a number of persons with fanciful names, who, in the style of the Hindoo chronology, reigned for thousands of years, until the appearance of Fohy, who, it is said, invented the arts of music, numbers, &c., and taught his subjects to live in a civilized state. He inhabited what is now the northern province of Shensy, anciently the country of *Tsin*,

* Royal Asiat. Trans., vol. i., *Memoir concerning the Chinese.*

or *Chin*, whence some derive the word China, by which the empire has been for ages designated in India. *Fohy* (often absurdly confounded with *Fo*, or Buddha) and his two successors are styled the "Three Emperors," and reputed the inventors of all the arts and accommodations of life. Of these, Shin-noong, or the "divine husbandman," instructed his people in agriculture; and Hoang-ty divided all the lands into groups of nine equal squares, of which the middle one was to be cultivated in common for the benefit of the state. He is said likewise to have invented the mode of noting the cycle of sixty years, the foundation of the Chinese system of chronology. The series of cycles is at least made to extend back to the time in which he is reputed to have lived, about 2600 years before Christ: but it is obvious that there could be no difficulty in calculating it much farther back than even that, had the inventors so pleased; and this date is therefore no certain proof of antiquity.

To the "three emperors" succeeded the "five sovereigns," and the designations seem equally arbitrary and fanciful in both cases, being in fact distinctions without a difference. The fictitious character of this early period might be proved in abundance of instances, and it is the worst feature of Du Halde's compilation that it sets every thing down without comment, and is filled with general and unmeaning eulogies out of Chinese works, whatever may be the subject of description. He observes that one of these *five sovereigns* regulated the calendar, "and desired to begin the year on the first day of the month in which the sun should be nearest the 15th degree of Aquarius, for which he is called the author and father of the ephemeris. He chose the time when the sun passes through the middle of this sign, because it is *the season in which the earth is adorned with plants, trees renew their verdure, and all nature seems reanimated:"*—this of course must mean the spring season. Now the person alluded to is said to have lived more than 2000 years before Christ, and, according to the usual mode of calculating the precession of the equinoxes, the sun must have passed through the 15th of Aquarius, in his time, somewhere about the *middle of December*. In a Chinese historian this strange blunder is not surprising, and only shows the character of their earlier records; but it ought to have been corrected in a European work.

Yaou and *Shun*, the last two of the five sovereigns, were the patterns of all Chinese emperors. To Yaou is attributed the intercalation (in their lunar year) of an additional lunar month seven times in every nineteen years; the number of days in seven lunations being nearly equal to nineteen multiplied by *eleven*, which last is the number of days by which the lunar year falls short of the solar. Yaou is said to have set aside his own son, and chosen Shun to be his successor, on account of his virtues. The choice of the reigning emperor is the rule of succession at the present day, and it is seldom that the eldest son succeeds in preference to the rest. To the age of Shun the Chinese refer their tradition of an extensive flooding of the lands, which by some has been identified with the Mosaic deluge. It was for his merit in draining the country, or drawing off the waters of the great inundation, in which he was employed eight years, that "Yu the great" was chosen by Shun for his successor.

He commenced the period called *Hea*, upwards of 2100 years before Christ. Yu is described as nine cubits in height, and it is stated that "the skies rained gold for three days;" which certainly (as Dr. Morrison observes) "lessens the credit of the history of this period." In fact, the whole of the long space of time included under Hea and Shâng is full of the marvellous. *Chow-wâng*, however, the last of the Shâng (about 1100 years before Christ), was a tyrant, by all accounts, not more remarkable for his cruelty or extravagances than many other tyrants have been. Frequent allusion is made to him in Chinese books, as well as to his wife, and various stories are related of their crimes. One of the emperor's relations having ventured to remonstrate with him, the cruel monarch ordered his heart to be brought to him for inspection, observing, that he wished to see in what respects the heart of a sage differed from those of common men. With the Chinese, the heart is the seat of the *mind*.

At length Woo-wong, literally "the martial king," was called upon to depose the tyrant, and all the people turned against the latter. When no hopes were left, he arrayed himself in his splendour, and, retiring to his palace, set fire to it and perished, like another Sardanapalus, in the flames. When the conqueror entered, the first object he perceived was the guilty queen, whom he put to death with his own hand, and immediately became the first of the dynasty *Chow*. This forms the subject of a portion of the *Shooking*, one of the five classical books delivered down by Confucius.

The Chinese have no existing records older than the compilations of *Confucius*, who was nearly contemporary with Herodotus, the father of Grecian history, and to whom Pope has given a very lofty niche in his Temple of Fame :—

> " Superior and alone Confucius stood,
> Who taught that useful science—to be good."

The *five classics* and the *four books*, which were bequeathed by that teacher or by his disciples, contain what is now known of the early traditions or records of the country. The period of authentic history may be considered as dating from the race of *Chow*, in whose time Confucius himself lived; for, although it might be going too far to condemn all that precedes that period as absolutely fabulous, it is still so much mixed up with fable as hardly to deserve the name of history. In his work called Chun-tsieu (*spring* and *autumn*, because written between those seasons) Confucius gives the annals of his own times, and relates the wars of the several petty states against each other. The southern half of the present empire (to the south of the Yangtse-keang) was then in a state of entire barbarism; and the northern half, extending from that river to the confines of Tartary, was divided among a number of petty independent states, derived from a common origin, but engaged in perpetual hostilities with each other.

The period of Chow, comprising above eight centuries, and extending down to 240 B. C., was distinguished, not only by the birth of Confucius, but by the appearance, in China, of Laou-keun, and, in India, of Fo, or Buddha, who were destined to give rise to the two sects which, subordinate to that of Confucius himself, have influenced rather than divided the population of China ever since. The estimation, however, which they have respectively enjoyed has been very different. The memory and the doctrines of Confucius have met with almost uninterrupted veneration to the present time; they have even retained their supremacy over the native worship of the Tartar dynasty; while the absurd superstitions of the other two have been alternately embraced and despised by the different sovereigns of the country. The mummeries of the Buddhists are a parallel to the worst parts of Roman Catholicism; and the disciples of Laou-keun combine a variety of superstitions; each sect, at the same time, being plainly a corruption of something that was better in its origin. We shall have to speak of these more in detail hereafter, under the head of Religions.

Confucius was respected by the sovereigns of nearly all the independent states of China, and was employed as minister by one of them. After his death, which happened B. C. 477, at the age of seventy-three, a series of sanguinary contests arose among the petty kingdoms, which gave to this period of history the name of *Chen-kuo*, or the "contending nations," and proved in after-times the ruin of the race of *Chow*. The King of *Tsin* had long been growing powerful at the expense of the neighbouring states: he fought against six other nations, and, after a course of successes, compelled them all to acknowledge his supremacy. The chief government began now to assume the aspect of an *empire*, which comprehended that half of modern China lying to the north of the great *Keang*; but which, after the lapse of a few centuries, was doomed again to be split into several parts.

The *first emperor* (which is implied by the title Chy-hoang-ty) being troubled by the incursions of the Tartars on the northern frontier, rendered himself for ever famous by the erection of the vast *wall*, which has now stood for 2000 years, extending along a space of 1500 miles, from the Gulf of Peking to Western Tartary. It has been estimated that this monstrous monument of human labour contains materials sufficient to surround the whole globe, on one of its largest circles, with a wall several feet in height. Another act of the same emperor entitled him to a different species of fame. He ordered that all the books of the learned, including the writings of Confucius, should be cast into the flames; many, of course, escaped this sentence, through the zeal of those who cultivated learning; but it is said that upwards of 400 persons, who attempted to evade or oppose the order, were burnt with the books they wished to save. It is not easy to explain the fantastic wickedness of such an act on any common principles; but one reason alleged for it is, the jealousy that this foolish emperor entertained of the fame of his progenitors, and the wish he indulged that posterity should hear of none before himself.

About the year 201 B. C., the race of Hân succeeded to the sovereignty, and commenced one of the most celebrated periods of Chinese history. It was now that the Tartars, by their predatory warfare, became the source of endless disquiet to the more polished and peaceful Chinese, by whom they were in vain propitiated with alliances and tribute. They were the *Hing-kuo* (erratic nations), against whom the first emperor had vainly built the wall; and under the name of Heung-noo (Huns) they constantly appear in the histories or fictions of that period. The first emperors of this race endeavoured to make friends of the Tartar chiefs by giving them their daughters in marriage. "The disgrace," says an historian of that period, "could not be exceeded—from this time China lost her honour." In the reign of Yuenty, the ninth emperor, the Tartars having been provoked by the punishment of two of their leaders, who had transgressed the boundaries of the great wall in hunting, the empire was again invaded, and a princess demanded and yielded in marriage. This forms the subject of one of the hundred plays of Yuen, an English version of which was printed by the Oriental Translation Committee in 1829, under the name of the "Sorrows of Hân." The impolitic system of buying off the barbarians, which commenced so early, terminated many centuries afterward in the overthrow of the empire.

The seventeenth emperor of Hân, by name *Ho-ty*, is said to have had considerable intercourse with the west. It is even recorded that one of his envoys reached *Tatsin*, or Arabia. It is certain that eunuchs, those fertile sources of trouble to his successors, were introduced during his reign, and it may be inferred that he borrowed them from western Asia, about A. D. 95. The reigns of the last two emperors of Hân were disturbed by the machinations of the eunuchs, and by the wars with the rebels called Hoang-kin, or Yellow Caps. At this time so little was left of the sovereign authority, that the emperors are frequently designated by the mere term *Choo*, or lord.

The period of the *San-kuo*, or "Three States," into which the country was divided towards the close of Hân, about A. D. 184, is a favourite subject of the historical plays and romances of the Chinese. A work, designated particularly by the above name, is much prized and very popular among them, and a manuscript translation of it in Latin, by one of the Catholic missionaries, exists in the library of the Royal Asiatic Society. Extracts from it might be made interesting, but the whole is perhaps too voluminous to bear an English translation in print. It is, however, as little stuffed with extravagances as could be expected from an Oriental history; and, except that it is in prose, bears a resemblance in some of its features to the Iliad, especially in what Lord Chesterfield calls "the porter-like language" of the heroes. These heroes excel all moderns in strength and prowess, and make exchanges after the fashion of Glaucus and Diomed, Hector and Ajax. One shows his liberality in horses, another in a weight of silver, or *iron* :—

> And steel well tempered, and refulgent gold."

Society seems to have been in much the same state, split into something like feudal principalities, hanging loosely together under the questionable authority of one head. That great step in civilization, the invention of printing (which arose in China about the tenth century of our era), had not yet taken place, and even the manufacture of paper had not long been introduced.

The leader of *Wei*, one of the three states, having at length obtained the sovereignty, established the capital in his own country, Honân, and commenced the dynasty called *Tsin*, A. D. 260. Having taken warning from the distractions arising from the interference of eunuchs and women in affairs of government during the period of the three states, a kind of salique-law was passed, that "queens should not reign, nor assist in public matters"—a good law, adds the historian, and worthy of being an example: it was, however, soon afterward abrogated in practice. It has been concluded, not without probability, that the name China, Sina, or Tsina, was taken from the dynasty of Tsin. The first emperor, or founder, is said to have had political transactions with Fergana, a province of Sogdiana, and to have received a Roman embassy.

On the conclusion of this race of sovereigns, in A. D. 416, China became divided into two principal kingdoms, Nanking being the capital of the southern one, and Honân of the northern. For about 200 years afterward five successive races (*woo-tae*) rapidly followed each other, and the salutary rule of hereditary succession being constantly violated by the strongest, the whole history of the period is a mere record of contests and crimes. At length, in A. D. 585, the north and south were united for the first time into one empire, of which the capital was fixed at Honân. The last of the five contending races was soon after deposed by *Ly-yuen*, who founded, in A. D. 622, the dynasty of *Tâng*.

Tae-tsoong, the second emperor of this race, was one of the most celebrated in China; his maxims are constantly quoted in books, and his temperance and love of justice considered as patterns. There is reason to believe that certain Christians of the Nestorian church first came to China in his reign, about A. D. 640. It is recorded that foreigners arrived, having fair hair and blue eyes. According to the Jesuits, whom Du Halde has quoted, a stone monument was found at *Sy-gân-foo* in Shensy, A.D. 1625, with the cross, an abstract of the Christian law, and the names of 72 preachers in Syriac characters, bearing the fore-mentioned date. It has been urged that this discovery may have been a pious fraud on the part of the holy fathers; but it is not easy to assign any adequate motive for such a forgery, and the evidence seems upon the whole in its favour.

One of the most remarkable circumstances in the history of Tâng is the extraordinary power which the eunuchs of the palace arrogated to themselves. The third emperor was so besotted by one of his wives, that he left her invested with sovereign power at his death, contrary to the enactment before made and provided. She reigned for above 20 years absolutely, leaving her son emperor; and this vicious and troubled period is another example quoted by the Chinese of the mischiefs which result to public affairs from the management of women. During her reign the eunuchs gathered fresh force, and for a considerable time had the choice of the emperors, and the control of their actions. The influence of such singular rulers must of course be referred to the operations of intrigue. The uncontrolled access which their condition gave them to all parts of the palace, and to the company of both sexes, was greatly calculated to facilitate their projects: and projects of mischief and disorder were the most likely ones to be formed by those who were cut off from the ties of kindred, and sufficiently disposed to regard the rest of mankind as their enemies. The awe of state was not long felt by such as were the immediate attendants, and perhaps the companions, of the sovereign, in his private haunts; and, that barrier once passed, the approaches of insolence and usurpation might advance unchecked. The power of the eunuchs was at length destroyed by the last emperor of the race, who in great measure extirpated them, through the assistance of a powerful leader, whose aid he requested. This person fulfilled his commission, but subsequently killed the emperor and his heir, and, after a course of atrocious cruelties, put an end to the dynasty Tâng, A. D. 897.

The whole country was once more thrown into a state of war and confusion, with several aspirants to the sovereignty. This period, which lasted about fifty-three years, is called in Chinese histories the *How Wootae*, or "latter five successions." The Tartar people of the region now called Leaoutung, at the eastern extremity of the great wall, encouraged by the unsettled and divided condition of the empire, gave much trouble by their incursions.

These turbulent portions of the Chinese annals, which were now soon to give way to a settled oriental despotism, bear many features of a feudal cast about them. We think we can perceive in the book of Meng-tse, or Mencius (as his name has been Latinized by the Jesuits), that the original government of China approached in some degree to that description. "The sovereign, the Koong, the How, the Pĕ, and the Nân, constituted five ranks. The sovereign had the immediate government of 100 ly; the Koong and How each of 100 ly; the Pĕ 70; and the Nân 50 ly."—(*Hea-meng*, ch. x.) We read in their histories of grants of land to certain officers of state, and of government and military lands, in which may be perceived a resemblance to the feudal fiefs or benefices. Whatever may have been the tenure in former times, the emperor is now, as in most oriental countries, regarded as the ultimate owner of *all* lands, from which he receives a tax of about 10 per cent.

After a succession of civil wars, Tae-tsoo, the first emperor of the *Soong* dynasty, was raised to the throne by the military leaders, in consequence of the minority of the real heir, who was only seven years of age, A. D. 950. Being about to engage the Eastern Tartars, they did not wish to be ruled by a child, who could not appreciate their services. They accordingly fixed on a servant of the deceased emperor, and immediately despatched messengers, who found him overcome with wine, and in that state communicated their message. The history adds, that, "before he had time to reply, the yellow robe was already applied to his person." Substitute purple for yellow, and this might be taken for the translation of some passages in Tacitus or Suetonius.

The art of printing having been invented just previous to this dynasty, about five hundred years before it was known to us, the multiplication of books, the instruments of learning, was a principal cause of the literary character of the age of Soong; to the same cause may be attributed the increased fulness of the records of this period, from whence the really interesting thread of Chinese history commences. Our lights now multiply fast, and the Tartars begin to take a considerable share in the national transactions. In fact, the whole history of this polished but unwarlike race is a series of disgraceful acts of compromise with the Eastern Tartars, called *Kin* (the origin of the Manchows, or present reigning family), until the Mongols, or Western Tartars, took possession of the empire under Koblai Khan.

In the reign of Chin-tsoong, the third emperor of Soong, the Eastern Tartars, having laid siege to a town near Peking, were forced to treat, but still obtained advantageous terms, with a large annual donative of money and silk. The pacific disposition of Jin-tsoong, the fourth emperor, gave them farther encouragement, and a disgraceful treaty was the consequence. Ten districts to the south of the wall being claimed by them, they received an annual quit-rent of 200,000 taëls, and a quantity of silk. To complete his disgrace, the emperor called himself a *tributary*, making use of the term *Nă-koong*.

Shin-tsoong, the sixth emperor, is described as having hastened the fall of his race by attending to the absurd suggestions of a minister, who was for reverting to the antiquated maxims of *Yaou* and *Shun*, names which may properly be said to belong rather to the mythology than the history of the empire. At length Wei-tsoong, the eighth sovereign in succession, enslaved himself to the eunuchs, and soon experienced the consequences of his weakness and imbecility. The Eastern Tartars advanced apace, took possession of a part of northern China, and threatened the whole country: they were destined, however, to be checked, not by the Chinese, but the Mongols. These inhabited the countries which extend from the northwestern provinces of China to Thibet and Sarmacand. They had already conquered India, and being now called in against the *Kin* or Eastern Tartars, they soon subdued both them and the enervated Chinese, whom they had been invited to protect.

The Mongols might be said to be masters of the northern half of modern China from the year 1234. The *Kin*, who until then had occupied a part of the provinces bordering on the wall, were attacked on one side by the Chinese, and on the other by the Mongols, under the command of the famous Pĕ-yen (*hundred-eyes*, or Argus), who is mentioned by Marco Polo, and the correctness of whose name is of itself a sufficient proof of the genuineness of that early traveller's narrative. Their principal city was taken, and the death of their prince put an end for the present to the Eastern Tartars; but the remnant became the stock from whence grew the Manchows, who afterward conquered China, and who hold it to this day in subjection.

When Koblai Khan had possessed himself of the northern part of the empire, he took occasion of the infancy of the reigning Chinese emperor to use an argument convenient to his purpose. "Your family," said he, "owes its rise to the minority of the last emperor of the preceding house; it is therefore just that the remains of Soong should give place to another family." The famous Pĕ-yen pursued the Chinese army first to Fokien, and afterward to Hoey-chow, in Canton province. Great cruelty was exercised on the vanquished, and it is recorded that "the blood of the people flowed in sounding torrents." The remains of the Chinese court betook themselves to the sea near Canton, and perished, A. D. 1281.

On the accession of Koblai Khan, the first of the *Yuen* dynasty, the favourite religion of the Tartars being that of Buddha, or Fo, of which the grand lama of Thibet is the head, an order was promulgated to burn all the books of the Taou sect. An exception was suggested in favour of the Taou-tĕ-king, as the only really inspired writing of that religion; but the order was made peremptory to burn them all. The historian, a Confucian, observes that his majesty, who favoured Buddhism, and those of his predecessors who had encouraged the other persuasion, were equally erroneous and partial; both doctrines should have been extinguished. Buddhism, in fact, has never flourished as it did under the Mongol Tartar race.

Koblai fixed the seat of government at Peking, or Kambalu, as it is styled by Marco Polo, after the Tartars. As the most effectual remedy for the sterility of the plain in which that capital is situated, he constructed the vast *canal*, extending south a distance of about 300 leagues into the most fertile provinces, and serving as an easy conveyance for their products, independently of a sea navigation. This great work, which is more particularly described in its proper place, was a benefit to China, by itself sufficient to redeem in some measure the injustice and violence by which the Mongol possessed himself of the empire.

The northern portion of China was now known by the name Kathai, or Cathay, the appellation invariably given to it by the Venetian traveller. The southern was styled Manjee, which is evidently a corruption of *Mantsze*, originally applied to the barbarians of the south. There is a portion of Ava bordering on China at this day called Manchegee, which probably has the same derivation. Notwithstanding the great qualities of Koblai, which were calculated to lay the foundations of a permanent dominion, the degeneracy of his successors was such as to cause the empire to pass out of the hands of the Mongol race in a little more than eighty years' time. There is scarcely any thing worthy of notice in their annals, save the rapid and excessive degeneracy of these Tartar princes. Koblai had wisely adopted the political institutions of China; but those who followed him surpassed the Chinese themselves in their luxury and effeminacy. Enervated by the climate and vices of the south, they quickly lost the courage and hardihood which had put the country in possession of their ancestors; and Shunty, the ninth emperor in succession, was compelled to resign the empire to a Chinese.

It is worthy of remark, that, of the score of dynasties which have followed each other, all established themselves on the vices, luxury, or indolence of their immediate forerunners. The present Manchow race has already shown no unequivocal symptoms of degeneracy. The two greatest princes by whom it has been distinguished, Kanghy and Kienloong, sedulously maintained the ancient habits of their Tartar subjects by frequent hunting excursions beyond the wall, in which they individually bore no small share of the fatigue and danger. The late emperor, Keaking, and the present one have, on the other hand, been remarkable for their comparative indolence; and the reigns of both have exhibited a mere succession of revolts and troubles. The following is part of an edict issued by the reigning monarch in 1824:—"With reference to the autumnal hunt of the present year, I ought to follow the established custom of my predecessors; but, at the same time, it is necessary to be guided by the circumstances of the times, and to act in conformity to them. The expedition to Je-ho (Zhehol) is also ordered to be put off for this year. It is an involuntary source of vexation to me: I should not think of adopting this measure from a love of ease and indulgence." Since that date, however, the same course has been repeated under various pretexts. The Manchow rule has already lasted much longer than the Mongol, and, from all present appearances, a bold Chinese adventurer might perhaps succeed in overthrowing it.

The first emperor of the *Ming* dynasty, which expelled the Mongols in 1366, had been servant to a monastery of bonzes, or priests of Buddha. Having joined a numerous body of revolters, he soon became their leader, and, after making himself master of some provinces in the south, at length defeated a part of the emperor's troops in a great battle. The Chinese now flocked to him from all parts; and, having crossed the Yellow river, he forced *Shunty* to fly northward, where he died soon after, leaving the empire in possession of the successful Chinese, who assumed the sovereignty with the title of *Tae-tsoo*, or "great ancestor."

The new emperor endeavoured to establish his capital at Foongyang-foo, his native city, but was obliged, from its local disadvantages, to give it up, and adopt Nanking instead; erecting Peking into a principality for one of his younger sons, Yoong-lŏ. When this prince succeeded as third emperor of his family, the capital was transferred in 1408 to Peking; a principal reason perhaps being the necessity of keeping the Eastern Tartars in check. Nanking was still occupied by the *heir*, with a distinct set of tribunals, and this shows more confidence than is commonly displayed under Asiatic despotisms. It was in the same reign that Timour, or Tamerlane, died on his way to the conquest of China, in the year 1405.

During the reign of Hoong-hy, the fourth emperor of the Ming family, a great conflagration of the palace melted together a mixture of valuable metals, and from this compound were constructed numbers of vases, which are highly valued at the present day. In this, the reader may perceive an origin somewhat similar to that of the famous Corinthian brass. Some of the Chinese vases so highly esteemed were seen by the British embassy near Nanking in 1816. It is a common practice, however, at present, to put the name of the above emperor on vases which have no pretensions whatever to this antique value.

It was in the same dynasty that the Portuguese, as we have already seen, came to China, and obtained, about the middle of the sixteenth century, their imperfect tenure of Macao; and it was also under the *Ming* race that the Jesuits established themselves in China. The zeal and address with which these intelligent and adventurous men opened a way for themselves and their mission, are deserving of high praise; and the knowledge which some of them obtained of the language, manners, and institutions of the country, has never, perhaps, been surpassed by any other Europeans. Had it not been for the narrow-minded bigotry and intolerance with which some of the popes, and the monks whom they deputed to China, frustrated the labours of the more sober-minded Jesuits, Europeans and their religion might at this day enjoy a very different footing in the empire.

In the year 1618, Wanliĕ, the thirteenth emperor of the Chinese dynasty, being on the throne, a war commenced with the Eastern Tartars, who now called their country (the present Mougden) Manchow, which means "the full region." We have before seen that, just previous to the Mongol conquest, and during the latter end of the Soong dynasty, these Eastern Tartars, under the name of *Kin*, or the "golden" race, had subdued some portion of the north of China, but were driven out by the Mongols. When the last of the Mongols, descendants of Koblai Khan, were expelled from China by the founder of the *Ming*, or Chinese race, they sought a refuge among the Eastern Tartars, and from their intermarriages with the natives sprung the Bogdoi khans, or Manchow princes, who were destined to expel the Ming. It is in this manner that the emperors of the present dynasty derive their descent from Koblai Khan.

It was Tien-ming, the lineal ancestor of the family now reigning, who in the time of Wanliĕ drew up a paper containing seven subjects of grievance, on the ground of which he formally attacked China, with the view of doing himself justice. He entered the province of Peking at the head of 50,000 men, and was preparing to besiege the capital, when he was repulsed, and compelled to retire for a while to Leaoutung, north of the great wall. His title *Tien-ming* literally means "Heaven's decree." The contest was subsequently resumed, and lasted with various success until the last emperor of Ming succeeded in 1627. This prince seemed insensible to the danger which threatened him, and, instead of repelling the Tartars, estranged his own subjects by his ill conduct, driving at length a portion of them to revolt. The leader of the rebels subdued the provinces Honân and Shensy, and murdered the principal mandarins; but, in order to gain their assistance, he freed the people from all taxes and contributions. The success of this policy soon enabled him to invest Peking with a very large army. The emperor, preferring death to being taken by the rebels, retired with his only daughter, whom he first stabbed, and then put an end to his own existence with a cord, A. D. 1643. Thus perished the last Chinese emperor; and the spot where he died was pointed out to the late Sir George Staunton in 1793.* The way in which a comparatively small nation of Tartars possessed themselves of China will now appear.

On the death of the emperor, the usurper met with universal submission, both at Peking and in the provinces, with the exception of the general Woosankwei, who commanded an army near Eastern Tartary. The latter fortified himself in a city which he commanded, and was presently besieged by the successful rebel, who showed him his father in chains, threatening to put him to death if the town was not surrendered. The father exhorted his son to hold out, and submitted to his fate: upon which Woosankwei, to revenge his death, as well as that of the emperor, made peace with the Manchows, and called them in to his assistance against the rebels. The usurper was in this manner soon defeated; but the Tartar king, proceeding to the capital, was so well received there, and conducted matters with such dexterity, that he at length found no difficulty in taking upon himself the sovereignty. Being seized with a mortal sickness, he had time to appoint his son Shunchy, then a boy, as his successor, A. D. 1644, and thus commenced the Manchow Tartar dynasty, of which the sixth emperor is now reigning.

Several cities of the south still held out against this foreign government, and particularly the maritime province of Fokien, which was not subdued

* Embassy, vol. ii., p. 121.

until some years afterward. The conquered Chinese were now compelled to shave the thick hair, which their nation had been accustomed to wear from the most ancient times as a cherished ornament, and to betake themselves to the Tartar fashion of a long platted tress, or tail. In other respects, too, they were commanded to adopt the Tartar habit on pain of death; and many are said to have died in preference to submission. Their new rulers must, indeed, have felt themselves sufficiently strong before they issued such an order. Many are the changes which may be made in despotic countries, without the notice, or even knowledge, of the larger portion of the community; but an entire alteration in the national costume affects every individual equally, from the highest to the lowest, and is perhaps, of all others, the most open and degrading mark of conquest. It can never be submitted to except by a people who are thoroughly subdued, nor ever imposed except by a government that feels itself able to carry a measure, which is perhaps resorted to principally for the purpose of trying, or of breaking, the spirit of the conquered. The ancient Chinese costume is now very exactly represented on the stage of their theatre, to which it is exclusively confined.

Such was the repugnance of the Chinese to the Tartar rule, that, during the eighteen years of the first emperor's reign, a portion of the south remained unsubdued, and a very formidable opponent to the new dynasty existed on the sea. This was Ching-she-loong, father to the maritime leader Koshinga, whom we have already had occasion to mention as the person who took Formosa from the Dutch. According to the policy always adopted, of effecting by compromise what cannot be accomplished by force, Shunchy offered him honours and rewards at Peking, on condition that he would submit. The father accepted the invitation, leaving his fleet with his son, and was well received; but Koshinga remained true to the Chinese cause, and subsequently co-operated with the adherents to the late dynasty on shore, committing great ravages with his fleet along the coast. Kang-hy, the second Tartar emperor, adopted the vigorous measure of compelling his subjects in the six maritime provinces to retire thirty Chinese *ly*, or three leagues inward from the coast, on pain of death. Thus, at the expense of destruction to a number of towns and villages, and of loss to the inhabitants, the power and resources of Koshinga were reduced, and his grandson was at length prevailed on to give up Formosa to the emperor, and accept the gift of a title for himself, A. D. 1683.

The final establishment of the Manchow Tartars in China is doubtless attributable, in no small measure, to the personal character of Kang-hy, who was perhaps the greatest monarch that ever ruled the country, and who had the singular fortune to reign for sixty years. By his hunting excursions beyond the great wall, when he really proceeded at the head of a large army, he kept up the military character of the Tartars; while at the same time his vigilant care was not wanting in the south. During the year 1689, he proceeded along the grand canal to Nanking, and thence to the famous city of Soochow. At that opulent and luxurious place it is said that carpets and silk stuffs being laid along the streets by the inhabitants, the emperor dismounted, and made his train do the same, proceeding thus to the palace on foot, in order that the people's property might not be injured.

His liberal and enlightened policy was strikingly displayed on two occasions of foreign intercourse. First, in the boundary and commercial treaty with Russia, of which Père Gerbillon has given an account, and which was consequent on a dispute that occurred at the frontier station of Yacsa. Gerbillon was sent by Kang-hy (whose numerous favours to the Catholic mission have already been noticed) to assist the negotiation as translator; and his detail of the expedition is given in the fourth volume of Du Halde. The mission proceeded in 1688, but circumstances prevented its completion until the following year; for the Eleuths or Kalmucs being then at war with the Kalka Tartars, and the route of the expedition lying along the country of the latter, it was thought prudent at first to return. The second instance is that embassy in 1713 to the Khan of the Tourgouth Tartars, then settled on the north bank of the Caspian, of which a translated account has been given by the present Sir George Staunton from the original Chinese. This is the most remote expedition that has ever been undertaken from China in modern times; and the details of the journey, with the emperor's own instructions for the conduct of his ambassador, are especially curious. Kang-hy subsequently gained considerable glory by the conquest of the above-mentioned Eleuths, who had long given great trouble in the regions about Thibet; and the exploits and triumphs of the emperor's army having been portrayed by a French missionary, in a series of skilful drawings, these were sent by the desire of Kang-hy to Paris, and there engraved on copper-plates. They contain a very faithful representation of Chinese and Tartar costumes and court ceremonies, and are by far the best things of the kind in existence.

Yoong-ching, the immediate successor of this great emperor, was remarkable for little else than for his violent persecution of the Catholic priests, who had certainly rendered themselves sufficiently noxious by their imprudent conduct to the rulers of China. Kien-loong, who succeeded in 1736, and who, like his great predecessor, Kang-hy, had the unusual fortune to reign for sixty years, was no unworthy inheritor of the fame and dominion of his grandfather. He encouraged the Chinese learning by cultivating it in his own person, and some of his poetical compositions are considered to possess intrinsic merit, independently of their being the productions of an emperor. The principal military transaction of his reign, remarkable upon the whole for its peaceful and prosperous course, was an expedition against the *Meaou-tse*, the race of mountaineers already described on the borders of Kuei-chow, and not far removed from the Canton province. The emperor boasted that they were subdued; but there is reason to believe that this hardy people, intrenched in the natural fortifications of their rude and precipitous mountains, lost little of the real independence which they had enjoyed for ages, and that they were "*triumphati magis quam victi.*" They have never submitted to the Tartar tonsure, the most conclusive mark of conquest; and their renewed acts of hostility, as late as the year 1832, gave serious alarm and trouble to the Peking government.

The first British embassy ever sent to China was received by Kien-loong in 1793, and the liberal conduct of that monarch, in dispensing with the performance of the prostration on the part of Lord Macartney, contrasts strongly with the petty species of trickery by which that Tartar act of homage, called the Kŏ-tow, was sought to be extorted from Lord Amherst in 1816, by his successor Kea-king; or rather by the ministers, for the emperor subsequently disavowed his knowledge of their proceedings. It has been reasonably supposed that Kien-loong, at the end of a long and prosperous reign, felt sufficiently assured of his own power and greatness to dispense with such a ceremony; and that the authority of his son having been shaken by frequent insurrections, and even by some attempts against his life, this circumstance rendered him, or at least his court more tenacious of external forms.

It has been ascertained, however, that the agency of the provincial government of Canton was powerfully exerted against the last embassy.

When the reign of Kien-loong, like that of his grandfather, had in 1795 reached the unusual term of sixty years, which just completes a revolution of the Chinese cycle, he resigned the throne to his son, with the title of emperor, while he reserved to himself that of the *supreme emperor*, though he retired altogether from state affairs, and lived but a short time afterward. Kea-king was ill calculated to maintain the imperial dignity after such a monarch as his father. Serra, a Catholic missionary, many years employed at Peking, obtained a very particular account of his habits, which were extremely profligate, and may account for the risks to which his life was exposed from assassins. After the early morning audience, from which no emperor can excuse himself, and having despatched the business submitted to him, he generally retired to the company of players, and afterward drank to excess. He would frequently proceed with players to the interior of the palace, and it was remarked that his two younger sons bore no resemblance to himself or to each other. He went so far as to carry the comedians with him when he proceeded to sacrifice at the temples of Heaven and Earth. This, with other circumstances, was noticed in a memorial by the famous *Soong-keun*, or Soong-tajin, one of the censors, and the conductor and friend of Lord Macartney while in China. When summoned by the emperor, and asked what punishment he deserved, he answered, "A slow and ignominious death." When told to choose another, he said, "beheading;" and, on a third occasion, he chose "strangling."* He was ordered to retire, and on the following day the court appointed him

* The three gradations of capital punishment.

governor of the Chinese Siberia, the region of Tartary to which criminals are exiled; thus (as Serra observes) acknowledging his rectitude, though unable to bear his censure.

When the reign of Kea-king, unmarked by any events except the suppression of some formidable revolts and conspiracies, had reached the twenty-fourth year, the occurrence of the sixtieth anniversary of the emperor's age was celebrated by a universal jubilee throughout the empire. Even with private individuals, the attainment of the sixtieth year (a revolution of the cycle) is marked by a particular celebration. In 1819 the national jubilee was observed, as usual, by a remission of all arrears of land-tax; by a general pardon or mitigation of punishment to criminals; and by the admission of double the usual number of candidates to degrees at the public examinations. The celebration of one man's age by two or three *hundred millions* of people is rather an imposing festival, and could happen to none but the Emperor of China. Kea-king, however, only survived it by a single year; and his death, in 1820, was the occasion of some curious information being obtained relative to the mode of succession, and other particulars.

The emperor's *will*, a very singular document, was published to the people. In it was this passage:—" The Yellow river has, from the remotest ages, been China's sorrow. Whenever the mouth of the stream has been impeded by sand-banks, it has, higher up its course, created alarm by overflowing the country. On such occasions I have not spared the imperial treasury to embank the river, and restore the waters to their former channel. Since a former repair of the river was completed six or seven years of tranquillity had elapsed, when last year, in the autumn, the excessive rains caused an unusual rise of the water, and in Honân the river burst its banks at several points, both on the south and north sides. The stream Woo-chy forced a passage to the sea, and the mischief done was immense. During the spring of this year, just as those who conducted the repair of the banks had reported that the work was finished, the southern bank at Ee-foong again gave way." The mention of this subject in the emperor's will is a sufficient proof of its importance If the science of European engineers could put an effectual stop to the evil, it would be the most important physical benefit that was ever conferred on the empire; but the illiberal jealousy of China is not likely to let the experiment be very soon tried. Even the European trade at Canton is annually taxed to meet the repairs of the Yellow river.

The emperor's *will* proceeds to state the merits of his second son, the present sovereign, Taou-kuâng, in having shot two of the assassins who entered the palace in 1813, which was the reason of his selection. It has been even supposed that Kea-king's death was hastened by some discontented person of high rank, who had been lately disgraced in consequence of the mysterious loss of an official seal. The emperor's death was announced to the several provinces by despatches written with *blue* ink, the mourning colour. All persons of condition were required to take the red silk ornament from their caps, with the ball or button of rank: all subjects of China, without exception, were called upon to forbear from shaving their heads for one hundred days, within which period none might marry, or play on musical instruments, or perform any sacrifice.

The personal character of the present emperor is much better than that of his father, but the lofty title which he chose for his reign, *Taou-kuâng*, "the glory of reason," has hardly been supported. The most disgraceful act of his administration was the murder, in 1828, of the Mahometan Tartar prince

Chinese Military Station, with Soldiers.

Jehanghir, who had surrendered himself in reliance on the faith of promises. It is supposed, indeed, that the reduction of those tribes towards Cashgar, effected by the aid of the Mongol Tartars that intervene, was marked by more than the usual share of Chinese treachery and craft. This war was a source of serious anxiety and expense to the emperor, whose reign has been infested by a continual succession of public calamities, and by more revolts and insurrections than have been known since the time of the first emperor of the Manchow dynasty. Subsequent to the termination of the troubles with the independent mountaineers northwest of Canton, which has been mentioned in another chapter, a very singular paper was written by a Chinese, stating the submission of the enemy to be a mere imposition on the emperor by his officers, and a public disgrace. He said that the imperial commissioners had expended 500,000 taëls of silver for a sham surrender and the appearance of victory, and wondered at their audacity in receiving the rewards of peacocks' feathers and other marks of favour. The money was represented to have been thrown away, for the mountaineers had disowned the authority of those who accepted it, and remained as independent as ever.

There must be a good deal of truth in this, or a Chinese would hardly have exposed himself to the risk of being the author; and it is a singular picture of the existing state of the empire. Many have been led by the events of recent years to surmise that the end of the Tartar dominion in China is at hand; its establishment and continuance are certainly facts not much less extraordinary (when the disproportion of the conquerors to the conquered is considered) than the British dominion in India; and the Mongol race were driven out by the Chinese after a much shorter possession than the Manchows have already enjoyed. These have had the prudence and wisdom to leave the Chinese in possession of their own forms and institutions in most instances, and to mould those of the Tartars to them; but distinctions sufficiently broad are still maintained to prevent the amalgamation of the original people with their masters. A symptom of weakness in the government is its extreme dread of numerous associations among the people; one of which, the Triad Society, has for its known object the expulsion of the Manchows.

An insurrection broke out in the Island of Formosa towards the close of 1832, accompanied by the death of a large portion of the troops, and of the greater number of mandarins on the spot, and the origin of it was attributed to the oppression of the emperor's government. A Tartar general, after the lapse of a few months, was despatched in all haste from Peking, with power to take troops from the different provinces at his need, and in a short time it was heard that the insurrection was over, and the troops countermanded. This sudden restoration of tranquillity was hardly less surprising, after violence had proceeded to such lengths, than the speedy submission of the mountaineers; but it was never clearly ascertained whether it was effected by force, or by the divisions of the inhabitants; or whether money had been used, as in the case of the mountaineers, to supply the place of arms.

The last emperor, Kea-king, showed a very determined aversion and hostility to the Roman Catholic religion, and numerous persecutions took place in his reign. The present monarch, by all appearances, inherited the same disposition from his father. He had not succeeded many weeks to the throne, when one of his high officers evinced his zeal by an accusation against certain Chinese who had been detected in the practice of what is called the "religion of the western ocean." A still more unequivocal proof exists in the expulsion from Peking of the very last of those European missionaries who, for their astronomical knowledge, had been attached in succession, for about 200 years, to that tribunal or board whose business it is to observe the motions of the heavenly bodies, and to construct the imperial calendar. It is probable that the present Chinese astronomers have acquired sufficient practical knowledge for the rough calculation of eclipses, and other routine matters of the same kind: but in the course of time another generation may perhaps require a fresh inoculation of science from Europe, and it will then befit Protestant missionaries to imitate the learning and enterprise of their Catholic predecessors,—but to avoid their want of moderation, and their disputes with each other about trifles.

CHAPTER VI.

GOVERNMENT AND LEGISLATION.

Paternal Authority the principle of Chinese Rule.—Malversations at Canton, in some degree an exception to the Empire at large.—Despotism tempered by influence of Public Opinion.—Motives to Education.—Reverence for Age.—Wealth has Influence, but is little respected.—Real Aristocracy official, and not hereditary.—The Emperor—is High Priest.—Ministers.—Machinery of Government.—Checks on Magistrates.—Civil Officers superior to Military.—Low art of War.—Guns cast by Missionaries.—Penal Code of China.—Merits and Defects.—Arrangement.—Punishments.—Privileges and Exemptions. — Crimes. — Character of Code. — Testimonies, foreign and domestic, in favour of its practical results.—Chinese recognise sanctions superior to absolute will of Emperor.

MONTESQUIEU has somewhere the following remark :—"*Heureux le peuple dont l'histoire est ennuyeuse ;*" and, if this be the characteristic of Chinese history, if we find the even current of its annals for a long time past less troubled by disorder and anarchy than can be stated of most other countries, we must look for the causes in the fundamental principles of its government, and in the maxims by which this is administered. It is well known that *parental authority* is the model or type of political rule in China—that natural restraint to which almost every man finds himself subject at the earliest dawn of his perceptions. Influenced, perhaps, by a consideration of the lasting force of early impressions on the human mind, the legislators of the country have thought that they should best provide for the stability of their fabric by basing it on that principle which is the most natural and familiar to every one from infancy, and the least likely ever to be called in question.

Whether or not this was the design with which the patriarchal form has been so long perpetuated in China, it seems certain that, being at once the most obvious and the simplest, it has for that reason been the *first* that has existed among the various societies of mankind. The North American tribes call all rulers "fathers." However well calculated to promote the union and welfare of small tribes or nations, the example of China, perhaps, in some respects, demonstrates that in large empires, where the supreme authority must be exercised almost entirely by distant delegation, it is liable to degenerate into a mere fiction, excellently calculated to strengthen and perpetuate the hand of despotism, but retaining little of the paternal character beyond its absolute authority. It is the policy of the Chinese government to grant to fathers over their children the *patria potestas* in full force, as the example and the sanction of its own power.

There is nothing more remarkable in their ritual and in their criminal code, than the exact parallel which is studiously kept up between the relations in which every person stands to his own parents and to the emperor. For similar offences against both, he suffers similar punishments; at the death of both he mourns the same time, and goes the same period unshaven; and both possess nearly the same power over his person. Thus he is bred up to civil obedience, "*tenero ab ungui*," with every chance of proving a *quiet* subject at least. Such institutions certainly do not denote the existence of much liberty; but if peaceful obedience and universal order be the sole objects in view, they argue, on the part of the governors, some knowledge of human nature, and an adaptation of the means to the end.

In the book of Sacred Instructions, addressed to

the people, founded on their ancient writings, and read publicly by the principal magistrates on the days that correspond to the new and full moon, the sixteen discourses of which it consists are *headed* by that which teaches the duties of children to parents, of juniors to elders, and (thence) of the people to the government. The principle is extended thus in a quotation from the sacred books :—"In our general conduct, not to be orderly is to fail in filial duty; in serving our sovereign, not to be faithful is to fail in filial duty; in acting as a magistrate, not to be careful is to fail in filial duty; in the intercourse of friends, not to be sincere is to fail in filial duty; in arms and in war, not to be brave is to fail in filial duty." The claims of elders are enforced thus :—"The duty to parents and the duty to elders are indeed similar in obligation; for he who can be a pious son will also prove an obedient younger brother; and he who is *both* will, while at home, prove an honest and orderly subject, and in active service, from home, a courageous and faithful soldier. . . . May you all, O soldiers and people, conform to these our instructions, evincing your good dispositions by your conduct and actions, each fulfilling his duty as a son and a junior, according to the example which is left you by the wise and holy men of former times. The wisdom of the ancient emperors, Yaou and Shun, had its foundation in these essential ties of human society. Mencius has said, 'Were all men to honour their kindred and respect their elders, the world would be at peace.'"

But the government does not confine itself to preaching; domestic rebellion is treated in nearly all respects as treason; being in fact *petit treason*. A special edict of the last emperor went beyond the established law in a case which occurred in one of the central provinces. A man and his wife had beaten and otherwise severely ill-used the mother of the former. This being reported by the viceroy to Peking, it was determined to enforce in a signal manner the fundamental principle of the empire. The very place where it occurred was anathematized, as it were, and made accursed. The principal offenders were put to death; the mother of the wife was bambooed, branded, and exiled for her daughter's crime; the scholars of the district for three years were not permitted to attend the public examination, and their promotion thereby stopped; the magistrates were deprived of their office and banished. The house in which the offenders dwelt was dug up from the foundations. "Let the viceroy," the edict adds, "make known this proclamation, and let it be dispersed through the whole empire, that the people may all learn it. And if there be any rebellious children who oppose, beat, or degrade their parents, they shall be punished in like manner. If ye people indeed know the renovating principle, then fear and obey the imperial will, nor look on this as empty declamation. For now, according to this case of *Teng-chen*, wherever there are the like I resolve to condemn them, and from my heart strictly charge you to beware. I instruct the magistrates of every province severely to warn the heads of families and elders of villages; and on the 2d and 16th of every month to read the Sacred Instructions, in order to show the importance of the relations of life, that persons may not rebel against their parents—*for I intend to render the empire filial.*" This was addressed to a population estimated commonly at 300,000,000.

"The vital and universally operating principle of the Chinese government," says Sir George Staunton, "is the duty of submission to parental authority, whether vested in the parents themselves, or in their representatives; and this, although usually described under the pleasing appellation of filial piety, is much more properly to be considered as a general rule of action than as the expression of any particular sentiment of affection. It may easily be traced even in the earliest of their records; it is inculcated with the greatest force in the writings of the first of their philosophers and legislators; it has survived each successive dynasty, and all the various changes and revolutions which the state has undergone; and it continues to this day powerfully enforced both by positive laws and by public opinion.

"A government constituted upon the basis of parental authority, thus highly estimated and extensively applied, has certainly the advantage of being directly sanctioned by the immutable and ever-operating laws of nature, and must thereby acquire a degree of firmness and durability to which governments, founded on the fortuitous superiority of particular individuals, either in strength or abilities, and continued only through the hereditary influence of particular families, can never be expected to attain. Parental authority and prerogative seem to be, obviously, the most respectable of titles, and parental regard and affection the most amiable of characters, with which sovereign and magisterial power can be invested; and are those under which it is natural to suppose it may most easily be perpetuated. By such principles the Chinese have been distinguished ever since their first existence as a nation; by such ties the vast and increasing population of China is still united as one people, subject to one supreme government, and uniform in its habits, manners, and language. In this state, in spite of every internal and external convulsion, it may possibly very long continue."

It is the business of the first of the "Four Books" of Confucius to inculcate, that from the knowledge and government of *one's self* must proceed the proper economy and government of a family; from the government of a family, that of a province and of a kingdom. The emperor is called the father of the empire; the viceroy, of the province over which he presides; and the mandarin, of the city which he governs; and the father of every family is the absolute and responsible ruler of his own household. Social peace and order being deemed the one thing needful, this object is very steadily and consistently pursued. The system derives some of its efficacy from the *habitual* and universal inculcation of obedience and deference, in unbroken series, from one end of society to the other; beginning in the relation of children to their parents, continuing through that of the young to the aged, of the uneducated to the educated, and terminating in that of the people to their rulers.

The great wealth of the empire, the cheerful and indefatigable industry of the people, and their unconquerable attachment to their country, are all of them circumstances which prove, that, if the government is jealous in guarding its rights, it is not altogether ignorant or unmindful of its duties. We are no unqualified admirers of the Chinese system, but would willingly explain, if possible, some of the causes which tend to the production of results whose existence nobody pretends to deny. In practice there is of course a great deal of inevitable abuse; but upon the whole, and with relation to ultimate effects, the machine works well: and we repeat that the surest proofs of this are apparent on the very face of the most cheerfully industrious and orderly, and the most wealthy, nation of Asia. It may be observed that we make great account of the circumstance of *cheerful* industry; because this characteristic, which is the first to strike all visiters of China, is the best proof in the world that the people possess their full share of the results of their own labour. Men do not toil either willingly or effectively for hard masters.

It would be a very rash conclusion to form any estimate of the insecurity of property *generally* from what is observed at Canton among those connected with the *foreign trade*, and especially the Hong merchants. These persons are instruments in the hands of a cautious government, which, not wishing to come into immediate collision with foreigners, uses them in the manner of a sponge, that, after being allowed to absorb the gains of a licensed monopoly, is made regularly to yield up its contents, by what is very correctly termed "squeezing." The rulers of China consider foreigners fair game: they have no sympathy with them, and, what is more, they diligently and systematically labour to destroy all sympathy on the part of their subjects, by representing the strangers to them in every light that is the most contemptible and odious. There is an annual edict or proclamation displayed at Canton at the commencement of the commercial season, accusing the foreigners of the most horrible practices, and desiring the people to have as little to say to them as possible. We have already seen that the professed rule is to govern them "like beasts," and not as the subjects of the empire. With perfect consistency, therefore, they are denied the equal benefits and protection of the known laws of the country, condemned to death for accidental homicide, and executed without the emperor's warrant. These are their real subjects of complaint in China; and whenever the accumulation of wrong shall have proved, by exact calculation, that it is more profitable, according to merely commercial principles, to remonstrate than to submit, these will form a righteous and equitable ground of quarrel.

But to return to the Hong merchants and others at Canton: there is in fact a set of laws existing under this jealous Tartar government, which makes all transactions of Chinese with foreigners, without an express license, *traitorous*—that is the word—and it forms a terrible engine of extortion; for the construction of the terms of the license, as well as of the particular regulations from time to time enacted, opens a wide field for injustice under the forms of law. This is the only solution of the anomaly, that at Canton, in a country where there is a written code with numerous provisions against extortion and oppression, and with severe denunciations against the abuse of power, there is still so much of the evil apparently existing. But it is the foreigner that pays, after all; the Hong merchants are the *véritables vaches à lait*, the real milch cows, but the foreign trade is the pasture in which they range. One of the ablest of their body many years since obtained the express authority of the local government for the Consoo, or body of Hong merchants, to levy charges at its own discretion on the foreign trade, for the avowed purpose of paying the demands of the mandarins. Other annual charges were levied to defray debts of individual merchants to foreigners, and, the debts being liquidated, the charges are *continued.* But for these abuses, the fair trade of Canton would be much more profitable than it is; and if they increase, it will die a natural death.

The same system cannot by any means be practised where *natives only* are concerned; and, if it could, the country would present a very different appearance. Extraordinary wealth is of course exposed to danger, *feriuntque summos fulmina montes*, or, as the Chinese express it, "the elephant is killed on account of his ivory." But they have another saying, that "happiness consists in a level or medium station;" and it is certain that the bulk of the native population enjoys the results of its industry with a very fair degree of security, or it would not be so industrious.

There are some curious practical anomalies which one is not prepared to find under a despotism. The people sometimes hold public meetings by advertisement, for the express purpose of addressing the magistrate, and this without being punished. The influence of public opinion seems indicated by this practice; together with that frequent custom of placarding and lampooning (though of course anonymously) noxious officers. Honours are rendered to a just magistrate, and addresses presented to him on his departure by the people; testimonies which are highly valued. These must be ranked with the exceptions to the *theories* of governments, of which Hume treats when he mentions, among other instances, the impressment of seamen in England; which is a departure from liberty, as the cases above mentioned are from despotism. It may be added, that there is no established censorship of the press in China, nor any limitations but those which the interests of social peace and order seem to render necessary. If these are endangered, the process of the government is of course more summary than even an information filed by the attorney-general.

It is deserving of remark, that the general prosperity and peace of China have been very much promoted by the diffusion of intelligence and education through the lower classes. Among the countless millions that constitute the empire, almost every man can read and write sufficiently for the ordinary purposes of life, and a respectable share of these acquirements goes low down in the scale of society. Of the sixteen discourses which are periodically read to the people, the eighth inculcates the necessity of a general acquaintance with the penal laws, which are printed purposely in a cheap form. They argue, that as men cannot properly be punished for what they do not know, so likewise they will be less liable to incur the penalty if they are made duly acquainted with the prohibition. This seems a very necessary branch of what has been called "*preventive* justice, upon every principle of reason, of humanity, and of sound policy, preferable in all respects to *punishing* justice."*

The general diffusion of education must be attributed to the influence of almost every motive of fear or hope that can operate on the human mind; it is inculcated by positive precepts, and encouraged by an open competition for the highest rewards. One of the strongest motives to every Chinese to educate his sons must be the consciousness that he is liable to punishment for their crimes at any period of their lives, as well as to reward for their merits: parents are often promoted by the acts of their sons Montesquieu, in violently condemning the liability to punishment,† seems to have been unaware, or unmindful, that it is in some measure the result of that absolute power which is through life intrusted to the father; and that such a trust, with some show of reason, carries with it a proportionate responsibility. He is not only punished, but rewarded too, according as he has administered this trust. How such a system must operate as a motive to education, is sufficiently obvious; and the only question is, whether the amount of personal liberty sacrificed is balanced by the amount of public benefit gained. So sensible are they of the importance of education, that the language is full of domestic or of state maxims in reference to it. "Bend the mulberry-tree when it is young."—"Without education in families, how are governors for the people to be obtained?"—and so on. Every town has its public place of instruction, and wealthy families have private tutors.

As regards the peaceful and orderly character by which the Chinese, as a nation, are distinguished, there is much truth in another remark of Montesquieu, namely, that the government had this object in view when it prescribed a certain code of cere-

* Blackstone, b. iv., c. 18.

† Book vi., c. 20.

monies and behaviour to its subjects; "a very proper method of inspiring mild and gentle dispositions, of maintaining peace and good order, and of banishing all the vices which spring from an asperity of temper." They certainly are, upon the whole, among the most good-humoured people in the world, and the most peaceable; and the chief causes of this must be sought for in their political and social institutions. Of the sixteen lectures periodically delivered to the people, the second is "on union and concord among kindred;" the third, "on concord and agreement among neighbours;" the ninth, "on mutual forbearance;" the sixteenth, "on reconciling animosities." Here perhaps we may perceive also the sources of their characteristic timidity, which is accompanied by its natural associate, the disposition to cunning and fraud.

The Chinese have lived so much in peace, that they have acquired by habit and education a more than common horror of political disorder. "Better be a dog in peace than a man in anarchy," is a common maxim. "It is a general rule," they say, "that the worst of men are fondest of change and commotion, hoping that they may thereby benefit themselves; but by adherence to a steady, quiet system, affairs proceed without confusion, and bad men have nothing to gain." They are, in short, a *nation of incurable conservatives*. At the same time, that only check of Asiatic despotism—the endurance of the people—appears from their history to have exercised a salutary influence. The first emperor of the Ming family observed, "The bowstring drawn violently will break; the people pressed hard will rebel." Another sovereign observed to his heir, "You see that the boat in which we sit is supported by the water, which at the same time is able, if roused, to overwhelm it: remember that the water represents the people, and the emperor only the boat." Amid all the internal revolutions of

China, it is deserving of remark, that no single instance has ever occurred of an attempt to change the *form* of that pure monarchy which is founded in, or derived from, patriarchal authority. The only object has been, in most cases, the destruction of a tyrant; or, when the country was divided into several states, the acquisition of universal power by the head of one of them.

This people has, perhaps, derived some advantage from the habit of reserving its respect exclusively for those objects which may be considered as the original and legitimate sources of that feeling. We think there is much truth in the observations of Mr. Rogers, in a note to one of his poems:—"Age was anciently synonymous with power; and we may always observe that the old are held in more or less honour, as men are more or less virtuous. Among us, and wherever birth and possession give rank and authority, the young and the profligate are seen continually above the old and the worthy: their age can never find its due respect; but among many of the ancient nations it was otherwise, and they reaped the benefit of it. 'Rien ne maintient plus les mœurs qu'une extrême subordination des jeunes gens envers les vieillards. Les uns et les autres seront contenus: ceux-là par le respect qu'ils auront pour les vieillards, et ceux-ci par le respect qu'ils auront pour eux-mêmes.' "—(*Montesquieu.*) We have before mentioned that the Chinese possess this antiquated habit; but their regard for age, even, is secondary to their respect for learning. "In learning," says their maxim, "age and youth go for nothing: the best informed takes the precedence." The chief source of rank and consideration in China is certainly cultivated talent; and, whatever may be the character of the learning on which it is exercised, this at least is a more legitimate as well as more beneficial object of respect than the vulgar pretensions of wealth and fashion, or the accidental ones of mere birth.

Wealth alone, though it has of course some necessary influence, is looked upon with less respect, comparatively, than perhaps in any other country; and this *because* all distinction and rank arise almost entirely from educated talent. The choice of official persons, who form the real aristocracy of the country, is guided, with a very few exceptions, by the possession of those qualities, and the country is therefore as ably ruled as it could be under the circumstances. "Les lettrés (observed a correspondent of ours from Peking) ainsi honorés par les Hân, ont acquis un grand ascendant sur le peuple; la politique s'en est emparé dans toutes les dynasties, et c'est sans doute à cette réunion des esprits que la Chine doit son bonheur, sa paix, et sa prosperité." The official aristocracy, content with their solid rank and power, aim at no external display; on the contrary, a certain affectation, on their part, of patriarchal simplicity, operates as a sumptuary law, and gives a corresponding tone to the habits of the people. We are bound to admit that some evils result from this: superfluous wealth, in the hands of the vulgar possessors of it, is driven to find a vent occasionally in the gratification of private sensuality.

Superfluous wealth, however, is no very common occurrence in China. A man's sons divide his property between them, or rather live upon it in common, and the only right of primogeniture seems to consist in the eldest being a sort of steward or trustee for the estate. The temptations to immoderate accumulation are not so great as with us, nor the opportunities for it so frequent, where the ordinary channels of commerce are liable neither to such spring-tides, nor to such violent ebbs. We must repeat that the fortunes made by hoppos and Hong merchants at Canton are no examples whatever of the usual state of things in the empire, in cases where natives only are concerned. The real aristocracy of the country being official, and not hereditary, there are no families to be perpetuated by a system of entails; and, if a man were willing to transmit his possessions in the shape of endless settlements, the law will not let him.

It is an observation of Hume, that "the absence of any hereditary aristocracy may secure the intestine tranquillity of the state, by making it impossible for faction or rebellion to find any powerful heads." This, we fancy, is exactly the principle on which the Chinese government is so jealous of any undue perpetuation of greatness in families.* There are certain hereditary titles, descending one step in rank through five generations, and the privilege of wearing the yellow and red girdles, which serve to distinguish the numerous descendants of the imperial family; but these, though they are certainly a class of titular nobility, are far from being the real aristocracy of the country, and, without personal merit, they are little considered.† The Chinese have a saying, that, "by learning, the sons of the common people become great; without learning, the sons of the great become mingled with the mass of the people."

All real rank of consequence being determined by talent, the test of this is afforded at the public examinations. These are open to the poorest persons; and only some classes, as menial servants, comedians, and the lowest agents of the police, are excluded. The government seems to consider that its own stability is best secured by placing the greatest talent, if not always the purest virtue, in offices of trust. With a view to promoting the efficiency

* There is a law in their penal code denouncing death not only to him who recommends the elevation of a civil officer to an hereditary title, but to him in whose favour the recommendation is made.

† Du Halde observes, "they have no lands; and, as the emperor cannot give them all pensions, some live in great poverty."

of their standing army, the Manchow Tartar emperors have established a military examination, in which the relative merit of mandarins in martial exercises is distinguished by similar grades.

It is time, however, that we proceed to consider the actual machinery of government, commencing with the supreme head, the emperor. His titles are the " Son of Heaven," the "Ten thousand Years." He is worshipped with divine honours, and with the attribute of ubiquity throughout the empire. The following is from an eyewitness to the celebration of the emperor's birthday at Peking,* and the ceremony is universal and simultaneous through the chief cities of China. "The first day was consecrated to the purpose of rendering a solemn, sacred, and devout homage to the supreme majesty of the emperor. The princes, tributaries, ambassadors, great officers of state, and principal mandarins, were assembled in a vast hall, and upon particular notice were introduced into an inner building, bearing at least the semblance of a temple. It was chiefly furnished with great instruments of music, among which were sets of cylindrical bells, suspended in a line from ornamented frames of wood, and gradually diminishing in size from one extremity to the other, and also triangular pieces of metal, arranged in the same order as the bells. To the sound of these instruments, a slow and solemn hymn was sung by eunuchs, who had such a command over their voices as to resemble the effect of the musical glasses at a distance. The performers were directed in gliding from one tone to another by the striking of a shrill and sonorous cymbal; and the judges of music among the gentlemen of the embassy were much pleased with their execution. The whole had indeed a grand effect. During the performance, and at particular signals, nine times re-

* Staunton, vol. ii., p. 255.

peated, all the persons present prostrated themselves nine times, except the ambassador and his suite, who made a profound obeisance. But he whom it was meant to honour continued, as if it were in imitation of the Deity, invisible the whole time. The awful impression made upon the minds of men by this apparent worship of a fellow-mortal was not to be effaced by any immediate scenes of sport or gayety, which were postponed to the following day.

The emperor worships Heaven, and the people worship the emperor. It is remarkable that with all this the sovereign, in styling himself, uses occasionally such a term of affected humility as "the imperfect man;" which presents a contrast to the inflated and self-laudatory expressions of most oriental monarchs. Every device of state, however, is used to keep up by habit the impression of awe. No person whatever can pass before the outer gate of the palace in any vehicle or on horseback. The vacant throne, or a screen of yellow silk, is equally worshipped with his actual presence. An imperial despatch is received in the provinces with offerings of incense and prostration, looking towards Peking. There is a paved walk to the principal audience-hall, on which none can tread but the emperor. At the same time, as if his transcendent majesty could derive no increase from personal decorations, he is distinguished from his court, unlike most Asiatic sovereigns, by being more plainly clad than those by whom he is surrounded. In Lord Macartney's mission, while the crowd of mandarins was covered with embroidery and splendour, the emperor appeared in a dress of plain brown silk, and a black velvet cap with a single pearl in front. Yellow, as the imperial colour, would seem at present rather to distinguish things pertaining to his use, or connected with him in other ways, than to constitute a part of his actual garments, except perhaps on very great occasions. The sovereign of China has the absolute disposal of the succession, and, if he pleases, can name his heir out of his own family. This has descended from time immemorial; and the ancient monarchs, Yaou and Shun, are famous examples of such a mode of selection. The imperial authority or sanction to all public acts is conveyed by the impression of a seal, some inches square, and composed of jade, a greenish white stone, called by the Chinese *Yu*. Any particular directions or remarks by the emperor himself are added in red, commonly styled "the vermilion pencil." All imperial edicts of a special nature, after being addressed to the proper tribunal, or other authority, are promulged in the Peking Gazette, which contains nothing but what relates to the supreme government; that is, either reports to the emperor, or mandates from him. It is death to falsify any paper therein contained: but it must be observed, that these special edicts of the sovereign, as applicable to the exigences of particular cases, either in aggravation or mitigation of punishment, are not allowed to be applied as precedents in penal jurisdiction.* There is more wisdom in this rule than in that which gave to the rescripts of the Roman emperors, in individual cases, the force of perpetual laws,—a system which has very properly been called "arguing from particulars to generals."

As Pontifex Maximus, or high-priest of the empire, the "Son of Heaven" alone, with his immediate representatives, sacrifices in the government temples, with victims and incense. These rites, preceded as they are by fasting and purification, bear a perfect resemblance to the offerings with which we are familiar in the history of antiquity. No hierarchy is maintained at the public expense, nor any priesthood attached to the Confucian or

* Penal Code, Sect. 415.

government religion, as the sovereign and his great officers perform that part. The two religious orders of Fo and Taou, which are only *tolerated*, and not maintained, by the government, derive support entirely from their own funds, or from voluntary private contributions. This remark must of course be confined to China; for in Mongol Tartary the emperor finds it expedient to show more favour to the lamas of the Buddhist hierarchy, on account of their influence over the people of those extensive regions. It is a striking circumstance that the Confucian persuasion has continued supreme in China, though the conquerors of the country were not Confucians.

The emperor's principal ministers form the Nuy-kŏ, or "interior council chamber," and the chief counsellors are four in number, two Tartars and two Chinese, the former always taking precedence: they all bear the titles of Choong-t'hang and Kŏ-laou, written by the Jesuits Colao. Below these are a number of assessors, who, together with them, form the great council of state. The body whence these chief ministers are generally selected is the Imperial College, or National Institute, of the Hân-lin. If there is any thing which can be called a hierarchy of the state religion (which we have already stated the government does not maintain in a special shape), it is this Hân-lin. In his memoirs of Napoleon, Bourrienne relates a very characteristic trait: in the classification of his private library, the emperor arranged the Bible under the head of political works. Just in the same spirit the Chinese government makes religion an engine, or rather a part, of political rule. The sovereign is high-priest, and his ministers are the members of the hierarchy; and the sacred books of Confucius are studied and expounded by the Hân-lin college, which in this respect is a species of Sorbonne. Besides the supreme council of the emperor already mentioned, there is the Keun-ky-tâ-chin, a body of privy-counsellors, for occasions when secrecy and despatch may be particularly required. The person called Duke Ho, in Lord Amherst's embassy, was one of these.

The Lew-poo, or six boards for the conduct of government business in detail, are, 1. The Board of Official Appointments, which takes cognizance of the conduct of all civil officers; 2. The Board of Revenue, which regulates all fiscal matters; 3. The Board of Rites and Ceremonies; 4. The Military Board; 5. The Supreme Court of Criminal Jurisdiction; 6. The Board of Public Works. These have all subordinate offices under them; as, for instance, the Astronomical Board is attached to the third, the ritual being regulated by the calendar.

The Lyfân-yuen may be literally rendered by the "office for foreign affairs." As its name imports, it has charge of the external relations of the empire. One of the presidents was deputed to receive the British embassy in 1816, and they consist always of Manchow or Mongol Tartars, no Chinese ever being employed. A very peculiar feature of the government is next observable in the Too-chă yuen, or office of censors, of which the members are generally styled Yu-she. There are two presidents, a Tartar and a Chinese, and the members consist in all of about forty or fifty, of which several are sent to various parts of the empire, as imperial inspectors, or perhaps, more properly speaking, spies. By the ancient custom of the empire they are privileged to present any advice or remonstrance to the sovereign without danger of losing their lives; but they are frequently degraded or punished when their addresses are unpalatable. An example of the office, and the fate of one of these, occurs at the commencement of the romance of the "Fortunate Union," published by the Oriental Translation Committee. A living example, however, is conspicuous in Soong-ta-jin, the conductor of Lord Macartney's embassy, who, at a very advanced age, is in a state of what may be styled respectable disgrace, for the boldness and honesty with which he has always spoken out.

The foregoing are the principal organs of the imperial government at Peking. The provinces are placed under the principal charge, either singly of a fooyuen, or governor, or two provinces together are made subject to a tsoong-tŏ, or "general governor," who has fooyuens under him for each single province. Canton and Kuâng-sy, adjoining, are together subject to the tsoong-tŏ, commonly called the Viceroy of Canton. In each of these governments there is a chief criminal judge and a treasurer, the latter having usually cognizance of civil suits, but his especial business being the charge of the territorial revenue. The salt department is sufficiently important to be under the particular management of the yen-yun-sse, or "salt-mandarin," as he is called at Canton; the Chinese government, like so many others, having reserved to itself the monopoly of this necessary of life.

The separate cities and districts of each province, in the three ranks of Foo, Chow, and Hien, are under the charge of their respective magistrates, who take their rank from the cities they govern. The total number of civil magistrates throughout China is estimated at 14,000. The importance of the European trade at Canton has given rise to the special appointment there of the hae-kuân, or commissioner of the customs, who is called by Europeans hoppo, a corruption of hoo-poo, the board of revenue at Peking. He is generally some Tartar favourite of the emperor, sent down to make his fortune by the foreign trade, and he generally contrives to do this rapidly, by squeezing the Hong merchants, over whom he has entire control.

A red book (being literally one with a red cover),

in six small volumes, is printed quarterly by authority, containing the name, birthplace, and other particulars relating to every official person in the empire. No individual can hold a magistracy in his own province; and each public officer is changed periodically, to prevent growing connexions and liaisons with those under his government. A son, a brother, or any other very near relation, cannot hold office under a corresponding relative. Once in three years the viceroy of each province forwards, to the board of civil appointments, the name of every officer under his government down to a hien's deputy, with remarks on their conduct and character, which have all been received from the immediate superiors of each :—a plan not unlike that which has lately been adopted in the civil government of British India. According to this report, every officer is raised or degraded so many degrees. Each magistrate is obliged to state, in the catalogue of his titles, the number of steps that he has been either raised or degraded. The offences of great officers are tried by imperial commissioners, specially appointed. Disturbances or rebellions in a province are never forgiven to a governor or viceroy. The governor of Canton, who only one year before had obtained signal marks of the emperor's favour, was ruined in 1832 by the rebellion or irruption of the mountaineers in the northwest, though he was quite innocent of any blame on the occasion.

The relative degrees of civil and military officers are partly distinguished by the colour of the ball which they wear at the apex or point of their conical caps. These are red, light blue, dark blue, crystal, white stone, and gold; and, with some modifications, they serve to distinguish what are called the "nine ranks." Each ball is accompanied by its corresponding badge, which is a piece of silk embroidery, about a foot square, with the representation of a bird, or other device, on both the breast and back of the ceremonial habit, together with a necklace of very large "court-beads" descending to the waist.

These mere outward decorations, however, are not infallible signs of the real rank of the wearer, for the bare permission to assume the dress, without any of the powers or privileges of an officer of government, may be purchased for a large sum of money. The only benefit derived is this, that, in case of a breach of the law, the individual cannot be punished *on the spot*, nor until he has been formally deprived of his ball, or button, a process which is not long in performing. Any Hong merchant at Canton, who should have purchased leave to wear the blue ball on his cap, may be cited to appear by a magistrate of the lowest grade, who wears only a gold or rather a gilt one, and, if really criminal, he may be deprived of his finery and punished with the bamboo like any unprivileged person.

It may be considered as one proof of social advancement on the part of the Chinese, that the civil authority is generally superior to the military, and that letters always rank above arms, in spite even of the manner in which the Tartars obtained the empire. In this respect China may be said to have subdued her conquerors. A military mandarin of the highest grade may be often seen on foot, when a civil officer of middling rank would be considered as degraded unless in a chair with four bearers; the others are not allowed chairs, but may ride. The present dynasty, as an encouragement to its army, established examinations, or rather trials, in the military art (as in riding and shooting with the bow), at which the candidates are ranked for promotion in three degrees like the civilians, though of course they can never come in competition with each other. The value which they attach to personal strength and dexterity in a commander, and the rank which the bow and arrow hold in their estimation, seem to prove clearly that the military art is not beyond its infancy among the Chinese.

Mandarin seated in a Sedan.—From Staunton.

All the military of the empire are under the management of their proper tribunal or board at Peking, the power of which, however, is jealously checked by a dependance on some of the others; as the Board of Revenue must supply the funds, and the Board of Public Works the *matériel*, of the army. The trusty Tartar troops are ranged under the eight standards; viz., the yellow, white, red, and blue, and each of these colours bordered by one of the others. The green flag distinguishes the Chinese troops. Each of the Tartar standards is said to consist of 10,000 men, making a standing army of 80,000. There is, besides, the local militia spread through the provinces; but this, from all that has been observed of it, is such a ragged and undisciplined rout, as to be fit for little more than the purposes of a police.

Including this militia, the whole number receiving pay throughout the empire has been estimated at 700,000, of which by far the largest portion are fixed to their native districts, cultivating the land, or following some other private pursuit. This circumstance, in a peaceful country, makes the profession of a militia-man an object of solicitude, as it provides something over and above a man's ordinary means. How ill-calculated it must be to produce efficient soldiers need scarcely be argued. The reasons adduced by Adam Smith, in his third volume, to prove the superiority of the militia of a barbarous nation over that of a civilized one, are quite conclusive on the subject, and best illustrated by the conquest of this very country by the Manchows, a mere maniple of a nation.

The missionaries themselves, quoted by Du Halde, who were much more accustomed to magnify than diminish the merit of any thing Chinese, seemed to be aware of the inferiority of these troops as soldiers. "They are not comparable," it is observed, "to our troops in Europe for either courage or discipline, and they are easily disordered and put to the rout. Besides that the Chinese are naturally effeminate, and the Tartars are almost become Chinese, the profound peace they have enjoyed does not give them occasion to become warlike." Several circumstances conduce to prevent China from deriving such advantage as she might to her military power, from the actual amount of her opulence and population. First, that pride and conceit, which are a bar to all improvement in the arts, and, among the rest, the art of war. Secondly, that jealousy of the Chinese population, which prevents the Tartar government from making of it such efficient troops as it might. Thirdly, that overwhelming superiority which the empire possesses over the petty and barbarous states on its frontiers; and which, in having prevented aggressions on it, has precluded the practice and experience so necessary to make good soldiers.

The long and successful resistance of the Meaoutse, a race of barbarians in the mountainous parts of the interior of China itself, and their independence at the present time, attest the weakness of Chinese military resources, and the very moderate efficiency of troops, which are seldom employed in any thing more formidable than the suppression of a revolt in some starving province, and thus engaged, as it were, in fighting with shadows. The Canton troops in 1832 were defeated by the mountaineers on the borders, and in fact proved utterly worthless from the general use of opium, and the absence of practice and discipline. This on land: but their navy is even worse. The long and successful career of the Ladrones, or pirates, in the vicinity of Canton, who were, after all, subdued only by the *honours* conferred on their chief as the price of his submission, is sufficient evidence on this point.

The abuses and malversation, on the part of military officers intrusted with funds for the provision of soldiers, appear to be frequent; and there is reason to suppose that some of the assumed militia of China are little better than men of straw, whose allotted funds are misapplied, if not after the example, yet in the manner, of that eminent commander Sir John Falstaff. It must have been to some such system that our embassy in 1816 was indebted for the ludicrous scenes exhibited in its progress. The emperor's edicts ordained that the troops should wear "an imposing aspect;" but, on approaching a town or station, numbers of fellows might be seen scouring along the banks of the river, laden with jackets and accoutrements, which were clapped on the backs of those who had been pressed for the occasion, and who betrayed, from under their assumed habiliments, the primitive dirt and rags of their condition.

Very few mounted soldiers were seen by either of our embassies; and, whatever may be their actual amount, they are said to be nearly all Tartars. A great difference seems to exist between the pay of Tartars and Chinese. One of the former, being a foot-soldier, is allowed two taëls per month, or about fivepence a day, with an allowance of rice; one of the latter, only one taël and six tenths, without the rice. The reasons for this difference may be the following:—First, that the Tartar in China belongs to a standing army, at a distance from his home, and dependant solely on his profession; while the other is commonly, if not always, a militia-man, carrying on his own occupations when off duty. Secondly, some allowance may be made for the national partiality of the governing power, and the necessity of attaching its confidential servants by liberality.

The most common uniform of the military is a jacket of blue turned up with red, or red bordered with white, over a long petticoat of blue. The cap is either of rattan or strips of bamboo painted, being in a conical shape, and well suited to ward off a blow; though on some occasions they wear a cap of cloth and silk, similar to that of the mandarins, without the ball or button at the top. Some few are defended by a clumsy-looking quilted armour of cloth, studded with metal buttons, which descends in a long petticoat, and gives the wearer the appearance of one who could neither fight nor fly. The helmet is of iron, in the shape of an inverted funnel, having a point at the top, to which is attached a bunch of silk or horse-hair.

The principal arms of the cavalry are bows and arrows, the bow being of elastic wood and horn combined, with a string of silk strongly twisted and wrought. The strength of their bows is estimated by the weight required to bend them, varying from about eighty pounds to a hundred weight. The string, in shooting, is held behind an agate or stone ring on the right thumb, the first joint of which is

Chinese Shield.—From an original drawing in the India House.

bent forward and confined by the middle joint of the forefinger being pressed upon it. Their swords

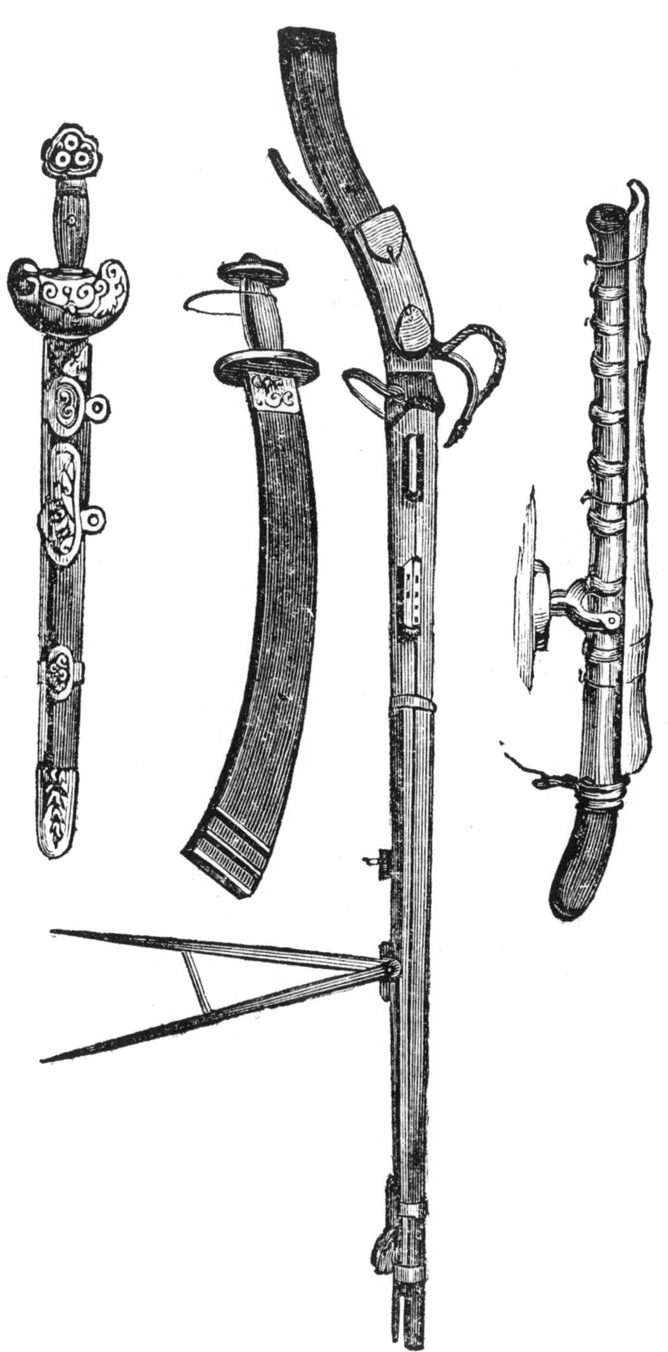

Instruments of War.

are generally ill-made, and their matchlocks considered by them as inferior weapons to the bow and arrow, which they may perhaps be, considering their appearance and make. Some are provided with shields, constructed of rattan turned spirally round a centre.

With regard to the use of artillery, Du Halde observes with apparent reason, that, "though the knowledge of gunpowder is very ancient in China, artillery is but modern." It is clear that, as late as 1621, the city of Macao was invited to send three guns to Peking, with men to manage them, against the Tartars; and equally certain that, under the last emperor of the Chinese dynasty, about the year 1636, when the empire was threatened by the Manchows, the Jesuits at Peking were desired by the emperor to instruct his people in casting some cannon. But the most successful operator in this way was the famous Ferdinand Verbiest, under whose inspection some hundred pieces of artillery were constructed for the Tartar emperor Kâng-hy, towards the end of the seventeenth century. This was made a subject of accusation against the Jesuits at Rome; but they defended themselves by arguing that it promoted the cause of Christianity, by making their services necessary to the Chinese government. It is certain that, during the course of three centuries, no mission has ever succeeded for a time so well as theirs, but that at present there are not a dozen European missionaries in the interior, among a population estimated at more than 300,000,000 of souls.

The highest military rank is that of a tseang-keun, or Tartar general, one of whom has charge of the regular troops in Canton province: this post can never be filled by a Chinese, but secondary commands may. Below these are subordinate officers, promoted in regular order from the lowest grade, according to their physical strength, and their skill in shooting with the bow, combined with the activity and zeal which they may occasionally display in cases of civil commotion or revolt. One very singular feature we must not forget to notice, in regard to the military officers of China. They are all subject to corporal punishment, and very often experience it, together with the punishment of the cangue, or moveable pillory, consisting of a heavy frame of wood, sometimes upwards of a hundred pounds in weight, with holes for the head and hands. This parental allotment of a certain quantum of flagellation and personal exposure, is occasionally the fate of the highest officers, and, upon the whole, must be regarded as a very odd way of improving their military character. It must be observed, however, that enterprising courage is not considered as a merit in Chinese tactics. They have a maxim, that "rash and arrogant soldiers must be defeated," which may be allowed to contain some truth; and the chief virtue of their strategy is extreme caution and love of craft, not without a large share of perfidy and falsehood: so that to treat with a Chinese general, and expect him to fulfil his engagements, would be altogether a miscalculation.

We may now turn our attention to that very efficient engine for the control of its vast and densely-thronged population, the penal code of China; and this deserves the more particular notice, as affording the best data for correctly estimating the character of the people to whom it has been adapted. The most perfect code of laws in the abstract is unavailing and useless, if not congenial to the dispositions and habits of those for whom it is formed; and, without keeping this in view, we might be apt to deny to the criminal laws of China the share of praise to which they are justly entitled, after making due abatement for their plain and undeniable defects. The following testimony in their favour, from a very able critique* on Sir George Staunton's version of the Leu-lee, must be considered as praise of a high kind:—"The most remarkable thing in this code is its great reasonableness, clearness, and consistency; the business-like brevity and directness of the various provisions, and the plainness and moderation of the language in which they are expressed. There is nothing here of the monstrous *verbiage* of most other Asiatic productions; none of the superstitious deliration, the miserable incoherence, the tremendous *nonsequiturs* and eternal repetitions of those oracular performances; nothing even of the turgid adulation, the accumulated epithets, and fatiguing self-praise of other Eastern despotisms; but a clear, concise, and distinct series of enactments, savouring throughout of practical judgment and European good sense, and, if not always conformable to our improved notions of expediency in this country, in general approaching to them more nearly than the codes of most other nations."

After this fair tribute, the evident defects of the system, being in some measure those of the state of society in which it originated, may be pointed out. There is, in the first place, a constant meddling with, and anxiety to compel the performance of, those relative duties which are better left to the operation of any other sanctions than positive laws. The evil of this perpetual interference of the law to enforce the practice of virtues, which in great measure cease to be such on being made compulsory, is to diminish their beneficial influence on the mind; and it is on the same principle that compulsory charity, even, has been condemned (though without sufficient reason), as it exists among us in the instance of the poor-laws. The Chinese carry their care beyond this life: for any person who is convicted of neglecting his occasional visits to the

* Edinburgh Review, August, 1810.

tombs of his ancestors is subject to punishment. A second defect which we may notice is that minute attention to trifles, and that excessive care to provide for every possible shade of difference that may arise between one case and another, which is so opposed to the European maxim, "*de minimis non curat lex.*" The Chinese, however, still stop short of the Hindoo institutes of Menu, which provide for some rare and singular contingences. For instance, the inheritance of a son being a whole, and that of a daughter a half, there is a peculiar sagacity and foresight in directing that the portion of an *hermaphrodite* shall be half of the one, and half of the other, or three fourths! A third defect is the occasional manifestation of a jealous fear, on the part of the government, lest, in the execution of its enactments, the judge should ever find himself impeded or hampered by too great clearness of definition, or the subject derive too much protection from the distinct statement of crime and punishment. Hence those vague generalities by which the benefits of a written code are in a great measure annulled. The following enactment is a specimen:—"Whoever is guilty of *improper conduct*, and such as is contrary to the *spirit* of the laws, though not a breach of any specific article, shall be punished at the least with forty blows; and, when the *impropriety* is of a *serious nature*, with eighty blows." The Chinese may justly say that it is "difficult to escape from the net of the law," when its meshes are thus closed against the exit of the minutest of the fry.

One feature of the criminal code, inseparable from the nature of the government from which it sprang, is the remorseless and unrelenting cruelty and injustice which mark all its provisions against the crime of treason. Nothing perhaps could more strongly show the different tempers of despotism and freedom, than the contrast between the Chinese law of high treason and our own. In China, every species of advantage and protection afforded to the criminal, in ordinary cases of a capital nature, is taken away from the traitor; in England, every possible safeguard is afforded him. It is well known that, with us, the prisoner must be furnished, at least ten days before his trial, with a copy of his endictment, a list of witnesses, and a list of the panel, or those from whom the jury are to be chosen. Then, again, he may challenge or object to as many as thirty-five of the panel in making up the jury; he cannot be convicted with less than two legal witnesses; and he may employ counsel in his defence. Now, in China, not a single circumstance of indulgence or safety to the criminal, in capital cases, is ever stated throughout the whole code, without this addition, "*except* in cases of high treason." The slenderness of the protection is only to be paralleled by the barbarity of the punishment, and, as in other absolute despotisms, the innocent family of the offender is consigned to destruction.* In 1803, an attempt was made on the life of the emperor by a single assassin. He was condemned to a lingering death, and his sons, "being of a tender age," to be strangled! Going back to the patriarchal origin of the government, the Chinese derive a sanction for their law of treason from their sacred books. These enjoin it on a son to pursue the author of his father's death to extremity; and Confucius himself tells him "not to live under the same heaven with the slayer of his father." The extension of this rule to the sovereign is, in the mind of every Chinese, a matter of course.

The arrangement of the penal code is extremely

* Among the Persians and Macedonians, not only the criminals convicted of treason, but all their relations and friends, were put to death. The posterity of Marius's faction were disqualified, by a law of Sylla, from advancing themselves by their own merit to estates and offices.—*Yorke's Considerations on the Law of Forfeiture.*

methodical and lucid. The first head is composed principally of general definitions and explanations in reference to the whole code; and the six following, which constitute the body of the work, correspond exactly to the Six Supreme Boards or Tribunals at Peking, being in fact the best illustrations of the respective duties and functions of those councils. In that light they may be briefly presented to the reader.

The division concerning the *Administration of Civil Offices* corresponds to the first of the Supreme Tribunals before noticed, whose title may be expressed by "the Board of Civil Appointments." Its two books treat, 1. Of the System of Government. 2. Of the Conduct of Officers.

The next comprehends *Fiscal and Statistical Laws*, and answers to the Board of Revenue at Peking. Its seven books comprise, 1. The Enrolment of the People. 2. Lands and Tenements. 3. Marriage (in its statistical relations). 4. Public Property. 5. Duties and Customs. 6. Private Property. 7. Sales and Markets.

The third treats of the *Ritual Laws*, and comes of course under the Tribunals of Rites and Ceremonies. The two books of this division treat, 1. Of Sacred Rites. 2. Miscellaneous Observances.

The division concerning *Military Laws* belongs to the Tribunal of War, or Military Board, and contains five books. 1. The Protection of the Palace. 2. The Regulation of the Army. 3. The Protection of the Frontier. 4. Military Horses and Cattle. 5. Expresses and Public Posts.

The next comprehends *Criminal Laws*, and pertains to the "Tribunal of Punishments," being by far the most considerable portion, and comprising eleven books. The principal heads are, Treason, Robbery, and Theft, Murder and Homicide of various kinds, Criminal Intercourse, Disturbing Graves, Quarrelling and Fighting, and Incendiarism.

The last division of the code, treating of *Public Works*, and coming under the appropriate Board at Peking, contains only two books. 1. Public Buildings. 2. Public Ways.

With regard to the punishments by which these laws are enforced, it is important to observe that very unfounded notions have been prevalent as to the caprice or cruelty which can be exercised towards criminals. Some vulgar daubs, commonly sold at Canton, and representing the punishment of the damned in the Buddhist hell, have been absurdly styled "Chinese punishments," and confounded with the true ones. There is in the first division of the code a very strict definition of all the legal pains and penalties to which the subject is liable, and even the application of torture in forcing evidence is strictly limited in its extent and application. History indeed relates the extraordinary contrivances of cruelty adopted by different tyrants previous to the formation of a distinct and written code; but this is common to nearly all countries.

The most general instrument of punishment is the bamboo, whose dimensions are exactly defined. The number of blows, attached *gradatim* with such precision to every individual offence, answers the purpose of a scale or measurement of the degrees of crime; and this punishment being often commutable for fine or otherwise, the apparent quantity of flagellation is of course greater than the real. A small hollow cylinder, full of tallies or slips of wood, stands before the judge, and according to the nature of the offence he takes out a certain number, and throws them on the floor of the court. These are taken up by the attendants, and five blows nominally, but in reality only four, inflicted for each.* This mitigation goes to the emperor's credit, being called "imperial favour," and it is in strict conform-

* The ceremony of the bamboo is described in the "Fortunate Union," vol. ii., p. 62.

ity with the Chinese maxim, that, "in enacting laws, rigour is necessary; in executing them, mercy;" although the converse has been of late generally maintained among ourselves—in *theory* at least.

The next punishment is the *Kea*, or Cangue, which has been called the wooden collar, being a species of walking pillory, in which the prisoner is paraded, with his offence inscribed. It is sometimes worn for a month together, and as the hand cannot be put to the mouth, the wearer must be fed by others. After this comes, in the first place, temporary banishment, to a distance not exceeding fifty leagues from the prisoner's home; and then exile beyond the Chinese frontier, either temporary or for life. Tartars are punished by an equal number of blows with the whip instead of the bamboo, and, in ordinary cases, with the Cangue instead of banishment.

The three capital punishments are, 1. strangulation; 2. for greater crimes, decollation; 3. for treason, parricide (which ranks as petit treason), sacrilege, &c., that mode of execution called *Ling-chy*, "a disgraceful and lingering death," which Europeans have somewhat incorrectly styled *cutting into ten thousand pieces*. The heads of robbers and murderers are publicly exposed in a cage suspended on a pole.

Chinese prisons are very severe, and, as there is no *Habeas corpus* Act, the most frequent instruments of judicial injustice are prolonged imprisonments. Nothing tends more effectually to deter from crime than the prospect of incarceration in those miserable abodes, which the Chinese emphatically style Ty-yŏ, or *hell*, and the severity of which is increased by the confinement being solitary. Women in ordinary cases enjoy the fortunate exemption of being placed, as criminals, in the custody of their nearest relations, who are answerable for them, and in this manner they escape the farther contamination of vice in a prison. The legal mode of torture, in

Punishment of Wooden Collar.—From Staunton.

forcing evidence, is to squeeze the ankles or the fingers between three sticks, tied triangularly; the former being applied to male, and the latter to female prisoners. Oaths are never required, nor even admitted, in judicial proceedings; but very severe punishments are attached to falsehood in evidence.

Ten *privileged classes* are enumerated in the introductory division of the code, who cannot be tried and punished without a special reference to the emperor. The grounds of exemption (which, as usual, are denied in treason) consist, generally, in relationship to the imperial line, or in high character and station. Throughout cases where the crime is less than capital, any person under fifteen years of age, or above seventy, is allowed to redeem himself from punishment by a fine. A species of *king's evidence* is permitted in cases of thieving and robbery, with a view to the recovery of the lost goods: in fact, something more than mere pardon is offered; as the accomplice who informs is entitled to the reward attached to the discovery of the criminals. This, however, extends only to the *first offence*.

The law distinguishes, in most cases, between principals and accessaries *before* the fact, punishing the latter one degree less severely than the former; and in this respect it differs from our own system, by which accessaries *before* the fact are punished as principals; *after* the fact, merely as concealers of what they ought to have revealed. In treason, however, as usual, the Chinese law punishes both principals and accessaries, and their innocent relations, with a sweeping severity. Where the safety of the emperor or the stability of the government is not involved, milder and more benevolent traits are frequently discernible in this code. With a view, for instance, to promote kindred and domestic ties, it is provided that relatives and servants, living under the same roof, shall in ordinary cases be held innocent, though they conceal the offences of their fellow-inmates, or even assist in effecting their escape. This was probably enacted in conformity with that precept of Confucius :—"The father may conceal the offences of his son, and the son those of his father—uprightness consists with this."—(*Hea-Lun*, ch. 13.)

The desire entertained and professed by the Chinese government, that its subjects should be generally *acquainted* with the laws of the empire, has given rise to something not unlike our benefit of clergy. It is enacted that all those private individuals who are found capable of explaining the nature, or comprehending the objects of the laws, shall receive pardon for all offences resulting from accident (and not malice), or imputable to them only in consequence of the guilt of others, provided it be the *first offence*, and not implicated with any act of treason or rebellion. A considerable portion of the sixth division of the code is devoted to providing for justice in the administration of legal punishments, and establishing safeguards for the subject. Severe penalties are denounced against officers of government for unjust imprisonment, delay of justice, cruelty, &c. A species of bail is allowed to minor offenders in case of sickness, and they are exempted, or released from imprisonment, on sufficient security being given for their return. Torture is forbidden to be exercised on persons above seventy, or under fifteen, as well as on those labouring under permanent disease. Women can never be imprisoned except for capital offences, or for adultery. Torture and death cannot be inflicted on a pregnant woman until one hundred days after her confinement, in consideration, we presume, of the infant.

The condition of slavery in China is broadly marked by the absence of rights and immunities pertaining to those who are subjects, without being slaves. The law regards the former class with less care, and affords less protection to them, than to their masters. Every offence is aggravated or diminished in its penalty, according as it is committed by a slave towards a freeman, or *vice versâ*. For a slave to kill his master, is punished with lingering death, as petit treason; while the converse of the case is not even capital. We find the same distinctions existing in the early history of Europe, in respect to the comparative personal rights of freemen and slaves. But, besides domestic slavery, it seems that for some infractions of the laws a whole family is sometimes condemned to public servitude, as appears from Section CXL. of the penal code. Personal service, too, is frequently levied by the government as a species of taxation on the lowest class, or that which has nothing but its labour to contribute. The comparative uncertainty of this, notwithstanding sundry enactments against its abuse, is a great evil; and both our embassies had reason to regret that they were the innocent occasions of much oppression and ill-usage to the poor people who were pressed by the mandarins to track their boats.

Robbery, with the concerted use of offensive weapons, is punished with death, however small may be the amount taken; and, if a burglar be killed by him whose house he invades, it is deemed an act of justifiable homicide. An intimation conveyed to the local magistrate of Macao that the English were aware of this part of the law, and prepared to take advantage of it, had the good effect of preventing night robberies, which until then had been frequent. Simple stealing is punished only with the bamboo and with exile, on a scale proportioned to the amount; and there is reason to believe that death is *never* inflicted, whatever may be the value of the thing stolen. Theft among near relations is punished with less severity than ordinary stealing; and Sir George Staunton explains this, by its being the violation of a right not perfectly exclusive, since the thief, according to the Chinese system of clubbing in families, being part owner of the thing stolen, infringes only that *qualified* interest which each individual has in his share of the family property. Consistently enough with this principle, we may add that the thief seems to be more severely punished in proportion as the relationship becomes more distant, as having a smaller share of the property, and therefore violating a more exclusive right. But then it must be remarked that the rule does not apply to servants stealing from their masters, a crime which in China is also punished less severely than ordinary theft. The case is quite different among us in England, and with apparent reason, on the principle of its being a violation of necessary confidence, in addition to the violation of property.

The Chinese law of *homicide* derives additional interest from the circumstance of British subjects having on several occasions become obnoxious to it at Canton, and from its forming a very important subject of consideration in the establishment of our novel relations with the local government at that place. With its characteristic love of order and horror of tumults, the national code treats affrays with unusual severity. Killing in an affray, and killing with a regular weapon, without reference to any intent either expressed or implied, are punished with strangling. Killing by pure accident, that is, not in an affray, nor with a weapon, and where there was no previous knowledge of probable consequences, is redeemable by a fine of about 4*l.* to the relations of the deceased.

With regard to affrays, it must however be observed, that a limit is allowed to the period of responsibility, in all cases where the homicide was evidently not preconcerted. When a person is wounded with only the hands or a stick, twenty days constitute the term of responsibility, after which the death of the sufferer does not make the offence capital. With a sharp instrument, fire, or scalding water, the term is extended to thirty days. In case of gun-shot wounds, to forty days; of broken bones or very violent wounds, fifty days. As the translator of the Leu-lee observes, the judicious application of the knowledge of this particular law once contributed to extricate the company's servants in China from very serious difficulties in the case of a native killed by a sailor. The situation of the English at Canton in respect to homicides will be particularly noticed in another place.

Fathers have virtually the power of life and death over their children; for, even if they kill them designedly, they are subject to only the chastisement of the bamboo, and a year's banishment; if struck by them, to no punishment at all. The penalty for striking parents, or for cursing them, is death, as among the Hebrews.—(Exod. xxi.) In practice, it does not appear that this absolute power bestowed on fathers is productive of evil; the natural feeling being, upon the whole, a sufficient security against its abuse.

The law of China is so tenacious of order, and so anxious to prevent the chance of homicide from quarrels, that some punishment is attached to the mere act of striking another with the hand or foot; —not as a private, but as a public offence. Though of course this cannot, in the generality of cases, be acted upon, it may account partly for the common spectacle of two Chinese jumping about, and vociferating their mutual reproaches for an incredible time without coming to blows. This noisy gesticulation seems to answer the purpose of a moral safety-valve and is certainly more harmless than actual hostilities, though perhaps more disagreeable to the neighbours, inasmuch as it lasts longer. The responsible elder of the village or district (divided always into tithings and hundreds) often interposes on these occasions, and restores quiet. The law also provides some punishment for opprobrious language, on the ground of its having "a tendency to produce quarrels and affrays;" or, as assumed by the English law in the criminal prosecution for libel, tending to a breach of the *king's peace*.

That portion of the Chinese code which relates to fiscal or statistical matters, to the tenure of lands and to inheritance, will be noticed elsewhere; but we may mention the subject of *debts* in this place. A period is allowed by law, on the expiration of which the debtor becomes liable to the bamboo if his obligations are not discharged. A creditor sometimes quarters himself and his family on his debtor, and, provided that this is done without violence and tumult, the civil authority does not interfere. One of the insolvent Hong merchants had in this manner to entertain some of his Chinese creditors, until the representations to the government of those Europeans who had claims against him occasioned his banishment into Tartary; it being a much greater offence to owe money to a foreigner than to a native. The true reason of this is, the anxiety of that cautious government to prevent the recurrence of the trouble which it has in former times experienced, from the embarrassing claims and demands of strangers, and no real sense of justice towards them.

The able critique on the code, which we have already quoted, proceeds to say, "When we turn from the ravings of the Zendavesta, or the Puranas, to the tone of sense and of business of this Chinese collection, we seem to be passing from darkness to light—from the drivellings of dotage to the exercise of an improved understanding: and redundant and minute as these laws are in many particulars, we scarcely know any European code that is at once so copious and so consistent, or that is nearly so free from intricacy, bigotry, and fiction. In every thing relating to political freedom, or individual independence, it is, indeed, wofully defective; but for the repression of disorder, and the gentle coercion of a vast population, it appears to us to be, in general, equally mild and efficacious." The defects are of course inherent in all *despotisms*, under which the legislator is not embarrassed by those considerations which in free states render every new law a problem, involving the greatest quantity of good to the public at the least expense of liberty to the individual; and which, in countries where there is more liberty than moral instruction, or where men are better acquainted with their *rights* than with their *duties*, must always render the business of government a difficult task.

It has been reasonably proposed by Sir George Staunton to estimate the Chinese legislation by its results, "to judge of the tree by its fruits, some of which (he observes) we shall find to be wholly inconsistent with the hypothesis of a very bad government, or a very vicious state of society." On this subject he quotes his colleague* in the commission of the last British embassy, "whose extensive acquaintance with Persia and India rendered him a peculiarly competent judge of comparative merit in this case. He pronounces China superior to the other countries of Asia, both in the arts of government, and the general aspect of society; and adds, that the laws are more generally known, and more equally administered; that those examples of oppression, accompanied with infliction of barbarous punishment, which offend the eye and distress the feelings of the most hurried traveller in other Asiatic countries, are scarcely to be met with in China; that the proportion which the middling orders bear to the other classes of the community appeared considerable; that, compared with Turkey, Persia, and

* Mr. Ellis, now ambassador to Persia, with whom the writer of this travelled through China, and always heard him express the same sentiments.

parts of India, an impression was produced highly favourable to the comparative situation of the lower orders."

"These statements," adds Sir George, "proceeding from a writer whose general opinions are certainly not very favourable to the government or people of China, have the greater weight. I should be disposed to add my own testimony to the same facts and in the same spirit. In the course of our journey through the Chinese empire, on the occasion of that embassy, I can recall to my recollection (the seaport of Canton of course excepted) but very few instances of beggary or abject misery among the lower classes, or of splendid extravagance among the higher; and I conceived myself enabled to trace almost universally throughout China the unequivocal signs of an industrious, thriving, and contented people."

Chinese law, with all its faults, is comparative perfection when contrasted with that of Japan, as described by Kœmpfer. "I have often wondered," says he, "at the brief and laconic style of those tablets which are hung up on the roads to notify the emperor's pleasure. There is no reason given how it came about that such a law was made; no mention of the lawgiver's view and intention; nor any graduated penalty put upon the violation thereof. The bare transgression of the law is capital, without any regard to the degree or heinousness of the crime, or the favourable circumstances the offender's case may be attended with." Some such comparison, perhaps, suggested the complacent reflections of *Tienkeeshĕ*, a Chinese, who thus wrote:—"I felicitate myself that I was born in China! It constantly occurs to me, what if I had been born beyond the sea, in some remote part of the earth, where the cold freezes, or the heat scorches; where the people are clothed with the leaves of plants, eat wood, dwell in the wilderness, lie in holes of the earth, are far removed from the converting maxims of the ancient kings, and are ignorant of the domestic relations. Though born as one of the generation of men, I should not have been different from a beast. But how happily I have been born in China! I have a house to live in, have drink and food, and commodious furniture. I have clothing and caps, and infinite blessings. Truly the highest felicity is mine."*

The country cannot, upon the whole, be very ill-governed, whose subjects write in this style. But it is a still more remarkable fact, that the following is a popular maxim of the Chinese, and one frequently quoted by them:—"To violate THE LAW is the same crime in the emperor as in a subject." This plainly intimates that there are certain sanctions which the people in general look upon as superior to the will of the sovereign himself. These are contained in their sacred books, whose principle is literally, *salus populi suprema lex*; as we shall see when we come to consider them hereafter. However much this principle may at times be violated under the pressure of a foreign Tartar dominion, it nevertheless continues to be recognised, and must doubtless exercise more or less influence on the conduct of the government.

* Chinese Gleaner, vol. I., p. 190.

CHAPTER VII.

CHARACTER AND MANNERS.

Chinese appear at Canton in their worst phase.—Instance of Gratitude.—Good and bad Traits.—Pride and Ignorance.—Age and high Station most honoured.—Regard to Kindred and Birthplace.—Real extent of Infanticide.—Physical Characteristics. — Personal Appearance. — Caprices of National Taste.—Primitive Features.—Degeneracy of Imperial Kindred.—Highest Honours open to Talent and Learning.—Absence of Ostentation.—Condition of Female Sex.—But one legal Wife.—Marriage.—Ceremonies attending it.—Children. —Education.—Funeral Rites.—Periods of Mourning.

Most of the good and bad traits of the Chinese character may, as usual, be traced to the advantages or faults of their social system. If those principles of government and those laws, of which we have given a slight sketch, have the effect of imbuing them with some of the vices connected with timidity of character, which are particularly disesteemed in Europe, it is only fair to give them credit, on the other hand, for the valuable qualities which they do really possess. The Chinese have, upon the whole, been under-estimated, or, rather, unfairly despised, on the score of their moral attributes. The reason of this has probably been, the extremely unfavourable aspect in which they have appeared to the generality of observers at Canton: just as if any one should attempt to form an estimate of *our* national character in England, from that peculiar phase under which it may present itself at some commercial seaport.

It is, in fact, a matter of astonishment, that the Chinese people at Canton are no worse than we find them. They are well acquainted with that maxim of their government, by which it openly professes to "rule barbarians by misrule, like *beasts*, and not like native subjects;" and they are perpetually supplied by the local authorities with every motive to behave towards strangers as if they were really a degraded order of beings. The natural consequence is, that their conduct to Europeans is very different from their conduct among themselves. Except when under the influence of either interest or of fear, they are often haughty and insolent to strangers, as well as fraudulent; and such is the effect of opinion among them, that even in cases where interest may persuade them to servility, this will not be exhibited in the presence of a countryman. A beggar has often been seen who, though he would bend his knee very readily to European passengers when unobserved, refrained altogether from it while Chinese were passing by. It was some time before the very coolies, the lowest class of servants, would condescend to carry a lantern before a European at night; and still longer before they could be induced, by any wages, to convey him in a sedan even at Macao, where it is permitted. Is it surprising, then, that they reconcile it, without much difficulty, to their feelings, to overreach and ill-use occasionally these creatures of an inferior rank, who, as their government phrases it, come to benefit by "the transforming influence of Chinese civilization;" or, rather, is it *not* very surprising that so general a course of honesty and good faith, and so many instances of kindness and generosity, even, have been experienced in their intercourse with us? If we deny to the Chinese their fair advantages, on a view somewhat more extended than the precincts of Canton afford, and if we condemn them ignorantly, it is the precise fault which we have most to censure on their part. We in fact become as illiberal as themselves.

The following anecdote, from a miscellaneous volume* by Sir George Staunton, is a favourable specimen of Chinese character, as it has appeared even at Canton. A considerable merchant had some dealings with an American trader, who attempted to quit the port without discharging his debt, and would have succeeded but for the spirit and activity of a young officer of one of the company's ships. He boarded the American vessel when upon the point of sailing, and, by his remonstrances or otherwise, prevailed on the American to make a satisfactory arrangement with his creditor. In acknowledgment for this service, the Chinese merchant purchased from the young officer, in his several successive voyages to China, on very favourable terms, the whole of his commercial adventure. He might thus have been considered to have fulfilled any ordinary claim upon his gratitude; but he went farther than this. After some years he expressed his surprise to the officer that he had not yet obtained the command of a ship. The other replied, that it was a lucrative post, which could be obtained only by purchase, and at an expense of some thousand pounds, a sum wholly out of his power to raise. The Chinese merchant said he would remove that difficulty, and immediately gave him a draught for the amount, to be repaid at his convenience. The officer died on his voyage home, and the draught was never presented; but it was drawn on a house of great respectability, and would have been duly honoured.

The late Dr. Morrison formed a very fair estimate of a people with whom he was better acquainted than most Europeans. "In China," he observes, "there is much to blame, but something to learn. Education is there made as general as possible, and moral instruction is ranked above physical." The

* Notices of China, part ii.

consequence is, that industry, tranquillity, and content are unusually prevalent in the bulk of the population. The exceptions to this, in the tumults which arise from local distress in limited districts, are in some measure the consequence of the very means taken to prevent them. The Chinese are bad political economists: the government, instead of allowing the trade in grain to take its natural course, erects its own granaries, in which there is much inevitable abuse, and prohibits the business of the great corn-factor, who, in consulting his own interests, would much better relieve the dearth of one season by the redundancy of another. The people, who are taught to look to the public granaries for relief, and have been led by their patriarchal theory of government to refer the good which they enjoy to the emperor and his delegates, very naturally attribute the evil which they suffer to the same quarters; and the government, aware of the danger, is proportionately anxious to guard against it. If it fails, in the pursuit of an erroneous system, there is no room for surprise.

Notwithstanding that his power is absolute, the emperor himself on all occasions endeavours to prove that his conduct is based in reason, and originates in benevolence,—the truth of the argument being of course a distinct affair. From the habits in which they are brought up, as well as from the operation of certain positive laws already noticed, the people are more ready to reason with each other than to resort to the *ultima ratio* of force. The advantageous features of their character, as mildness, docility, industry, peaceableness, subordination, and respect for the aged, are accompanied by the vices of specious insincerity, falsehood, with mutual distrust, and jealousy. Lying and deceit, being generally the refuge of the weak and timid, have been held in Europe to be the most disgraceful vices, ever since the influence of those feudal institutions, under which strength and courage were the things most valued. The Chinese at any time do not attach the same degree of disgrace to deceit; and least of all do they discountenance it towards Europeans at Canton. A true calculation of their own interest makes most of the merchants of that place sufficiently scrupulous in their commercial engagements, but on all other points "the foreign devil," as they call him, is fair game. Many a Chinese of Canton, in his intercourse with a stranger, would seem occasionally to have an abstract love of falsehood and trickery, independently of any thing that he can gain by it; and he will appear sometimes to volunteer a lie, when it would be just the same to him to tell the truth. Mr. Barrow has attributed their national insincerity to a motive which no doubt operates with the *higher* classes, as much as an ignorant contempt, and a mischievous malignity, do with the rabble. "As a direct refusal," he observes, "to any request would betray a want of good-breeding, every proposal finds their immediate acquiescence: they promise without hesitation, but generally disappoint by the invention of some slight pretence or plausible objection: they have no proper sense of the obligations of truth." This renders all negotiations with them on public matters almost entirely fruitless, as no reliance whatever can be placed on them for the fulfilment of engagements. They dispense with faith towards foreigners in a manner truly Machiavelian.

The excellent observer above quoted remarked also the cheerful character and willing industry of the Chinese. This is in fact a most invaluable trait, and, like most other virtues, it brings its own reward: the display is not, however, limited to their own country. The superior character of the Chinese as *colonists*, in regard to intelligence, industry, and general sobriety, must be derived from their education, and from the influence of something good in their national system. Their government very justly regards education as omnipotent, and some share of it nearly every Chinese obtains. Their domestic discipline is all on the side of social order and universal industry.

The important advantages which they certainly possess, more especially in comparison with the adjoining countries, have given the Chinese the inordinate national pride so offensive to Europeans. These illusions of self-love, fostered by ignorance, have inspired them with notions of their country, in regard to the rest of the earth, quite analogous to those entertained by the old astronomers, of the earth relatively to the universe. They think it the centre of a system, and call it *choong-ku* , the central nation; nor is it a small increase of foreign intercourse and knowledge that will be required to set them right. The natural disposition of the people to despise strangers has been artfully promoted by the mandarins. A timid and miserable policy has led them to consider it their interest to increase the mutual dislike and disunion. Hence the slanderous proclamations exhibited by them against foreigners at Canton, and the penalties attached to a "traitorous intercourse" with Europeans. The most dangerous accusation against a native is that of being subject to foreign influence in *any* way.

There is a positive law against the use of things not sanctioned by custom; partly therefore from fear, partly from conceit, they are very little inclined to adopt foreign modes, or purchase foreign manufactures. Raw produce, or the *material* of manufactures, finds a better market among them; but the most marketable commodity of all is *dollars*. Indisputably superior as Europe is in science, and in the productions of science, yet to a Chinese, who sees few things brought from thence that really suit his peculiar and conventional wants, or that are in conformity with the usages enjoined by the ritual,—and who, until lately, heard little of the different states into which Europe is divided, but the indistinct rumour of their endless wars and massacres on a large scale,—it is not surprising if no very elevated picture presented itself, in comparison with his own immense and wealthy country, its hundreds of millions of industrious and intelligent people, and an uninterrupted peace of nearly 200 years, even if we go no farther than the Tartar invasion. Whatever there is of extreme poverty and destitution in the country, arises solely from the unusual degree in which the population is made to press against the means of subsistence, by causes which we shall notice hereafter; and not from any fault in the *distribution* of wealth, which is perhaps far more equal here than in any other country. There is much less inequality in the fortunes than in the ranks and conditions of men. The comparatively low estimation in which *mere* wealth is held, is a considerable moral advantage on the side of the Chinese; for—

> "Magnum pauperies opprobrium, jubet
> Quidvis et facere et pati."

Poverty is no reproach among them. The two things which they most respect are, station derived from personal merit, and the claims of venerable old age. The last was signally honoured by Kang-hy, the second emperor of the reigning family. An inferior officer, of more than a hundred years of age, having come to an audience to do homage, the emperor rose from his seat and met him, desiring the old man to stand up without ceremony, and telling him he paid this respect to his great age. According to that connexion which exists between the languages and the usages of nations, the ordinary address of civility and respect in China is *Laou-yay*, "Old, or venerable Father," which, as a mere form of speech, is often addressed to a person half the age of the speaker.

The peaceful and prudential character of the people may be traced to the influence and authority of age. In consequence of the individuals of succeeding generations living entirely under the power and control of the oldest surviving heads of families, the ignorant and inexperienced are guided by the more mature judgment of the elders, and the sallies of rashness and folly easily restrained. The effects of example and of early habit are equally visible in their conversation. The Chinese frequently get the better of Europeans, in a discussion, by imperturbable coolness and gravity. It is part of their policy to gain the advantage by letting their opponent work himself into a passion, and place himself in the wrong: hence the more than ordinary necessity of carefully preserving the temper with them. Gravity of demeanour is much affected, particularly by magistrates and persons of rank: it is styled *choong*, literally heavy, or *grave* (which, in its origin, means the same), in contradistinction to *king*, light, or *levity*. As this is, in some degree, promoted by a heavy, lumbering figure, it may be the origin of their partiality for bulkiness in men; while in women they admire such an opposite quality. Any under-sized individual, who does not fill his chair well, they jocularly style "short measure."

It is the discipline to which they are subject from earliest childhood, and the habit of controlling their ruder passions, that render crimes of violence so unfrequent among them. Robbery is very seldom accompanied by murder. Under real or supposed injury, however, they are sometimes found to be very revengeful, and on such occasions not at all scrupulous as to how they accomplish their purpose. Women will sometimes hang or drown themselves, merely to bring those with whom they have quarrelled into trouble. The people, quiet and sub missive as they are, will, when once roused by in tolerable oppression, rise *en masse* against a magistrate, and destroy him if they can. In such a case, should the obnoxious governor escape the vengeance of the populace, he seldom meets with any mercy at Peking, where revolts prove serious occurrences to those under whom they take place.

To the system of clubbing together in families—we might almost say in clans—is to be attributed that sacred regard to kindred which operates better than a public provision for the relief of the poor, and serves as one of the best means for the *distribution* of wealth; a valuable science, in which they perhaps beat our economists, though they do not equal them in the rules for its *creation*. Hence, too, that regard for the place of his birth, which always clings to a Chinese through life, often making him apply for leave to quit the honours and emoluments of office, and retire to his native village. The same feeling makes the colonists, who venture abroad in search of gain, return home as soon as they have acquired something like a competency, though at the risk of being oppressed under the forms of law for having left China. They have a popular saying, "If he who attains to honours or wealth never returns to his native place, he is like a finely-dressed person walking in the dark;"—it is all thrown away.

We have now touched briefly upon the leading features of the Chinese character, which will be viewed and appreciated according to the peculiar tastes and opinions of readers, but which, by most persons, must be allowed to contain an admixture, at least, of what is good and valuable. It remains to notice one important circumstance which has very naturally rendered this people obnoxious to severe censure—the infanticide* of female children. The presumed extent of this practice has been

* This subject is not mentioned in the penal code.

brought as an argument against the prevalence of parental feeling in China; but we believe that the amount of it has, by most writers, been overrated. No doubt but, in occasional instances of female births, infanticide does exist; but these cases certainly occur only in the chief cities, and the most crowded population, where the difficulty of subsistence takes away all hope from the poorest persons of being able to rear their offspring. The Chinese are in general peculiarly fond of their children, and the attachment seems to be mutual. The instances at Canton (a very crowded and populous place) of the bodies of infants being seen floating are not frequent, and may reasonably, in some cases, be attributed to accident, where such multitudes are brought up from their birth in small boats. There never was a more absurd blunder than to charge to infanticide those instances in which the infants are found floating with a hollow gourd about their persons, as if the gourd were a part of the system of exposure! Why, the very object of attaching these gourds to the children living in boats is to save them from the risk of being drowned, and to float them until they can be pulled out of the water. That children are sometimes found drowned, in spite of this precaution, is possible enough; but to consider the gourds as part and parcel of their fate, is about as reasonable and correct as if somebody should attribute all the deaths in England, from drowning, to the exertions of the Humane Society.*

The Roman Catholic fathers, with all their complete and intimate knowledge of China, had a trick

* Mons. de Guignes is quite right on this point. "Quant à ce que l'on dit qu'elles attachent une calabasse sur le dos des enfans pour les faire flotter plus long-tems, afin de donner le tems à quelque personne charitable de leur sauver la vie, elles ne le font que pour avoir elles-mêmes le moyen de les secourir dans le cas où ils tomberoient à la rivière."

of giving their own colouring to such matters as bore in any way upon the honour and glory of the mission. We have seen that they dealt now and then in *miracles;* the mere over-statement, therefore, of the practice of infanticide was natural enough, when connected with the object; and Du Halde gives a pompous account of the fruits of the missionary exertions. The merit, however, was peculiar, and of an equivocal kind; for, instead of attempting on most occasions to save the lives of the children doomed to be drowned, they or their proselytes walked about to the houses, baptizing the new-born infants previous to death—a cheap, rapid, and easy work of charity.

—" Licebit,
Injecto ter pulvere, curras."

In their physical characteristics, the Chinese are generally as superior to the nations which border on them as in other points. It has often been remarked, that a finer-shaped and more powerful race of men exist nowhere than the coolies, or porters of Canton, and the weights which they carry with ease on a bamboo, between two of them, would break down most others. The freedom of their dress gives a development to their limbs that renders many of the Chinese models for a sculptor. As sailors, they have been found always much stronger and more efficient than Lascars on board of English ships, though the obstacles which exist to their entering into foreign service prevent their being frequently engaged. During the war, the difficulty of manning the company's ships with English seamen was the occasion of great numbers being employed, though at a very heavy expense.

The superior physical character of the Chinese, in comparison with many other Asiatics, must in great measure be attributed to the general healthiness of their climate, notwithstanding the existence of very considerable, as well as rapid, vicissitudes of heat and cold. The extent to which cultivation and drainage have been carried in all the lower levels throughout the country, must, no doubt, have its share in the effect; and the general prevalence of active, as well as sober, habits in the bulk of the population, is another important circumstance. It may be observed here, that if that terrible scourge the *cholera* could be proved to have existed at all in China,* during the period in which it has occasioned such frightful ravages in other parts of the world, its extent and effects have been so inconsiderable as not to deserve serious notice. The idea which has prevailed in France, relative to the use of tea being a means of avoiding the disease, might seem to derive some corroboration from this general immunity in the country where tea is more extensively consumed than elsewhere.

When the cranium, or scull, of a Chinese is compared with those of a European and a negro, it is observable that what is called the *facial angle*, in the case of the first, is something of a medium between the other two; in other words, that the forehead and upper part of the face in the Chinese retire, or incline backward, rather more than in the European, but much less than in the African. The same remark holds in respect to the oblique insertion of the incisors, or front teeth. In the thickness of the lips the Chinese approaches, but by no means equals, the negro; nor is that feature at all so prominent as in the latter. The nose is flattened, and the nostrils expanded, in the Chinese, but not to the same extent as in the Ethiopian. In some points of physiology, the people whom we describe bear a considerable resemblance to the North American Indians. There is the same lank, black, and shining hair; the same obliquity of the eyes, and eye-

* The European shipping at Whampoa not included

brows turned upwards at the outer extremities; and a corresponding thinness and tufty growth of beard. The Chinese, too, is distinguished by a nearly total absence of hair from the surface of the body. In the smallness of the hands and feet, and of the bones of the body, compared with Europeans, he resembles the generality of Asiatics. We may remark here that the Esquimaux, as represented in the plates to Captain Lyon's voyage, bear a very striking similarity to the *Tân-kea*, or "boat-people" of the coast of China, who are treated by the government as a different race from those on shore, and not allowed to intermarry with them. Whether the miserable inhabitants of the cold regions to the north have thus migrated southward, along the coast, at some former periods, in search of a more genial climate, must be a mere matter of conjecture in the absence of positive proof.

Though the Chinese are allied to the Mongols in the general cast of their features, the harsher points of the latter are softened down in the former considerably. It would be a hopeless task to attempt to explain, on any certain grounds, the mode in which China first became peopled. The only thing like testimony that we possess, out of China, relating to this subject, is in the Institutes of Menu, as quoted by Sir William Jones. It is there written, that "many families of the military class, having gradually abandoned the ordinances of the Veda, and the company of Brahmins, lived in a state of degradation, as the *Chinas* and some other nations." A native historian certainly states that, at a period corresponding to 1200 years before Christ, "the Chinese nation was small and feeble, the Eastern foreigners (people between them and the east coast) numerous and strong," and that the former "gradually obtained a settlement in the middle of the country." This, as far as it goes, might be construed into a proof that

China, according to the opinion of Sir William Jones, was originally peopled in part from India.

But, however that may be, the position hazarded by De Guignes, that the Chinese were a colony from Egypt, seems hardly capable of sufficient support from testimony, either direct or circumstantial. Such a distant emigration could not have taken place without the knowledge and notice of the nations inhabiting the vast countries that intervene: besides which, there exists not the slightest shadow of resemblance between the hieroglyphics of Egypt and the Chinese characters. This point was first satisfactorily proved in a letter from Père Amiot at Peking to the Royal Society at London, which had applied to him for information. In one respect, indeed, we are ready to admit that there is a resemblance; but that is only in the *use* of the respective characters. The researches of Dr. Young first proved that the pictorial emblems of the sacred language of Egypt had been used in the Rosetta inscription, as symbols of *sound* in the expression of foreign names. Now, this is precisely what the Chinese do, from obvious necessity, in similar cases. Their monosyllabic characters are used to represent the sounds of foreigners' names, and either connected by a line along the side, or otherwise distinguished by a small mark, for the same reason that the Egyptians enclosed theirs in an oval ring, or cartouche.

But to return to our immediate subject. People in Europe have been strangely misled, in their notions of Chinese physiognomy and appearance, by the figures represented on those specimens of manufacture which proceed from Canton, and which are commonly in a style of broad caricature. A Chinese at Peking might as well form an idea of us from some of the performances of Cruikshank. The consequence has been, that a character of silly levity and farce has been associated, in the minds of many persons, with the most steady, considerate, and matter-of-fact people in the world, who in grave matters of business are often a match for the best of Europeans. Their features have perhaps less of the harsh angularity of the Tartar countenance in the south than at Peking. Among those who are not exposed to the climate, the complexion is fully as fair as that of Spaniards and Portuguese; but the sun has a powerful effect on their skins, and that upper portion of a man's person habitually exposed in the summer is often so different from the remainder, that, when stripped, he looks like the lower half of a European joined on to the upper moiety of an Asiatic. Up to the age of twenty they are often very good-looking, but soon after that period the prominent cheek-bones generally give a harshness to the features, as the roundness of youth wears off. With the progress of age the old men become in most cases extremely ugly, and the old women can only be described by Juvenal:—

——"Tales adspice rugas
Quales, umbriferos ubi pandit Tabraca saltus,
In vetulâ scalpit jam mater simia buccâ."

——"Such wrinkles see,
As in an Indian forest's solitude,
Some old ape scrubs amid her numerous brood."

A conjecture has already been offered in explanation of the very opposite characters of figure admired in the two sexes. A woman should be extremely slender and fragile in appearance; a man very stout,—not in those proportions that denote muscular strength, and what we call *condition*,—but corpulent, obese, alderman-like. It is fashionable in both men and women to allow the nails of the left hand to grow to an inordinate length, until they assume an appearance very like the claws of the bradypus, as represented in Sir Charles Bell's work on the "Hand." An English gentleman in China reasonably prohibited one of his servants from indulging in this piece of foppery, on the ground that fingers provided with such appendages could not possibly perform any work. The brittleness of the nail rendering it liable to break, they have been known sometimes to protect it, when very long, by means of thin slips of bamboo.

But the most unaccountable species of taste is that mutilation of the women's feet, for which the Chinese are so remarkable. Of the origin of this custom there is no very distinct account, except that it took place about the close of the Tâng dynasty, or the end of the ninth century of our era. The Tartars have had the good sense not to adopt this artificial deformity, and their ladies wear a shoe like that of the men, except that it has a white sole of still greater thickness. As it would seem next to impossible to refer to any notions of physical beauty, however arbitrary, such shocking mutilation as that produced by the cramping of the foot

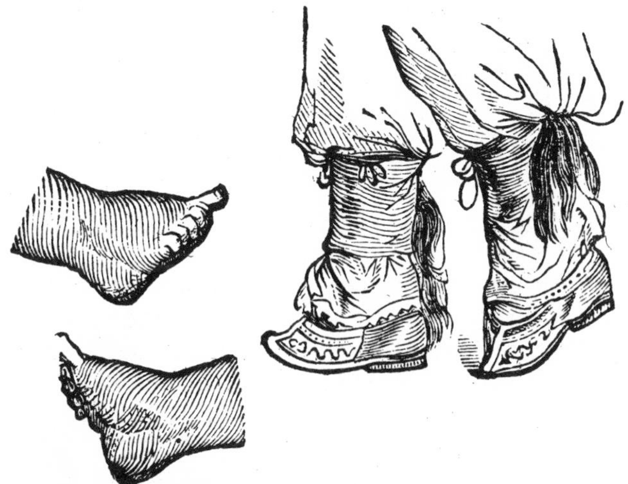

Small feet of a Chinese Lady.

in early childhood, it may partly be ascribed to the principle which dictates the fashion of long nails,

The idea conveyed by these is *exemption from labour;* and, as the small feet make cripples of the women, it is fair to conclude that the idea of gentility which they convey arises from a similar association. That appearance of helplessness which is induced by the mutilation they admire extremely, notwithstanding its very usual concomitant of sickliness; and the tottering gait of the poor women, as they hobble along upon the heel of the foot, they compare to the waving of a willow agitated by the breeze. We may add that this odious custom extends lower down in the scale of society than might have been expected from its disabling effect upon those who have to labour for their subsistence. If the custom was first imposed by the tyranny of the men, the women are fully revenged in the diminution of their charms and domestic usefulness.

In no instances have the folly and childishness of a large portion of mankind been more strikingly displayed than in those various, and occasionally very opposite, modes in which they have departed from the standard of nature, and sought distinction even in deformity. Thus, while one race of people crushes the feet of its children, another flattens their heads between two boards; and, while we in Europe admire the natural whiteness of the teeth, the Malays file off the enamel, and die them black, for the all-sufficient reason that dogs' teeth are white! A New Zealand chief has his distinctive coat of arms emblazoned on the skin of his face, as well as on his limbs; and an Esquimaux is nothing if he have not bits of stone stuffed through a hole in each cheek. Quite as absurd, and still more mischievous, is the infatuation which, among some Europeans, attaches beauty to that modification of the human figure which resembles the wasp, and compresses the waist until the very ribs have been distorted, and the functions of the vital organs irreparably disordered.

It is an interesting question to investigate how the Chinese are to be ranked with other nations in the comparative scale of civil society. We have already endeavoured to show in part, and have still to show, the considerable moral and political advantages which they actually possess, and which Sir George Staunton has, with his usual knowledge and ability, summed up as attributable "to the regard paid to the ties of kindred; to the sobriety, industry, and intelligence of the lower classes; to the nearly total absence of feudal rights and privileges; the equal distribution of landed property; to the indisposition of government to engage in schemes of foreign warfare and ambition; and to a system of penal laws the most clearly defined, comprehensive, and business-like of any, at least among *Asiatics*." It would be idle, on the other hand, to deny that they possess vices and defects peculiar to their own political and social condition.

It has been reasonably argued by the authority above quoted, that "a people whose written language is founded on the most ancient of principles, and the frame of whose government is essentially conformable to the patriarchal system of the first ages, must have segregated themselves from the rest of mankind before the period at which the symbolic was superseded by the alphabetic character, and the patriarchal by other forms of government." The same circumstances of government and language which denote the *antiquity* of the Chinese institutions, may, we think, account for their *durability*. The theory of government combining the *pater atque princeps*, which has always been the first to present itself to men's minds, if not the best in practice, may be the most plausible in principle; and the system of written characters, which cannot be altered with the readiness of our syllabic words (notoriously the subjects of caprice in most languages), may have given a considerable fixedness to the intellect of China, through the medium of its literature. Any one who has been in the habit of translating *into* Chinese, knows the difficulty of conveying *foreign ideas* in an intelligible shape.

There is another primitive characteristic to be noticed in the classification of the four ranks, or orders, into which the community of China is divided. These are, in the first place, the learned; secondly, husbandmen; thirdly, manufacturers; and fourthly, merchants. This arrangement seems sufficiently correct and philosophical, considered with a reference merely to the successive rise of those four orders in the progress of society. In the earliest ages, superior wisdom and knowledge, the result of old age and experience, constitute the principal claim to respect and distinction. As society advances, and as nomadic tribes become fixed to particular spots, they turn their attention to the cultivation of land. With the gradual increase of raw produce, the rise of towns, and the adoption of exchanges between town and country, follow manufactures; and lastly, with the growth of capital and the increase of manufactures, comes commerce, domestic and foreign.

But, by the time that a country has reached a certain point of advancement, this pristine arrangement (with the exception of the first class) must be considered as merely nominal, and perhaps, in some communities, rather as the inverse order in which the several classes will really stand in relation to each other. The influence of wealth—the consequence arising from superior possessions—will have its sway; and as manufactures may become a more fertile source of wealth than tillage, and commerce than manufactures, so the former may impart greater influence to those who pursue them respectively. Accordingly, we find, in China, that the poor cultivator of one of those small patches, to which the subdivision of inheritances tends to reduce the lands, derives little substantial benefit from the estimation in which his calling is affected to be held; even though the emperor himself once a year guides the plough. On the other hand, the opulent merchant contrives to obtain the services of those whom he can benefit by his wealth; even the acquaintance and good offices of persons in power, however low the nominal rank assigned to him in the theoretical institutions of the country. At the same time, the class of the *learned* retain their supremacy far above all, and fill the ranks of government.

Hereditary rank, without merit, is of little value to the possessor, as we have before noticed. The descendants of the Manchow family are ranked in *five* degrees, which, for that reason only, were distinguished by the Jesuits with the titles of the five orders of European nobility. These imperial descendants wear the yellow girdle, and, without any power whatever, have certain small revenues allotted to them for a subsistence. Of course, as they multiply, some of the remoter branches become reduced to a very indigent condition, when unaided by personal exertion and merit. At the fall of the last Chinese dynasty, a vast number of the ejected family dropped the yellow girdle, and sought for safety in a private condition. It is said that many of the representatives of the *Ming* race still remain; one of them was servant to several of the Jesuits; and, whenever it shall happen that rebellion succeeds against the Tartars, some of the number may probably be forthcoming.

The imperial relatives of the Tartar line being numerous, and withal brought up to a life of idleness, are in many cases ignorant, worthless, and dissipated; and it is possibly from some feeling of jealousy, as well as on account of their disorderly character, that they are kept under very strict control. The last British embassy had a specimen of their conduct and manners at Yuen-ming-yuen, as well as of the little ceremony with which they are occasionally treated. When they crowded, with a childish and uncivil curiosity, upon the English party, the principal person among the mandarins seized a whip, and, not satisfied with using that alone, actually *kicked* out the mob of yellow-girdles. In the previous mission of Lord Macartney, Mr. Barrow has related an instance of the meanness of one of these princes of the blood—no less a person than a grandson of the emperor—who sent him a paltry present, with a broad hint that his gold watch would be acceptable in return.

There are two lines of the imperial house of China; the first descended from the great conqueror himself, and the second from his collaterals, or his brothers and uncles. The first are called Tsoong-shĕ,* "ancestral house," and distinguished by a yellow girdle, and a bridle of the same colour. The second are styled Keolo (a Tartar word), and marked by a red sash and bridle. Every thing about their dress and equipage is subject to minute regulation. Some are decorated with the peacock's feather, and others allowed the privilege of the green sedan. There are rules concerning their establishments and retinue, and the number of eunuchs which each may employ. The greatest number of these allowed to any individual is eleven, the chief of whom wears a white ball or button on his cap. For the government of all the members of the imperial kindred there is a court, called the "office of the ancestral tribe." This is wholly distinct from the Chinese courts, and has its own laws and usages; and a wâng (called by the Jesuits *regulus*, or little king) is president of it.

The principal use of these imperial descendants

* Tsoong-jin Foo.

seems to be the formation of a courtly *apanage*, to swell the emperor's state. They are obliged, at the new and full moon, to attend the court, and arrange themselves in order, some within the audience-hall, and some without, at, or rather *before*, daybreak. When the emperor makes his appearance, they all fall prostrate and perform their adoration; and it was the party collected for this purpose at daybreak on the 29th August, 1816, which so greatly annoyed the English embassy by their importunate curiosity and uncourtly rudeness. It is their idle and useless life, and the absence of any motives for exertion, which make these persons frequently both ignorant and vicious, and extremely troublesome to the emperor. Many have been ordered away from Peking, and sent to Manchow Tartary, to be placed under the charge of the native chiefs, while others have been sentenced to perpetual solitary confinement. In 1819, one of the imperial clan, wearing a red girdle, found his way to Canton, where he had a relation by affinity officiating as the provincial judge. His plea for quitting the capital was extreme poverty, but the judge did not venture to house him. He was delivered in custody to the local authorities, and packed off again under military escort to Peking, where it is said he was shut up for the remainder of his life.

These persons are strongly contrasted, in point of intelligence, learning, and every other claim to respect, with the *official rulers* of China—its real aristocracy. The impartial distribution (with few exceptions) of state offices and magistracies to *all* who give evidence of superior learning or talent, without regard to birth or possessions, lies probably at the bottom of the greatness and prosperity of the empire. Nothing can be more true than the observations on this subject of the late Dr. Milne, an excellent Chinese scholar: "This principle has always been maintained; although, as may naturally be supposed, it has often in practice been departed from. Yet the existence of the principle, and its being acted on to a considerable extent, give every person in China (with the exception of menial servants, the lowest agents of the police, and comedians) a solid reason to be satisfied with the system. They are the ambitious who generally overturn governments; but in China there is a road open to the ambitious, without the dreadful alternative of revolutionizing the country. All that is required of a man is the very reasonable thing that he should give some proof of the possession of superior talents.

"The government affords him every three years, and occasionally oftener, an opportunity of displaying his attainments in a stipulated way; and, if it cannot give offices to all, it gives honours, and declares the successful candidate eligible to a situation either civil or military; and, finally, to the highest offices of the state, if his merits shall entitle him thereto. The present dynasty has frequently sold commissions both in the civil service and in the army, in order to supply its pecuniary wants; which circumstance gives much dissatisfaction to those who depend on their learning and knowledge for promotion; and this conduct is generally deemed disreputable. Those of the community who are raised above manual labour, or the drudgery of daily business, are occupied with what gratifies their laudable emulation, or their vanity and ambition; and from among these, when the state wants men, it selects the best talents of the whole country. I submit it, whether the principle and the system, which I have thus slightly exhibited, be not the great secret of the Chinese aggrandizement."

The superior honours paid to letters over arms must tend to make Chinese ambition run in a peaceful channel. At the annual meetings of the mandarins in the provincial capitals, to perform adoration before the emperor's shrine on his birthday, this difference is shown by the civil officers taking their places to the east (the higher station), and the others to the west. The civil mandarins look upon Confucius as their peculiar patron, and are in fact the high priesthood, whose sole privilege it is to sacrifice at his temples.

The lineal descendants of Confucius also have some hereditary honours. The head of this race is always distinguished by the title of koong, the highest of the five degrees before mentioned. He repairs to Peking once a year from Keŏ-fow Hien, in Shantung province, the birthplace of the great philosopher and statesman, and receives certain marks of distinction from the emperor. Père Bouvet, in 1693, found the governor of a *chow*, or city of the second order, in one of the southern provinces, bearing the same surname, and deriving his descent from the deified teacher of China, but he had earned his office by his learning, and not by his descent. The great limitation in the privileges of the various species of hereditary rank, and the continual subdivision of property among a man's numerous descendants, are the causes which prevent any individual becoming dangerous by his influence or wealth. The true aristocracy of China, its official rulers, are of course a constantly fluctuating body. The gentry of every province, below these, consist of the mandarins retired from employment, and all who have attained any of the three literary degrees, or the nine ranks distinguished by the ball on the cap. The merit of a son often elevates his parents, and posthumous titles of dignity are occasionally conferred on the ancestors for several generations.

Among the various causes which conduce to give to the upper classes in China their unostentatious character, and to prevent expensiveness being a *fashion* among them, we may observe that a sufficient reason exists for the absence of magnificence from the establishments of official persons, independently of its being their *policy* to affect simplicity. As none can exercise office in his birthplace, or patrimonial abode, he can have no motive to expend money on his official residence, from which he is liable at the shortest notice to be removed elsewhere; the longest period being generally three years. Hence official persons are commonly very shabby in every thing but their personal habiliments; their followers, even, being often dirty and ragged. The pride of external pomp and retinue is not allowed, on ordinary occasions, to any except the official aristocracy, and with these it consists rather in the *number* than in the *condition* of their attendants.

The intercourse of social life in all cases where women are confined to their homes, or to the company of their own sex, must of course suffer; and accordingly we find that in China it is cold, formal, and encumbered with the ponderous system of ceremonies, which have been transmitted from time immemorial. These, however, are occasionally cast off in those scenes of convivial excess into which exclusively male society is so apt to degenerate, when the recoil is sometimes as great on the side of license, as the previous restraint has been strict. It must be observed, however, in justice to the better class of Chinese, that these scenes are held in deserved disrepute, and prove always more or less injurious to a man's character.

Notwithstanding the general disadvantages on the side of the weaker sex here, in common with other Asiatic countries, its respectability is in some degree preserved by a certain extent of authority allowed to widows over their sons, and by the homage which these are obliged to pay to their mothers. The emperor himself performs the ceremonies of the *ko-tow* before his own mother, who receives them seated on a throne. They have a maxim that "a woman is thrice dependant; before marriage, on her father; after marriage, on her husband; when a widow, on her son;" but this seems to mean principally with reference to support and subsistence.

The ladies of the better class are instructed in embroidering, as well as painting on silk, and music is of course a favourite accomplishment. They are not often very deeply versed in letters, but celebrated instances are sometimes quoted of those who have been skilled in composing verses. The modesty of manner which is deemed so essential to the female character is heightened by their dress, frequently of magnificent materials, and in fashion extremely becoming. They reckon it indecorous in women of birth and breeding to show even their hands, and in touching or moving any thing these are generally covered by their long sleeves. The Chinese look upon the dress of the European ladies (as sometimes represented in drawings or paintings) with surprise, and they certainly present a considerable contrast to their own. Perhaps in both instances the just medium may in some measure be departed from, although in contrary directions.

There is no point on which greater misconception has prevailed than respecting the existence of universal polygamy in China. We will state the case exactly, from the preface to the translation of the "Fortunate Union," which is therein declared to be "a more faithful picture of Chinese manners, inasmuch as the hero espouses but *one wife*. It is not strictly true that their laws sanction *polygamy*, though they permit *concubinage*. A Chinese can have but one tsy, or wife, properly so called, who is distinguished by a title, espoused with ceremonies, and chosen from a rank of life totally different from his tsiĕ, or handmaids, of whom he may have as many or as few as he pleases; and, though the offspring of the latter possess many of the rights of legitimacy (ranking, however, after the children of the wife), this circumstance makes little difference as to the truth of the position. Even in the present romance, the profligate rival aims at effecting his union with the heroine, only by setting aside his previous marriage with her cousin as informal. Any Chinese fiction, therefore (and of these there are many), which describes a man espousing two wives, is in this respect no truer a picture of existing manners, than in respect to any other silly or amusing extravagance which it may happen to contain. In fact, the wife is of equal rank with the husband by birth, and espoused with regular marriage ceremonies; possessing, moreover, certain legal rights, such as they are; the handmaid is bought for money, and received into the house nearly like any other domestic. The principle on which Chinese law and custom admit the offspring of concubinage to legitimate rights is obvious; the importance which attaches in that country to the securing of male descendants. It is plain that the tsy and the tsiĕ stand to each other in very much the same relation as the Sarah and the Hagar of the Old Testament, and therefore the common expression *first* and *second wife*, which the translator himself has used on former occasions, in imitation of his predecessors, is hardly correct."

If a person has *sons* by his wife (for daughters never enter into the account), it is considered derogatory to take a handmaid at all; but, if he has not, it is of course allowable. Still, for every additional repetition, he sinks in personal respectability, and none, in any case, but the rich can afford it. But the strongest dissuasives to a prudent person, on these occasions, are the domestic jealousies that inevitably fill the household with confusion, and sometimes with crime. The Chinese have a maxim, that "nine women in ten are jealous," and they speak feelingly.

Without doubt it is a double calamity to a Chinese wife to be childless, and the sentiment of Creusa in the Greek play must be universal:—

> Καὶ τωνδ' ἁπάντων εσχατον πειση κακον
> ———————— εκ δουλης τινος
> Γυναίκος, εις σον δωμα δέσποτην αγειν.
>
> *Euripid.* (Ιων. 836.)

The feeling is very strongly portrayed in the drama called "An Heir in Old Age," translated from the Chinese into English, and from the English version into French. Here the spouse of an old man, who has only one daughter, in concert with her own child, and the young man to whom the latter is married, drives from the house a handmaid, who, being pregnant, is an object of unconquerable jealousy to all parties except the old man himself, who is anxiously expecting an heir. Both the woman and child are concealed for three years, after which the jealous feeling of the wife is overcome, only by the consideration that, without a male heir, they shall have nobody to sacrifice to their manes after death. This regard to the sepulchral rites, by the way, is another feeling not peculiar to China, but one powerfully developed in several of the Greek plays; as the Ajax, and the Choëphori, of Sophocles.

The women whom a rich Chinese takes in the event of his wife proving barren are generally purchased for a sum of money. They are of course from the lowest ranks, entering the family as domestic slaves; and the prevalence of this condition may be traced to the difficulty of subsistence in so thickly peopled a country, which leads many to sell their children, sometimes their wives, and even themselves. Men of high spirit and principle have been known to object to their daughters being handmaids even to the emperor himself; though of course this is an exception to the general rule.

When the sovereign has espoused an emperess with the usual ceremonies, he is supplied with handmaids from among the daughters of *Tartars* principally, selected on account of their beauty. On the death of an emperor, all these women are shut up in a secluded part of the palace, and debarred from marriage with any one. Marco Polo, with his usual fidelity, describes the process of selecting the Tartar ladies for the emperor, in the way that appears exactly to be followed at the present day.

Marriage among the Chinese, with every circumstance relating to it, is so fully described in the "Fortunate Union," that the curious reader may be referred for details to that specimen of Chinese literature and manners. It may be as well, in this place, to remark on the principal legal conditions of the married state, and then to describe the ceremonies attendant on the espousals. Their maxim is, that "a married woman can commit no crime; the responsibility rests with her husband." Throughout the Chinese law, obligations and penalties seem to be pretty fairly adjusted; excepting always in cases of *treason.* A child, a wife, or a dependant, being very much at the disposal of the father, husband, or master, is proportionately exempt from punishment when acting under their authority. A woman under marriage assumes her husband's surname. Marriage between all persons of the *name surname* being unlawful, this rule must of course include all descendants of the male branch for ever; and as, in so vast a population, there are not a great many more than one hundred surnames throughout the empire, the embarrassments that arise from so strict a law must be considerable. There is likewise a prohibition of wedlock between some of the nearest relations by affinity; and any marriage of an officer of government with an *actress* is void, the parties being, besides, punishable with sixty blows.

There are seven grounds of divorce, and some of

them are amusing. The first, barrenness, would seem to be superfluous, as there is a remedy provided in legal concubinage; but the truth is, that either resource, or perhaps both, are in a man's power at his option. The other causes of separation are, adultery, disobedience to the husband's parents, *talkativeness*, *thieving*, ill temper, and inveterate infirmities. Any of these, however, may be set aside by three circumstances; the wife having mourned for her husband's parents; the family having acquired wealth since the marriage; and the wife being without parents to receive her back. It is in all cases disreputable, and in some (as those of a particular rank) illegal, for a widow to marry again. Whenever a widow is herself unwilling, the law protects her; and should she act by the compulsion of parents or other relations, these are severely punishable. Widows, indeed, have a very powerful dissuasive from second wedlock, in being absolute mistresses of themselves and children so long as they remain in their existing condition.

From the Buddhists, who say that "those connected in a previous existence become united in this," the Chinese have borrowed the notion that marriage goes by destiny. A certain deity, whom they style *Yue-laou*, "the old man of the moon," unites with a silken cord (they relate) all predestined couples, after which nothing can prevent their ultimate union. Early marriages are promoted by every motive that can influence humanity, and we shall have to notice these particulars in treating of the excessive population of the country. Their maxim is, "there are three great acts of disregard to parents, and to die without progeny is the *chief*." The most essential circumstance in a respectable family alliance is, that there should be equality of rank and station on either side, or that "the gates*

* Mun-hoo teng-tuy.

should correspond," as the Chinese express it. The marriage is preceded by a negotiation called *ping*, conducted by agents or go-betweens, selected by the parents. The aid of judicial astrology is now called in, and the horoscopes of the two parties compared, under the title of the "eight characters," which express the year, month, day, and hour of the nativities of the intended couple. This being settled, presents are sent by the bridegroom in ratification of the union; but the bride in ordinary cases brings neither presents nor dower to her husband—*dotem non uxor marito, sed maritus uxori affert.* The choice of a lucky day is considered of such importance, that if the Kalèndar (in which all these matters are noticed with the science of a Partridge, Moore, or Sídrophel himself) should be unfavourable in its auguries, the ceremony is postponed for months. These superstitions are common to all times and countries. In the Iphigenia at Aulis, one of the plays of Euripides, we have an exact case in point. Clytemnestra says to her husband, who is deceiving her about their daughter, "On what day shall our child wed?"—to which he replies, "When the orb of a fortunate moon shall arrive."

The most appropriate and felicitous time for marriage is considered to be in spring, and the first moon of the Chinese year (February) is preferred. It is in this month that the peach-tree blossoms in China, and hence there are constant allusions to it in connexion with marriage. These verses, from the elegant pen of Sir William Jones, are a paraphrase of a literal translation which that indefatigable scholar obtained of a passage in the Chinese "Book of Odes."

"Sweet child of spring, the garden's queen,
Yon peach-tree charms the roving sight
Its fragrant leaves how richly green,
Its blossoms how divinely bright!

"So softly shines the beauteous bride,
By love and conscious virtue led,
O'er her new mansion to preside,
And placid joys around her spread."

Some time previous to the day fixed, the bridegroom is invested ceremoniously with a dress cap or bonnet, and takes an additional name. The bride, at the same time, whose hair had until this hung down in long tresses, has it turned up in the manner of married women, and fastened with bodkins. When the wedding-day arrives, the friends of the bridegroom send him presents in the morning, with their congratulations. Among the presents are live geese, which are emblematical of the concord of the married state, and some of these birds are always carried in the procession. The bride's relations likewise send her gifts, consisting chiefly of female finery; and her young sisters and friends of her own sex come and weep with her until it is time to leave the house of her parents. At length, when the evening arrives,* and the stars just begin to be visible, the bridegroom comes with an ornamented sedan, and a cavalcade of lanterns, music, &c., to fetch home his spouse. On their reaching his residence, the bride is carried into the house in the arms of the matrons who act as her friends, and lifted over a pan of charcoal at the door; the meaning of which ceremony is not clear, but which may have reference to the commencement of her household duties. She soon after issues from the bridal chamber with her attendants into the great hall, bearing the prepared Areca, or betel-nut, and invites the guests there assembled to partake of it. Having gone through some ceremonies in company with the bridegroom, she is led

* In accordance with an epithalamium in one of their ancient books, in which is this line, "The three stars shine on the gate."

back to her chamber, where she is unveiled by her future husband. A table is then spread, and the cup of alliance is drunk together by the young couple. Some fortunate matron, the mother of many children, then enters and pronounces a benediction, as well as going through the form of laying the nuptial bed. Meanwhile the party of friends in the hall make merry, and when the bridegroom joins them they either ply him with wine, or not, according to the character and grade of the company. When the hour of retirement arrives, they escort him to the door of the chamber in a body, and then disperse.

On the following day the new couple come forth to the great hall, where they adore the household gods, and pay their respects to their parents and nearest relations. They then return to their chamber, where they receive the visits of their young friends; and the whole of the first month is devoted in like manner to leisure and amusement. On the third day after the wedding, the bride proceeds in an ornamented sedan to visit her parents; and at length, when the month is expired, the bride's friends send her a particular head-dress; an entertainment is partaken of by the relations of both parties, and the marriage ceremonies are thereby concluded. On some occasions the bride is espoused at the house of her own parents, with some little difference in the forms. Both these modes are detailed in the novel of the Fortunate Union.

It may be remarked that, as so many parties are concerned in the conduct of the negotiations previous to marriage, and as the two persons principally interested never see each other the whole time, there is a door open to fraud and trickery, as well as to misunderstandings of all kinds. It cannot be supposed, however, nor indeed is it true in practice, that the bridegroom has *never* in any case *seen* his intended spouse previous to wedlock; though of course the separation of the sexes must prevent any intimate society between them. The law provides for most cases of dispute or of detected imposture, some of which enter into the plot of the novel already referred to. Both parties are called upon explicitly to make known to each other the existence of any bodily or constitutional defect; what the true age of each is; and whether they were born of a wife or a concubine; whether real offspring, or only adopted. Should there be any suppression of what is true, or any allegation of what is false, the penalties are severe. The Chinese law prohibits all marriages between subjects and foreigners, and even forbids any alliances between the unsubdued mountaineers, called Meaou-tse, in the interior of the empire, and its own people in the neighbouring plains.

When women prove childless, they pay adoration to the goddess Kuân-yin, a principal image in Buddhist temples, whose name means "heedful of prayers" (*ter vocata audit*), and whose functions seem compounded of those of Venus genetrix and Lucina. There is, however, the widest difference, in their estimation, between male and female offspring; the former are as eagerly desired as the latter are generally deprecated. Sons are considered in this country, where the power over them is so absolute through life, as a sure support, as well as a probable source of wealth or dignities, should they succeed in learning: but the grand object is the perpetuation of the race, to sacrifice at the family tombs. Without sons, a man lives without honour or satisfaction, and dies unhappy; and, as the only remedy, he is permitted to adopt the sons of his younger brothers. Sometimes, however, the extreme desire of male offspring leads parents to suborn the midwives to purchase a boy of some poor person, and substitute it for the girl just born. This is termed *tow loong, hoân foong*—"stealing a dragon in exchange for a phenix."

Their maxim is, that, as the emperor should have the care of a father for his people, a father should have the power of a sovereign over his family. A man is even able to sell his children for slaves, as appears from the constant practice. They do not subscribe to the precept of Rousseau—"*Quand chacun pourrait s'aliéner lui-même, il ne peut aliéner ses enfans.*" How completely the children of concubines pertain to the lawful wife is proved by this passage in the drama of "An Heir in Old Age," where, in addressing his wife, the old man says, "Seaou-mei is now pregnant; whether she produces a boy or a girl, the same will be your property; you may then hire out her services, or sell her, as it best pleases you." The handmaids are in fact only domestic slaves.

The birth of a son is of course an occasion of great rejoicing; the family or surname is first given, and then the "milk name," which is generally some diminutive of endearment. A month after the event, the relations and friends between them send the child a silver plate, on which are engraved the three words, "long-life, honours, felicity." The boy is lessoned in behaviour and in ceremonies from his earliest childhood, and at four or five he commences reading. The importance of general education was known so long since in China, that a work written before the Christian era speaks of the "*ancient* system of instruction," which required that every town and village, down to only a few families, should have a common school. The wealthy Chinese employ private teachers, and others send their sons to day-schools, which are so well attended that the fees paid by each boy are extremely small. In large towns there are *night* schools, of which those who are obliged to labour through the day avail themselves.

The sixteen discourses of the Emperor Yoong-ching, called the Sacred Edicts, commence with the domestic duties as the foundation of the political; and the eleventh treats of instructing the younger branches of a family. Dr. Morrison, in his dictionary, has given a selection from one hundred rules or maxims, to be observed at a school, some of which are extremely good. Among other points, the habit of *attention* is dwelt upon as of primary importance, and boys are warned against "repeating with the mouth while the heart (or mind) is thinking of something else." They are taught never to be satisfied with a confused or indistinct understanding of what they are learning, but to ask for explanations; and always to make a personal application to *themselves* of the precepts which they learn. Scholars are not often subjected to corporal punishments. The rule is to try the effects of rewards and of persuasion, until it is plain that these will not operate; after which it is the custom to disgrace a boy by making him remain on his knees at his seat before the whole school, or sometimes at the door, while a stick of incense (a sort of slow match) burns to a certain point: the last rosort is to flog him.

The object of the government, as Dr. Morrison justly observed, in making education general, is not to extend the bounds of knowledge, but to impart the knowledge already possessed to as large a portion as possible of the rising generation, and "to pluck out true talent" from the mass of the community for its own service. The advancement of learning, or discoveries in physical science, are not in its contemplation. It prescribes the books to be studied; a departure from which is *heterodoxy;* and discountenances all innovations that do not originate with itself. In this we may perceive one of the causes, not only of the stationary and unprogressive character of Chinese institutions, but likewise of their permanency and continuance.

The process of early instruction in the language is this: they first teach children a few of the principal characters (as the names of the chief objects in nature or art) exactly as we do the letters, by rude pictures, having the characters attached. Then follows the Santse-king, or "trimetrical classic," being a summary of infant erudition, conveyed in chiming lines of three words or feet. They soon after proceed to the "Four Books," which contain the doctrines of Confucius, and which, with the "Five classics" subsequently added, are in fact the Chinese scriptures. The Four Books they learn by heart entirely, and the whole business of the literary class is afterward to comment on them, or compose essays on their texts. Writing is taught by tracing the characters, with their hair pencil, on transparent paper placed over the copy, and they commence with very large characters in the first instance. Specimens of this species of caligraphy are contained in the Royal Asiatic Transactions. In lieu of slates, they generally use boards painted white to save paper, washing out the writing when finished. Instructers are of course very plentiful, on account of the numbers who enter the learned profession, and fail in attaining the higher degrees.

Every principal city is furnished with halls of examination, and the embassy of 1816 was lodged in one of these buildings, at Nânheung-foo, a town at the bottom of the pass which leads northward from Canton province. It consisted of a number of halls and courts, surrounded by separate cells for the candidates, who are admitted with nothing but blank paper and the implements of writing; a part of the system which corresponds with our college examinations. The students who succeed in their own district, at the annual examination, are ranked as *Sewtsae*, or bachelors, and according to their merits are draughted for farther advancement, until they become fitted for the triennial examination, held at the provincial capital, by an officer expressly deputed from the Hânlin college at Peking. The papers consist of moral and political essays on texts selected from the sacred books, as well as of verses on given subjects. Pains are taken to prevent the examiners from knowing the authors of the essays and poems; but of course this cannot always be effectual in shutting out abuse.

Those who succeed at the triennial examinations attain the rank of *kiu-jin*, which may be properly termed licentiate, as it qualifies for actual employment; and once in three years all these licentiates repair to Peking (their expenses being paid if necessary), to be examined for the *tsin-sse*, or doctor's degree, to which only thirty can be admitted at one time. From these doctors are selected the members of the Imperial college of Hânlin, after an examination held in the palace itself. These fortunate and illustrious persons form the body from whom the ministers of the emperor are generally chosen.

A man's sons may or may not be instrumental, by their literary success, in reflecting honour on their parents, or advancing them in worldly rank and prosperity; but the mere chance of this, joined to the heavy responsibility for their conduct, is a great inducement to fathers to bring them up with care, and may serve to account for the great and universal prevalence of a certain degree of education throughout the empire. Such is the demand on every individual for exertion, in a country so thickly peopled, that the children of the very lowest classes, whom extreme indigence precludes from the hope or chance of rising by learning, are trained to labour and to the cares of life almost from the time they can first walk. With a slight stick or pole, proportioned to their size, across their shoulders, young children are constantly seen trudging along with weights, sometimes much heavier than they ought to carry, or busily engaged in other serious employments, as the assistants of their parents. In a country where the youngest cannot afford to be idle, and where, as their proverb strongly expresses it, "to stop the hand is the way to stop the mouth," there is an air of staid gravity about some of the children quite unsuited to their years.

But it is not during his life only that a man looks for the services of his sons. It is his consolation, in declining years, to think that they will continue the performance of the prescribed rites in the hall of ancestors, and at the family tombs, when he is no more; and it is the absence of this prospect that makes the childless doubly miserable. The superstition derives influence from the importance attached by the government to this species of posthumous duty; a neglect of which is punishable, as we have seen, by the laws. Indeed, of all the subjects of their care, there are none which the Chinese so religiously attend to as the tombs of their ancestors, conceiving that any neglect is sure to be followed by worldly misfortune. It is almost the only thing that approaches to the character of a "religious sense" among them; for, throughout their idolatrous superstitions, there is a remarkable absence of reverence towards the idols and priests of the Buddha and Taou sects. The want of ceremony with which they treat their gods is not more surprising, however, than the apparently impious expressions which are occasionally used in the ancient classics of Europe towards the whole family of Olympus:—

"Tunc cum virguncula Juno!"

When a parent or elder relation among the Chinese dies, the event is formally announced to all the branches of the family; each side of the doors is distinguished by labels in white, which is the mourning colour. The lineal descendants of the deceased, clothed in coarse white cloth, with bandages of the same round their heads, sit weeping round the corpse on the ground, the women keeping up a dismal howl after the manner of the Irish. In the meantime the friends of the deceased appear with white coverlets of linen or silk, which are placed on the body; the eldest son, or next lineal male descendant, supported on each side by relations, and bearing in his hands a porcelain bowl containing two copper coins, now proceeds to the river, or the nearest well, or the wet ditch of the city, to "buy water," as it is termed. The ceremony must be performed by the *eldest son's son*, in preference to the second son, and entitles him to a double share of the property, which in other respects is divided equally among the sons. The form of washing the face and body with this water being completed, the deceased is dressed as in life, and laid in a coffin, of which the planks are from four to six inches in thickness, and the bottom strewed with quick-lime. On being closed, it is made air-tight by cement, being besides varnished on the inside and outside. A tablet is then placed on it, bearing inscribed the name and titles of the deceased, as they are afterward to be cut upon his tomb.

On the expiration of thrice seven, or twenty-one days, the funeral procession takes place, the tablet being conveyed in a gilded sedan or pavilion, with incense and offerings before it. It is accompanied by music closely resembling the Scottish bagpipe, with the continual repetition of three successive strokes on a sort of drum. The children and relations of both sexes follow in white, without much order or regularity, and, upon reaching the grave, the ceremonies and oblations commence. It being a part of their superstition that money and garments must be burnt for the use of the deceased in the world of spirits, these are, with a wise economy, represented by *paper*. The form of the tomb, whether large or small, is exactly that of a Greek Ω, which, if taken in the sense of "the end," is an odd accidental coincidence. Those of the rich and great are sometimes very large, and contain a considerable quantity of masonry, with figures of animals in stone. The whole detail of sepulchral rites, with the sentiments of the Chinese concerning the dead, is contained in the drama of "An Heir in Old Age."

After the interment, the tablet of the deceased is brought back in procession, and, if the family be rich, it is placed in the hall of ancestors; if poor, in some part of the house with incense before it. Twice in every year, in the spring and autumn, are the periods fixed for performing the rites to the dead, but the first is the principal period, and the only one commonly attended to. Unlike the generality of Chinese festivals, which are regulated by the moon (and therefore moveable), this is determined by the sun, and occurs annually 105 days after the winter solstice, i. e., the 5th of April. About that time (for a day or two before or after does not signify to them) the whole population of the town is seen trooping out in parties to the hills, to repair and sweep the tombs, and make offerings, leaving behind them, on their return home, long streamers of red and white paper, to mark the fulfilment of their rites. Whole ranges of hills, sprinkled with tombs, may at that season be seen covered with these testimonials of attention to the departed, fluttering in the wind and sunshine.

Such are the harmless, if not meritorious forms of respect for the dead, which the Jesuits wisely tolerated in their converts, knowing the consequences of outraging their most cherished prejudices; but the crowds of ignorant monks who flocked to the breach which those scientific and able men had opened, jealous, perhaps, at their success, brought this as a charge against them, until the point became one of serious controversy and reference to the pope. His holiness being determined to govern men's consciences at Peking, and supersede the emperor's authority over his subjects, espoused the bigoted and unwiser part, which of course led to the expulsion of the monks of all varieties, "black, white, and gray, with all their trumpery," and prevented those social and political mischiefs which have invariably attended their influence elsewhere. Such a strict persecution of the Romish converts followed, that, after the lapse of about three centuries, the number of them at the present day is as nothing in comparison with what it once was. The emperor said of their conduct, "This surely is as contradictory to reason and social order as the wild fury of a mad dog." With reference to one of their miracles (of which they were liberal), he adds, "it would appear to be a tale which their ingenuity has contrived; and, upon this principle, what is there we may not readily expect them to say or write?"

The body of a rich person is generally transported to his native province, however distant, but on the journey it is not permitted to pass through any walled town. We might take a lesson from their wholesome practice of allowing no interments within cities, and of confining them either to hills, or the most barren tracts unavailable for cultivation; thus consulting at once the health and the subsistence of the living. To perform "the rites at the *hills*" is synonymous with the *tombs* in Chinese. To such sanitary regulations, and to the antiseptic effects attending the constant burning of incense, crackers, &c., in every house, we may principally attribute the remarkable healthiness of Canton and other towns, notwithstanding the drawbacks of a dense population, hot climate, low site, indifferent drainage of houses, &c. Indeed, were it not for the comparative coldness of the climate in European cities where such abominations prevail, the gorging the earth with corpses until it refuses to cover them, and the filling of churches with dead bodies, might work effects sufficiently evident to all, to expel prejudices which,

> "*Sans* honorer les morts, font mourir les vivans."*

No corpse is ever allowed to be carried up a landing-place, or to pass through a gateway which can in any way be construed as pertaining to the emperor, on account of the supposed ill omen, concerning which the Chinese are so particular as seldom even to mention death except by a circumlocution, as "to become *immortal*," that is, in the modified sense of the Buddhists.

On the occasion of a deceased officer from a British ship being taken ashore for burial at Macao, the sailors were proceeding with the coffin up the steps leading to the Chinese custom-house, when the inmates of the latter turned out with sticks and staves to prevent them. The sailors being, as usual, quite ready to fight, particularly on an occasion when they supposed some insult was intended to the dead, it is likely that mischief might have ensued, if a person on the spot, who understood the prejudice, and explained it satisfactorily, had not prevented the effects of the misunderstanding.

The importance which the Chinese attach to the spot in which a body should be buried, is sometimes the occasion of extraordinary delay in the performance of the funeral ceremonies. A Hong merchant at Canton, who was the eldest son of the family, and had deferred for various superstitious reasons the interment of his father's body, was prosecuted at law by the next brother, and finally compelled to commit it to the tomb. The prin-

* Without honouring the dead, bring death to the living.

cipal scruples on these occasions arise from circumstances relative to the situation and aspect of the sepulchre, a sort of geomantic science, in which the same cheats who profess astrology affect to be adepts. Their calling is a sufficiently secure one, since it is as difficult to prove the *negative* as the *affirmative* of those propositions in which they deal; and the dead make no complaints, being on such points, as the doctor in Molière says, "*Les plus honnêtes gens du monde.*" The choice of a lucky spot is supposed to have a considerable influence on the fortunes of the survivers, and they will sometimes, after the lapse of many years, dig up the bones with care, and remove them to a distant and more favourable site. All tombs are sacred to *How-too*, "queen earth," an expression which has a most singular parallel, not only in the words, but the occasion of their use, in a passage of the Electra of Euripides, where Orestes, invoking the shade of his father at the tomb, adds,—

Καὶ γη τ'ανασσα, χειρας η διδώμ' εμας.*

"And thou, *queen earth*, to whom I stretch my hands."

The original and strict period of mourning (according to the ritual) is three years for a parent, but this is commonly reduced in practice to thrice nine, or twenty-seven months, during which an officer of the highest rank must retire to his house, unless under a particular dispensation from the emperor. The full period of three years must elapse before children can marry subsequent to the death of their parents. The colour of mourning is white, and dull gray, or ash, with round buttons of crystal or glass in lieu of gilt ones; the ornamental ball, denoting rank, is taken from the cap, as well as the tuft of crimson silk which falls over the latter. As the Chinese shave their heads, the neg-

* Electr. 677.

lect and desolation of mourning are indicated by letting the hair grow; for the same reason that some nations, who wore their hair long, have shaved it during that period. On the death of the emperor, the same observances are kept, by his hundreds of millions of subjects, as on the death of the parent of each individual; the whole empire remains unshaven for the space of one hundred days, while the period of mourning apparel lasts longer, and all officers of government take the ball and crimson silk from their caps. It is said that, on the death of Kâng-hy's emperess, four of her maids desired to be buried with her; but that wise monarch would not permit the exercise of this piece of Scythian barbarity, the practice of which he abolished for ever in favour of the more humane and civilized customs of the Chinese.

In regard to the succession to paternal property, the disposal of it by will is restricted except to the legal heirs; and we have seen that, to a very limited extent, there is a law of *primogeniture*, inasmuch as the eldest son, or he who "buys water" at the funeral rites, has a double portion. More correctly speaking, perhaps, the property may be said to descend to the eldest son* *in trust* for all the younger brothers, over whom he has a considerable authority, and who commonly live together and club their shares, by which means families in this over-peopled country are more easily subsisted than they would otherwise be, and every man's income is made to go the farthest possible. To this usage, and the necessity for it, may be attributed the constant exhortations of the emperor, in the book of "Sacred Edicts," relative to the preservation of union and concord among kindred and their families.

* Leu lee, sec. 78.

CHAPTER VIII.

MANNERS AND CUSTOMS.

The New Year.—Fireworks.—Contrariety of Usages and Notions to our own.—Festivals.—Meeting the Spring.—Encouragements to Husbandry.—Festival for the Dead.—Chinese Assumption. — Ceremonial Usages. — Diplomatic Forms. — Feasts and Entertainments.—Dinners.—Particular description of one.—Asiatic Politeness.—Articles of Food and Drink. —Taverns and Eating-houses.—Amusements.—Gambling.— Conviviality. — Kite-flying. — Imperial Hunts. — Skating at Peking.

There is, perhaps, no people in the world that keeps fewer holydays than the Chinese, among whose overflowing population the introduction of a Romish calendar of saints would be altogether disastrous. Some of their festivals are regulated by the sun, and are therefore fixed, as the winter solstice, and the period for visiting the tombs; but the greater number being dependant on the moon, become accordingly moveable. The principal, and almost the only *universal* season of leisure and rejoicing, is the new year, at which time, indeed, the whole empire may be said to be almost beside itself. On the approach of the new moon which falls nearest to the point when the sun is in the 15° of Aquarius (the commencement of the Chinese civil year), all public offices are closed for some ten days in advance, and the mandarins lock up their seals until the 20th of the first moon. On the night of the last day of the old year everybody sits up, and at the moment of midnight commences an interminable *feu de joie* of crackers strung together. Indeed, the consumption of this noisy species of firework is so enormous that the air becomes absolutely charged with nitre; and a governor of Canton once in vain endeavoured to suppress it, on the ground of the undue wastefulness of the practice, though it probably contributes to the healthiness of Chinese towns. From midnight until dawn, everybody is engaged in the performance of sacred rites, or in preparing his house for the solemnities of the new year. Many go through the ceremony of washing and bathing in warm water, in which are infused the aromatic leaves of the hoang-py, a fruit-tree. Every dwelling is swept and garnished, and the shrine of the household gods decorated with huge porcelain dishes or vases containing the fragrant gourd, the large citron, called by them "the hand of Buddha" (or Fo), and the flowers of the narcissus. The bulbs of this last are placed in pots or vases filled with smooth round pebbles and water, just so long before the time as to be in full blossom exactly at the new year. Early on the morning of the first day of the first moon, crowds repair to the different temples in their best attire, kindred and acquaintance meet, and visits are paid universally to offer the compliments of the season. A man on this day hardly knows his own domestics, so finely are they attired; and on all sides along the streets may be seen the bowings and half-kneelings, with the affected efforts to prevent them, which constitute a part of Chinese ceremonies of courtesy.

The large red tickets of congratulation which they send to each other on this occasion have a wood-cut, representing the three principal felicities in Chinese estimation, namely, offspring, official employment (or promotion), and long life. These are indicated by the figures of a child, a mandarin, and an aged figure accompanied by a stork, the emblem of longevity. For the space of the first three days it would be reckoned unlucky, if not criminal, to perform any work beyond what is required by the daily exigences of life, and many defer their occupations for about twenty days. At every house the visiter is received with ready cups of tea, and with the betel, as used in India and the Eastern islands. That nothing may interrupt the general festivity, the termination of the previous year is occupied in settling all outstanding money-accounts, and the discredit is so great of not being able to pay up at that period, that many will borrow, at a ruinous rate, of Peter, in order to satisfy the demands of Paul. It being the custom to kill great numbers of capons previous to the new year, an unhappy debtor, who cannot arrange with his creditors at that period, is said, in derision, to have "a capon's destiny."

The new year is the principal period for exchanging presents among friends. These commonly consist of delicacies, as rare fruits, sweetmeats, fine tea, and occasionally of silk stuffs for dresses, and ornaments of various kinds. These are accompanied by a list inscribed on a red ticket, which it is customary to return by the bearer, with this inscription, "received with thanks." The compliment is immediately to be returned by presents of the same kind and in the same manner, the servants who convey them always receiving a reward. It is an unpardonable insult to send back a batch of these new-year's gifts, though, if they are deemed too liberal, a selection may be made, and the rest returned, with this note beside them on the ticket, "The pearls are declined." The better kinds of fruit, tea, and other articles used on these occasions, are for the same reason styled "ceremonial, or present goods."

The first full moon of the new year is the Feast of Lanterns, being a display of ingenuity and taste in the construction and mechanism of an infinite variety of lanterns made of silk, varnish, horn, paper, and glass, some of them supplied with moving figures of men galloping on horseback, fighting, or performing various feats, together with numerous representations of beasts, birds, and other living creatures, the whole in full motion. The moving principle in these is the same with that of the smoke-jack, being a horizontal wheel turned by the draught of air created by the heat of the lamp. The circular motion is communicated in various directions by fine threads attached to the moving figures. The general effect is extremely good; though, as objects of real use, the Chinese lamps labour under the disadvantage of giving but a poor light, which arises in part from the opacity of the materials, and the superfluity of ornament, but principally from the badness of the lamp itself, which is simply a cotton wick immersed in a cup of oil; and they have no way of increasing the light except by adding to the number of wicks. They seem to admire our Argand lamps, but seldom use them, except in compliment to European guests; and, even when received as presents, they may frequently be seen laid by in a dusty corner.

The fireworks of the Chinese are sometimes ingenious and entertaining, rather, however, on account of the variety of moving figures which they exhibit, than the brilliancy or skill of the pyrotechny, which is inferior to our own. Their best thing of the kind is what Europeans call a *drum*, from its being a cylindrical case, in which is contained a multitude of figures folded into a small space, and so contrived as to drop in succession on strings, and remain suspended in motion, during the explosion of the various fireworks contained within the cylinder. They likewise contrive to make paper figures of boats to float and move upon the water, by means of a stream of fire issuing from the stern. Their rockets are bad, but blue lights they manufacture sufficiently well for the use of European ships.

In their diversions the Chinese have much of that childish character which distinguishes other

Asiatics. Science, as an amusement, may be said to be entirely wanting to them, and the intellect cannot be unbended from the pursuits of business by the rational conversation or occupations which distinguish the superior portions of European society. The mind under a despotism has few of those calls for exertion, among the bulk of the people, which in free states give it manly strength and vigour. Bearing no part in public transactions, and living in uninterrupted peace, the uniform insipidity of their existence is relieved by any, even the most frivolous and puerile amusements. This feature, as well as the very striking *contrariety* of Chinese customs, in comparison with our own, is given with sufficient correctness in the following passages from a little work printed at Macao, which are inserted here, divested of some of the buffoonery of the original :—

"On inquiring of the boatman in what direction Macao lay, I was answered, in the west-north, the wind, as I was informed, being east-south. We do not say so in Europe, thought I; but imagine my surprise when, in explaining the utility of the compass, the boatman added, that the needle pointed to the south! Desirous to change the subject, I remarked that I concluded he was about to proceed to some high festival, or merrimaking, as his dress was completely white. He told me, with a look of much dejection, that his only brother had died the week before, and that he was in the deepest mourning for him. On my landing, the first object that attracted my attention was a military mandarin, who wore an embroidered petticoat, with a string of beads round his neck, and who besides carried a fan; and it was with some dismay I observed him mount on the right side of his horse. I was surrounded by natives, all of whom had the hair shaven from the forepart of the head, while a portion of them permitted it to grow on their faces. On my way to the house prepared for my reception, I saw two Chinese boys discussing with much earnestness who should be the possessor of an orange. They debated the point with a vast variety of gesture, and at length, without venturing to fight about it, sat down and divided the orange equally between them.....At that moment my attention was drawn by several old Chinese, some of whom had gray beards, and nearly all of them huge goggling spectacles. A few were chirruping and chuckling to singing-birds, which they carried in bamboo cages, or perched on a stick; others were catching flies to feed the birds: the remainder of the party seemed to be delightfully employed in flying paper kites, while a group of boys were gravely looking on, and regarding these innocent occupations of their seniors with the most serious and gratified attention. ....I was resolute in my determination to persevere, and the next morning found me provided with a Chinese master, who happily understood English. I was fully prepared to be told that I was about to study a language without an alphabet, but was somewhat astonished, on his opening the Chinese volume, to find him begin at what I had all my life previously considered the end of the book. He read the date of the publication—'The fifth year, tenth month, twenty-third day.'—'We arrange our dates differently,' I observed; and begged that he would speak of their ceremonials. He commenced by saying, 'When you receive a distinguished guest, do not fail to place him on your left hand, for that is the seat of honour; and be cautious not to uncover the head, as it would be an unbecoming act of familiarity.' Hardly prepared for this blow to my established notions, I requested he would discourse of their philosophy. He reopened the volume, and read with becoming gravity, 'The most learned men are decidedly of opinion that the seat of the human understanding is the stomach.'* I seized the volume in despair, and rushed from the apartment."

A festival much honoured by the Chinese, and indicative of their ancient regard for agriculture, is that which takes place when the sun reaches the 15° of Aquarius. The governor of every capital city issues in state towards the eastern gate, to "meet the spring," which is represented by a procession bearing a huge clay figure of the buffalo, called by the Chinese "water-bullock" (from its propensity for muddy shallows), which is always used to drag their plough through the flooded rice-grounds. The train is attended by litters, on which are borne children fancifully dressed, and decorated with flowers, representing mythological personages; and the whole is accompanied by a band of musicians. When they have reached the governor's house, he delivers a discourse in his capacity of Priest of Spring, recommending the care of husbandry; and, after he has struck the clay buffalo thrice with a whip, the people fall upon it with stones, and break in pieces the image, whose hollow inside is filled with a multitude of smaller images in clay, for which they scramble. This ceremony bears some resemblance to the procession of the bull Apis in ancient Egypt, which was connected in like manner with the labours of agriculture and the hopes of an abundant season.

The emperor himself, at about the same period of the year, honours the profession of husbandry by going through the ceremony of holding the plough. Accompanied by some princes of the blood, and a selection of the principal ministers, he proceeds to a field set apart for the purpose, in the enclosure which surrounds the Temple of the Earth, where every thing has been duly prepared by regular hus-

* They place it in the *heart.*

bandmen in attendance. After certain sacrifices, consisting of grain which has been preserved from the produce of the same field, the emperor ploughs a few furrows, after which he is followed by the princes and ministers in order. The "five sorts of grain" are then sown, and when the emperor has viewed the completion of the work by the husbandmen present, the field is committed to the charge of an officer, whose business it is to collect and store the produce for sacrifices.

The same countenance and example which the emperor affords in person to the production of the principal materials of *food*, are given by the empress to the cultivation of the mulberry and the rearing of silk-worms, the sources whence they derive their chief substance for *clothing*, and the care of which for the most part comes under the female department. In the ninth moon, the empress proceeds with her principal ladies to sacrifice at the altar of the inventor of the silk manufacture; and when that ceremony is concluded, they collect a quantity of the mulberry-leaves, which are devoted to the nourishment of the imperial depot of silk-worms. Various other processes connected with the same business are gone through, as heating the cocoons in water, winding off the filament, &c.; and so the ceremony concludes. Of the sixteen "Sacred Edicts" addressed to the people, the fourth relates exclusively to the two foregoing subjects. "Attend (it is said) to your farms and mulberry-trees, that you may have sufficient food and clothing;" and they are reminded that, although only four of the provinces (all of them cut by the 30th parallel of latitude) produce silk in perfection, yet there are the equally useful materials elsewhere of hemp and cotton. "Thus different are the sources whence clothing is procured; but the duty of preparing it, as exemplified in the cultivation of the mulberry-tree, is one and the same." One of the emperors of the present dynasty caused a work to be published expressly in illustration of the two great departments of native industry. It is styled *Keng-chĕ Too*, "Illustrations of Husbandry and Weaving," and consists of numerous wood-cuts, representing the various processes in the production of rice and silk, with letter-press descriptions. The great preference which the rulers of China give to such kinds of industry over the pursuits of commerce, but especially *foreign* commerce, would seem to be dictated by a sentiment analogous to that which is conveyed in four of Goldsmith's lines :—

> "That trade's proud empire hastes to swift decay,
> As ocean sweeps the labour'd mole away ;
> While self-dependant states can time defy,
> As rocks resist the billows and the sky."

The principal public festivals of China that remain to be noticed are not numerous. The fifth day of the fifth moon, which usually occurs in June, is celebrated in a way which cannot fail to excite the attention of a visiter to Canton. Very long, narrow boats, built for the purpose, and manned by forty to sixty, and sometimes eighty men with paddles, who keep time to the beat of a gong, with which one of the crew stands up in the boat. These race against each other on the rivers with great heat and emulation, and accidents frequently occur from the upsetting or breaking of the "dragon-boats," as they are called from their great length. This constitutes one of the few athletic diversions of the Chinese.

On the first day of the seventh moon, or some time in the month of August, they have a festival for the benefit of their departed relatives in the world of spirits. It is not a domestic celebration, however, but a public one : large mat houses are erected, ornamented with lanterns and chandeliers, in which are placed images of the infernal deities, including *Yen-Wâng*, the Chinese Pluto. Priests of the Buddha sect are engaged to chant masses for the dead, offerings of food are presented, and large quantities of paper, representing clothes, are burnt, in order that they may pass into the other world for the use of the departed. On these occasions may be seen representations of the future state of the Buddhists, with the torments of the damned, and the various gradations of misery and happiness in the life to come. These celebrations being calculated to bring large numbers together, appear to consist in a great measure of feasting and entertainment; and they are said to have arisen from some tradition of a young man who went down to the nether world to bring back, not his wife, but (what is much more suitable to Chinese sentiment) his mother. According to the story, this Asiatic Orpheus was more successful than the Thracian.

We proceed now to their ordinary usages in social intercourse. The importance which the Chinese attach to ceremonies might perhaps be supposed to produce in them a constrained stiffness and formality of manner; but, notwithstanding the apparent encumbrance of ceremony prescribed on solemn occasions, our embassies have proved that persons of high authority and station are distinguished generally in their address by a dignified simplicity and ease. This does not, however, prevent their laying a great stress on precedence, especially on public occasions, where the spectators are numerous; and in the case of foreign embassies they will always do their utmost to maintain (as *they* think) the superiority of their own court by placing themselves before their guests. The following extract, from Sir George Staunton's unpublished journal of the last embassy, is in point: —"A message had come from the legate to say, that, as the passage of the next sluice on the canal was attended with some risk, the ambassador had better go on shore, and that he should be ready to receive his lordship in a tent on the following morning. To this it was returned for answer, that, if it was proposed to meet on any particular business, the ambassador would attend; but that otherwise he begged to decline it, having observed that the legate always assumed the highest seat, although in his visits to the ambassador the first place had invariably been given to him. Kuâng-Tajin replied by saying, that he did this merely because his situation obliged him: word was accordingly sent that his excellency would be glad to meet the poo-ching-sse, or treasurer, whose station did not oblige him to assume the highest seat. In the morning, after breakfast, three chairs arrived for the ambassador and commissioners, and on their way they crossed the sluice, which was to be passed by their boats, over a temporary range of boards. Immediately on the other side stood the tent, a neat structure of coloured cloth in stripes, which we were requested by the attendants to enter, and take our seats. The legate, attended by the treasurer, soon came in, and, after conversing for a short time on their legs, the ambassador requested that Kuâng-Tajin would sit down, saying he would waive all claims as a guest to the first place. The legate upon this proceeded to the first seat, and the treasurer, without the least ceremony, walked towards the *second*. On this the ambassador desired it might be intimated that, though he was ready to yield to the one, he would not consent to sit below the other; and the treasurer, rather than take the third place, marched out of the tent."

This incivility to Europeans is the more unpardonable, as among themselves it is the rule in general, during visits, to contend for the lowest seat, and they would be heartily ashamed of the opposite ill-breeding towards each other; but they view strangers as an inferior caste altogether. Their arm-chairs are always ranged in regular order, and, being very bulky and solid, like our oldfashioned seats of former times, they are not easily removed. "In Chinese apartments there is placed a broad couch, in size approaching to a bed, called a *kâng*. On the middle of this is planted a little table about a foot in height, intended to rest the arm, or place teacups upon. On either side of this little table, on the couch, sit the two principal persons, fronting the entrance; and from the ends of the couch, at right angles to it, descend two rows of arm-chairs for the other guests, who sit nearest to the couch, according to their rank."*

When any one proceeds in his chair to pay a visit, his attendants present his ticket at the gate, consisting of his name and titles written down the middle of a folded sheet of red paper, ornamented with gold leaf; and there is sometimes enough paper in these, when opened out like a screen, to extend across a room. If the visiter is in mourning, his ticket is white, with blue letters. According to the relative rank of the parties, the person visited comes out a greater or less distance to receive his guest, and, when they meet, their genuflections, and endeavours to prevent the same, are also according to rule. These matters are all so well understood by those who are bred up to them, that they occasion no embarrassment whatever to the Chinese. The ordinary salutation among equals is to join the closed hands, and lift them two or three times towards the head, saying, *Haou—tsing, tsing;* that is, "Are you well?—Hail, hail!" Hence is derived, we believe, the Canton jargon of *chin-chin*.

Soon after being seated, the attendants invariably enter with porcelain cups furnished with covers, in

* Morrison's Journal, 1816.

each of which, on removing the little saucer by which it is surmounted, appears a small quantity of fine tea-leaves, on which boiling water has been poured; and thus it is that they drink the infusion, without the addition of either sugar or milk. The delicate aroma of fine tea is no doubt more clearly distinguished in this mode of taking it, and a little habit leads many Europeans in China to relish the custom. Though the infusion is generally made in the cup, they occasionally use teapots of antique and tasteful shapes, which are not unfrequently made of tutenague externally, covering earthenware on the inside. At visits, a circular japanned tray is frequently brought in, having numerous compartments radiating from the centre, in which are a variety of sweetmeats or dried fruits. These are taken up with a small two-pronged fork of silver. On the conclusion of a visit, the host conducts his guest, if he wishes to do him high honour, even to his sedan, and there remains until he is carried off; but on ordinary occasions it is deemed sufficient to go as far as the top of the stone steps, if there are any, or merely to the door of the apartment.

Only mandarins, or official persons, can be carried by four bearers, or accompanied by a train of attendants: these are marshalled in two files before the chair. One pair of the myrmidons carry gongs, on which they strike at regular intervals; another pair utter, likewise at intervals, a long-drawn shout, or rather yell, to denote the approach of the great man; a third pair carry chains, which they jingle in concert, being in fact jailers or executioners, with high caps of iron wire, in which is stuck a gray feather. Then come two fellows with the usual bamboo, or bastinade; and the cortège is made up by the servants and other followers, some of whom carry red umbrellas of dignity, others large red boards, on which are inscribed in gilt characters the officer's titles. The populace who meet such a procession are not to denote their respect in any other way than by standing aside, with their arms hanging close to their sides, and their eyes on the ground. It is only when called or taken before a tribunal that they are obliged to kneel; and these are occasions which most Chinese are not very willing to seek.

English residents at Canton have occasionally had opportunities of taking a part in the formal dinners of the Chinese; but few have seen a solemn feast conferred by the emperor, which may be described from an unpublished journal of the last embassy. "The ambassador informed the gentlemen of his suite that he was going to perform the same salutation of respect, before the yellow screen, that he was accustomed to make to the vacant throne of his sovereign in the House of Lords. We were directed to keep our eyes on him, and do exactly as he did. A low solemn hymn of not unpleasing melody now commenced, and at the voice of a crier, the two imperial legates fell prostrate three times, and each time thrice struck the floor with their foreheads: a cranio-verberative sound being audible amid the deep silence which prevailed around. The ambassador and his suite, standing up in the meanwhile, made nine profound bows. Thus far we had got very well over the ground, without doing that which no representatives of *Chinese* majesty ever condescended to do to a foreigner, until Genghis Khân first *made* them. They here conceded to us the point on which they broke off with Count Golovkin, the Russian ambassador, though they yielded it to Lord Macartney.

"When the ceremony was over, the feast was brought in, and the theatrical entertainments commenced. The legates sat to the left, on an elevation of one step; and the ambassador and two commissioners on the same elevation to the right. The other Chinese grandees sat on the left, a little below the legates; and the gentlemen of the embassy to the right, below his lordship and the commissioners. The two lines thus faced each other down the room. As no chairs can be used where the emperor is present, or supposed to be so, the whole party sat cross-legged on cushions, with sartorial precision; but the mandarins, being bred to the trade, of course had the advantage of us. The tables were low in proportion, and, when we were all seated, a number of attendants placed on each table, holding only two guests, a large tray which fitted it, and contained a complete course, of which four in all were served. The first consisted of a rich soup; the second of sixteen round and narrow dishes containing salted meats and other relishes; the third of eight basins of birds'-nests, sharks'-fins, deer-sinews, and other viands supposed to be highly nourishing; the fourth of twelve bowls of stews immersed in a rich soup. The guests helped themselves with chopsticks, small spoons of porcelain fashioned like a child's pap-boat, and four-pronged forks of silver, small and straight; and, when they drank to each other, the warm wine was poured into little cups by the attendants, who at the same time bent one knee.

"At the other end of the hall where we sat, so as to be viewed by each person from his place down the two ranges of tables, proceeded the stage performances. The music was infernal, and the occasional crash of gongs might have roused Satan and his legions from their sleep on the sulphureous lake. Some pyrotechnic monsters, breathing fire and smoke, were among the dramatis personæ; but by far the best part of the scene was the tumbling—really superior in its kind. The strength and activity of one man were particularly eminent. Leaping from the ground, he performed a somerset in the air backward, and, after the first effort, continued to revolve in this manner with such velocity, that his head and feet, the extremities of revolution, were scarcely discernible."

An invitation to a private feast is conveyed some days before, by a crimson-coloured ticket, on which is inscribed the time appointed, and the guest is entreated to bestow "the illumination of his presence." The arrangement of the tables is the same as at the imperial entertainment, but they are of the ordinary height, and the party are seated on chairs, two at each table, so as to see the performances on the stage. The *matériel* of the dinner is much the same as before described; but, previous to its commencement, the host, standing up, drinks to his guests, and then invites them to begin upon the dishes before them. At a certain period of the entertainment, towards the close, the whole party rise at once, and drink to their host. Before the dramatic performance begins, one of the actors presents to the principal guest a list of plays, consisting perhaps of fifty or sixty different pieces; but they have these so well by heart, that they are ready to perform any one he may select. There is no scenery, and in this respect a great deal is left to the imagination of the spectators. The dresses, however, are extremely splendid, especially in heroical pieces, consisting of representations of different portions of their ancient history. The most objectionable part is the terrible din kept up by the instruments of music and the gongs, during those portions of the play which represent battles and tragical scenes.

The females of the household, meanwhile, who cannot take a part in the festivities of the table, look on from behind a trellis-work at one of the sides of the stage, with such of their friends of the same sex as may be invited on the occasion. A particular description of the Chinese drama will be given in its proper place; but we may observe here, that *dancing* is a thing almost entirely unknown to them, either on or off the stage. On one occasion, indeed, in the interval or space between the ranges of tables, we saw two children, showily dressed, go through a species of minuet, consisting of a regular figure to slow time, accompanied by a motion of the arms and head not ungraceful in effect.

A formal dinner, which begins about six o'clock in the evening, is generally protracted to a great length, the succession of dishes, or rather bowls, which follow each other appearing sometimes to be interminable. So little, however, is eaten of each, that the guests often continue tasting the contents of one after another until the very end. There seems to be little regularity in the timing of the different viands, but after the birds'-nest-soup (which is, in fact, a strong chicken-broth, in which that substance is introduced in long strips, after the manner of vermicelli), the peculiar delicacies which have already been mentioned, together with mutton, fish, game, and poultry, follow indiscriminately. The signal of the repast approaching its termination is the appearance of a bowl of rice for each person, and this is followed soon after by tea, in lieu of the wine. The whole is crowned by a course of fruits and sweetmeats, very much in the manner of our dessert.

The greater portion of cups, bowls, and saucers (for they have no flat plates of their own), which constitute the dinner service, consist of fine porcelain; but occasionally a few particular meats are served in silver or tutenague covers, under which is a spirit-lamp to keep them hot. The wine-cups, too, are sometimes of silver gilt, and of rather elegant vase-like shapes. The extreme smallness of these cups, joined to the weakness of the wine, which is always drunk warm, enables them to take a great number without being in the least affected, or at all exceeding the bounds of sobriety. On some occasions of peculiar ceremony, the feast is closed by a great cup scooped from the horn of the rhinoceros, which animal is said to exist in the forests of Yunnân and Kuâng-sy. We find in the works of Arabian writers that the same substance has often been used for the drinking-cups of Asiatic potentates, being supposed to sweat on the approach of poison, and therefore to be a safeguard against it. When the Mongols conquered the empire they probably introduced its use into China.

The following description of a Chinese dinner, from the pen of our friend Captain Laplace, of the French navy, although rather a long extract, is given with so much of the characteristic vivacity of his countrymen, and so well conveys the *first impression* of a scene not often attended by Europeans, that it is introduced without farther apology. "The first course was laid out in a great number of saucers of painted porcelain, and consisted of various relishes in a cold state, as salted earthworms, prepared and dried, but so cut up that I fortunately did not know what they were until I had swallowed them; salted or smoked fish, and ham, both of them cut into extremely small slices; besides which, there was what they called Japan leather, a sort of darkish skin, hard and tough, with a strong and far from agreeable taste, which seemed to have been macerated for some time in water. All these et cæteras, including among the number a liquor which I recognised to be soy, made from a Japan bean, and long since adopted by the wine-drinkers of Europe to revive their faded appetites or tastes, were used as seasoning to a great number of stews which were contained in bowls, and succeeded each other uninterruptedly. All the dishes without exception swam in soup. On one side figured pigeons'-eggs, cooked in gravy, together with ducks and fowls cut very small, and immersed in a dark-coloured sauce; on the other, little balls made of sharks'-fins, eggs prepared by heat, of which both the smell and taste seemed to us equally repulsive, immense grubs, a peculiar kind of sea-fish, crabs, and pounded shrimps.

"Seated at the right of our excellent Amphitryon,* I was the object of his whole attention, but nevertheless found myself considerably at a loss how to use the two little ivory sticks, tipped with silver, which, together with a knife that had a long, narrow, and thin blade, formed the whole of my eating apparatus. I had great difficulty in seizing my prey in the midst of those several bowls filled with gravy: in vain I tried to hold, in imitation of my host, this substitute for a fork between the thumb and the two first fingers of the right hand; for the cursed chop-sticks slipped aside every moment, leaving behind them the unhappy little morsel which I coveted. It is true that the master of the house came to the relief of my inexperience (by which he was much entertained) with his two instruments, the extremities of which, a few moments before, had touched a mouth, whence age, and the use of snuff and tobacco, had cruelly chased its good looks. I could very well have dispensed with such an auxiliary, for my stomach had already much ado to support the various ragouts, each one more surprising than another, which I had been obliged, *nolens volens*, to taste of. However, I contrived to eat with tolerable propriety a soup prepared with the famous birds'-nests, in which the Chinese are such epicures. The substance thus served up is reduced into very thin filaments, transparent as ising-glass, and resembling vermicelli, with little or no taste.† At first I was much puzzled to

* To some of our readers it may be necessary to explain that this word is used in French to express *host*, from the following popular verse of a comedy:—

"*Le véritable Amphitryon est l'Amphitryon* où l'on dine."

† It is generally accompanied with pigeons'-eggs, boiled hard, and eaten with soy.

find out how, with our chop-sticks, we should be able to taste of the various soups which composed the greater part of the dinner, and had already called to mind the fable of the fox and the stork, when our two Chinese entertainers, dipping at once into the bowls with the little saucer placed at the side of each guest, showed us how to get rid of the difficulty." We confess we were never witness to this slovenly manœuvre, as the Chinese tables are generally supplied with a species of spoon, of silver or porcelain, sufficiently convenient in shape.

" To the younger guests, naturally lively, such a crowd of novelties presented an inexhaustible fund of pleasantry, and, though unintelligible to the worthy Hong merchant and his brother, the jokes seemed to delight them not a bit the less. The wine in the meanwhile circulated freely, and the toasts followed each other in rapid succession. This liquor, which to my taste was by no means agreeable, is always taken hot; and in this state it approaches pretty nearly to Madeira in colour, as well as a little in taste; but it is not easy to get tipsy with it, for, in spite of the necessity of frequently attending to the invitations of my host, this wine did not in the least affect my head. We drank it in little gilt cups, having the shape of an antique vase, with two handles of perfect workmanship, and kept constantly filled by attendants holding large silver vessels like coffee-pots. The Chinese mode of pledging is singular enough, but has at the same time some little resemblance to the English. The person who wishes to do this courtesy to one or more guests gives them notice by an attendant; then, taking the full cup with both hands, he lifts it to the level of his mouth, and, after making a comical sign with his head, he drinks off the contents; he waits until the other party has done the same, and finally repeats the first nod of the head, holding the cup downward before him, to show it is quite empty.

"After all these good things, served one upon the other, of which it gave me pleasure to see the last, succeeded the second course, which was preceded by a little ceremony, of which the object seemed to me to be a trial of the guests' appetites. Upon the edges of four bowls, arranged in a square, three others were placed filled with stews, and surmounted by an eighth, which thus formed the summit of a pyramid; and the custom is to touch none of these, although invited by the host. On the refusal of the party, the whole disappeared, and the table was covered with articles in pastry and sugar, in the midst of which was a salad composed of the tender shoots of the bamboo, and some watery preparations that exhaled a most disagreeable odour.

"Up to this point, the relishes, of which I first spoke, had been the sole accompaniments of all the successive ragouts; they still served to season the bowls of plain rice, which the attendants now* for the first time placed before each of the guests. I regarded with an air of considerable embarrassment the two little sticks, with which, notwithstanding the experience acquired since the commencement of the repast, it seemed very doubtful whether I should be able to eat my rice grain by grain, according to the belief of Europeans regarding the Chinese custom. I therefore waited until my host should begin, to follow his example, foreseeing that, on this new occasion, some fresh discovery would serve to relieve us from the truly ludicrous embarrassment which we all displayed: in a word, our two Chinese, cleverly joining the ends of their chopsticks, plunged them into the bowls of rice, held up to the mouth, which was opened to its full extent, and thus easily shovelled in the rice, not by grains,

* It must be remembered that this was a formal dinner Rice forms a much more integral part of an every-day meal.

but by handfuls. Thus instructed, I might have followed their example; but I preferred making up with the other delicacies for the few attractions which, to my taste, had been displayed by the first course. The second lasted a much shorter time: the attendants cleared away every thing. Presently the table was strewed with flowers, which vied with each other in brilliancy; pretty baskets, filled with the same, were mixed with plates which contained a vast variety of delicious sweetmeats as well as cakes, of which the forms were as ingenious as they were varied. This display of the productions of nature and of art was equally agreeable to the eyes and the tastes of the guests: by the side of the yellow plantain was seen the *litchi*, of which the strong, rough, and bright crimson skin defends a stone enveloped in a whitish pulp, which for its fine aromatic taste is superior to most of the tropical fruits. Indigenous to the provinces which border on the Chinese Sea, the newly-gathered litchi presents to the inhabitants a wholesome and delicious food* during the summer, and forms, when dried, an excellent provision for the winter. With these fruits of the warm climates were mingled those of the temperate zone, brought at some expense from the northern provinces; as walnuts, chestnuts (small, and inferior to those of France), apples, grapes, and Peking pears, which last, though their lively colour and pleasant smell attracted the attention, proved to be tasteless, and even retained all the harshness of wild fruits. The conversation, frequently interrupted during the commencement of the repast, in order to do honour to the numerous pledges of our host, and to all the wonders of the Chinese kitchen assembled before us, became now general, and sufficiently noisy. My neighbour es-

* This is a very heating fruit, and known to be dangerous if taken in large quantities.

pecially, little accustomed to such lively mirth, was quite enchanted, and displayed his satisfaction by loud laughs, to which was perpetually joined the sonorous accompaniment of his somewhat overloaded stomach. According to the received usages of Chinese fashion, I ought to have followed this example, in testimony of a more than satisfied appetite, but my wish to gratify our excellent Amphitryon would not carry me quite so far. This custom, which in France would seem more than extraordinary, was however nothing new to myself, for I had already remarked it in the best societies at Manilla. Need I then to be surprised on finding the Chinese so little nice in their convivial habits, when our near neighbours the Spaniards have not yet cast off this remnant of the grossness of the olden time?"

This disagreeable custom would seem to be tolerated all over Asia, where it is considered as much a matter of course as coughing or sneezing. The curious part of the history is, that any ideas of *civility* or *politeness* should be attached to that which in England or France would be so differently received. "At length," adds our author, "we adjourned to the next room to take tea,—the indispensable commencement and close of all visits and ceremonies among the Chinese. According to custom, the servants presented it in porcelain cups, each of which was covered with a saucer-like top, which confines and prevents the aroma from evaporating. The boiling water had been poured over a few of the leaves, collected at the bottom of the cup; and the infusion, to which no sugar is ever added in China, exhaled a delicious fragrant odour, of which the best teas carried to Europe can scarcely give an idea."

It is remarkable that the grape, although abundant, is not used in this country for the production of wine, which is fermented from rice but nevertheless resembles some of our weaker white wines both in colour and flavour. The rice is soaked in water, with some other ingredients, for a considerable number of days. The liquor is then boiled, after which it is allowed to ferment, and subsequently drawn off clear from the bottom, to be put up in earthen jars, not unlike the amphoræ of the ancients still remaining to us. The residue is used in the distillation of a very strong spirit, little inferior in strength to pure alcohol, which they sometimes introduce in an extremely small cup at the close of their dinners. When good it resembles strong whiskey, both in its colourless appearance and its smoky flavour. The Tartars are said still to preserve a remnant of their pastoral state, in their predilection for a strong liquor which is distilled from mutton. One of the soups, too, presented at the imperial feast conferred on the last British embassy at Tien-tsin, was said to be composed of mare's milk and blood!

The Chinese are little addicted to drinking plain water, which in a considerable portion of the country is extremely bad. On the Peking river, several of the persons in the embassies suffered severely from its use, by which they were afflicted with dysenteries and other unpleasant symptoms. It was generally of a milky colour, and though cleared in some measure by being stirred with a bamboo, in the cleft of which a piece of alum had been stuck as a precipitate, it always retained a portion of its noxious qualities. It may fairly be surmised, that the badness of the water occasioned the first introduction, and subsequently the universal use, of tea as an article of drink. Notwithstanding their general repugnance to eating and drinking what is cold, none understand better than the Chinese of the North the use of ice during hot weather. Near to Peking, in the month of August, and when the thermometer stood above 80°, we constantly saw people carrying about supplies of this article of luxury. Two large lumps, whose solid thickness proved the lowness of the temperature which produced them, were suspended in shallow baskets at opposite ends of a pole, carried across the shoulders. Every vender of fruit at a stall either sold it in lumps, or used it in cooling his goods ; and the embassy was liberally supplied with ice for cooling wine. The mode of preserving it through the summer is the usual one, of depositing the ice at a sufficient depth in the ground, surrounding it with straw or other non-conducting substance, and draining off the wet.

The Chinese cookery has a much nearer resemblance to the French than the English, in the general use of ragouts and made-dishes, rather than plain articles of diet, as well as in the liberal introduction of vegetables into every preparation of meat. The expenses of the wealthy, as might be expected, run very much in the direction of sensual pleasures, among which the gastronomic hold a conspicuous place. Some of the articles, however, which they esteem as delicacies, would have few attractions for a European. Among others the larvæ of the sphinx-moth, as well as a grub which is bred in the sugarcane, are much relished. Their dishes are frequently cooked with the oil extracted from the *ricinus*, which yields the castor-oil of medicine; but, as it is used by them in the fresh state, and with some peculiar preparation, it has neither the strong detergent properties, nor the detestable taste, by which this oil is known in Europe.

The general prevalence of Buddhism among the population is perhaps one of the reasons that beef is scarcely ever used by them, though the multitudes of bullocks killed annually for the use of the European shipping proves that their religious scruples cannot be very strong. It must, however, be observed, that some absurd prejudices and maxims, not to say positive laws, have always existed against an extended consumption of flesh food. There are, accordingly, no people in the world that consume so little butcher's meat, or so much fish and vegetables. The rivers and coasts of this country are profusely productive of fish, and the people exercise the greatest ingenuity in catching them. Carp and mullet were observed by the last embassy in all the towns bordering on the route from Peking. It would be a mistake to suppose that the extension of cultivation had rendered game scarce. There are abundance of wooded hills and mountains as well as lakes, about which wild fowl, pheasants, red-legged partridges, and snipes, are plentiful. Wild geese are seen on the Canton river during winter in large flocks, as well as teal and wild ducks; and the woodcock is sometimes, though rarely, to be procured.

The most universal vegetable food in the empire, next to rice, is the *pĕ-tsae*, a species of brassica, which derives its name (white-cabbage) from being partially blanched, as celery is with us. By our embassies it was frequently used as a salad, and when fresh is little inferior to lettuce, which it greatly resembles as a plant. The most celebrated place for its production is the neighbourhood of Tien-tsin, where the soil is a loose, sandy alluvium. From thence it is conveyed, either in the fresh state or salted, to all parts of the country. They are said to preserve it fresh, either by planting in wet sand, or by burying it deep in the ground; and it is a popular remark, that the nine gates of Peking are blocked during the autumnal season with the vehicles bringing in the pĕ-tsae. Besides this vegetable, the northern provinces consume millet and the oil of sesamum as general articles of diet. Many of the cottagers were observed to possess the means of independent support in the patches of cultivation which surrounded their huts, being supplied in many cases with a small and simple mill, worked by an ass, for the expression of the sesamum-oil. The vegetable oils which are used to the southward are obtained from the *Camellia oleifera*, and the *Arachis hypogæa*, as well as the *Ricinus*.

As the embassies approached the south, the most common vegetables in use appeared to be the *Solanum melongena*, several species of gourds and cucumbers, the sweet potato, and one or two species of kidney-bean, of which in some cases they boil the young plants. Peas, too, which were introduced by the Dutch factory for their own use, appear sometimes at Chinese dinners in stews, being generally eaten in the pod, while this is young and tender. Near Macao the potato has become very common, but it does not spread so rapidly as might have been expected; for, after twenty years since its first introduction, this vegetable is far from being either plentiful or cheap at Canton, only eighty miles distant from the former place. Nothing, indeed, will ever supersede *rice* as the staple article of diet among the Chinese populace, whose predilection for it may be gathered from what Mr. Gutzlaff says in his journal: "Rice being very cheap in Siam, every (Chinese) sailor had provided a bag or two as a present to his family. In fact, the chief thing they wish and work for is rice: their domestic accounts are entirely regulated by the quantity of rice consumed; their meals according to the number of the bowls of it boiled; and their exertions according to the quantity wanted. Every substitute for this favourite food is considered meager, and indicative of the greatest wretchedness. When they cannot obtain a sufficient quantity to satisfy their appetites, they supply the deficiency with an equal weight of water.* Inquiring whether the western barbarians

* Making a sort of gruel of the rice.

eat rice, and finding me slow to give them an answer, they exclaimed, 'Oh! the steril regions of barbarians, which produce not the necessaries of life. Strange that the inhabitants have not long ago died of hunger!' I endeavoured to show them that we had substitutes for rice which were equal, if not superior to it; but all to no purpose; and they still maintained that it is rice only which can properly sustain the life of a human being."

If the rich should appear to be fantastic in the selection of their diet, the poor are no less indiscriminate in the supply of theirs. They will, in fact, eat nearly every thing that comes in their way; and, with one half of the prejudices of the Hindoos, a large portion of the Chinese population would perish with hunger. They make no difficulty whatever of dogs, cats, and even rats; and indeed the first of these are enumerated as a regular article of food in one of their ancient books. Among the rich themselves, a wild cat, previously prepared by feeding, is reckoned a delicacy. Chinese dogs are said to have a particular aversion for butchers, in consequence, no doubt, of the violation of those personal exemptions and privileges which the canine race are allowed to enjoy almost everywhere else.

As might be expected from the economical habits of the people, that great save-all, the pig, is universally reared about cottages, and its flesh is by far the commonest meat; the maxim is, "that a scholar does not quit his books, nor the poor man his pigs." If it be true that the frequent use of pork produces or predisposes to leprosy ("*cui id animal obnoxium,*" says Tacitus), the Chinese would go far to corroborate the truth of the observation, being very subject to that, as well as other cutaneous affections; but it must be remarked, at the same time, that their foul-feeding is *universal.* They contrive to rear ducks very cheaply, by making them hunt for their own food. Large quantities of the eggs are hatched artificially, and the ducks brought up by thousands in peculiar boats, where their lodging is constructed upon broad platforms, extending far beyond the sides of the boat. In this manner they are conveyed to different parts of the rivers, and turned out to seek their food upon the muddy banks and shoals. So well disciplined are these birds, that, upon a given signal, they follow their leaders with great regularity up the inclined board, by which they return to their habitation on the close of the day's feeding. The flesh is preserved by the bodies of the ducks being split open, flattened, and salted, and in this condition exposed to the dry northerly winds during the cold months.

The consumption of salted provisions is very general, and enables the government to draw a large revenue from the *gabelle* which it levies on salt. In consequence of the immense quantities of both sea and river fish which are daily caught, and the rapidly putrescent nature of that species of provision, a considerable portion is cured with salt, and dried in the sun, the *haut goût* which generally accompanies it being rather a recommendation to the taste of the Chinese. Indeed, it is one of their most favourite as well as universal articles of food; and they even overcame their prejudice, or indifference for whatever is foreign, on the occasion of salted cod being introduced for two or three years in English ships; the somewhat decayed condition in which it reached China being said to have been any thing but a drawback. This species of cargo, however, besides its disagreeable nature, and the injurious effect which it might have on more delicate articles of shipment, was found during the long voyage to breed a peculiar insect, which, from the readiness with which it bored into the planks and timbers of a ship, was considered as dangerous, and accordingly the import was greatly discontinued.

The middling and poorer classes are amply accommodated with taverns and eating-houses, where, for a very small sum, a hot breakfast or dinner may be obtained in a moment. There are some favourable specimens of these at Canton, to the west of the factories, built up to the height of two stories, and looking down the river. Such is the jealous inhospitality of the local government, or rather of the Hong merchants (who have charge of foreigners), that the owners of these taverns are strictly prohibited from entertaining Europeans; and they have often refused all offers from those who wished to try the entertainment which they afforded. Such of the Chinese of respectability as have not their families at Canton, frequently resort to these places in the evening, where they are provided with a comfortable dinner; and about the period of sunset the whole range is seen gayly lighted up through its several stories.

The public houses for the poorer people are generally open sheds, and on particular festivals these consist of a temporary structure of matting, with a boarded floor, fitted up with tables and benches, and affording the means of gambling and drinking to the dissolute portion of the lowest class. To the credit of the Chinese, as a nation, it must be stated that the proportion which this description of persons bears to their numerous population is not large. The seafaring inhabitants of Canton and Fokien are perhaps among the worst. The dangerous profession of these poor people, and their unsettled, wandering habits, tend together to give them the reckless and improvident character which is often found attached to the lower grades of the maritime profession in other countries. Mr. Gutzlaff has drawn a very revolting picture of the sailors who navigate the Chinese junks, and his account is no doubt in the main quite correct; but it must be observed, in general, of the gentlemen of his profession, both

Catholics and Protestants, that, accustomed habitually to view the heathen almost exclusively on the side of their spiritual wants, they have sometimes drawn rather too unfavourable a picture of their moral character. This, however, is more true of many others than of Mr. Gutzlaff, whose candour has occasionally done fair justice to the inhabitants of the Chinese empire on the score of their good qualities.

Though the lowest orders are certainly very prone to gambling, this is a vice which is chiefly confined to them. So much infamy attaches to the practice in any official or respectable station, and the law in such cases is so severe, that the better classes are happily exempt from it. This seems to be a point on which the *liberty* of the subject may in any community (where public opinion is ineffectual) be unceremoniously violated, very much to its own benefit, since true liberty consists in the power to do every thing except that which is plainly opposed to the general good. Those laudable inventions, dice, cards, and dominoes, are all of them known to the Chinese. Their cards are small pieces of pasteboard, about two inches long and an inch broad, with black and red characters on the faces. The idle and dissolute sometimes train quails for fighting, as the Malays do cocks; and even a species of cricket is occasionally made subservient to this cruel purpose.* The Chinese chess differs in board, men, and moves, from that of India, and cannot in any way be identified with it, except in being a game of skill, and not of chance.

They have two contrivances for the promotion of drinking at their merry-meetings. One of these, called *tsoey-moey*, consists in each person guessing at the number of fingers suddenly held up between

* Two of them are placed together in a bowl, and irritated until they tear each other to pieces.

himself and his adversary, and the penalty of the loser is each time to drink a cup of wine. In still, calm evenings, during the continuance of the Chinese festivals, the yells of the common people engaged at this tipsy sport are sometimes heard to drown all other noises. It is precisely the same as the game of *morra*, common among the lower orders in Italy at the present day, and derived by them from the Roman sport of "*micare digitis*," of which Cicero remarked, that "you must have great faith in the honesty of any man with whom you played in the dark;"—"*multâ fide opus est, ut cum aliquo in tenebris mices.*" The other festive scheme is a handsome bouquet of choice flowers, to be circulated quickly from hand to hand among the guests, while a rapid roll is kept up on a kettle-drum in an adjoining apartment. Whoever may chance to hold the flowers at the instant the drum stops, pays forfeit by drinking a cup of wine. It may be easily imagined that this rational amusement occasionally gives rise to scenes worthy of Sir Toby and his associates in the Twelfth Night.

In lieu of theatrical entertainments at their dinners, conjuring, sleight of hand, and other species of dexterity, are sometimes introduced for the diversion of the assembly. The conjurer has always an accomplice, as usual, who serves to distract the attention of the spectators. One of their best exhibitions of mere dexterity is where a common China saucer is spun on its bottom upon the end of a ratan cane, in a very surprising manner. The rapid revolution communicated to the saucer by the motion of the performer's wrist, through the medium of the flexible and elastic ratan, keeps it whirling round without falling, even though the cane is occasionally held nearly horizontally, and sometimes passed behind the back, or under the legs, of the exhibiter. It may be observed that the cup is seldom in danger of falling, except for the moment when the eye of the performer may be taken off from it.

Among their out-of-door amusements, a very common one is to play at shuttlecock with the *feet.* A circle of some half a dozen keep up in this manner the game between them with considerable dexterity, the thick soles of their shoes serving them in lieu of battledoors, and the hand being allowed occasionally to assist. In kite-flying the Chinese certainly excel all others, both in the various construction of their kites, and the heights to which they make them rise. They have a very thin, as well as tough, sort of paper, made of refuse silk, which, in combination with the split bamboo, is excellently adapted to the purpose. The kites are made to assume every possible shape; and, at some distance, it is impossible occasionally to distinguish them from real birds. By means of round holes, supplied with vibrating cords, or other substances, they contrive to produce a loud humming noise, something like that of a top, occasioned by the rapid passage of the air as it is opposed to the kite. At a particular season of the year, not only boys, but grown men, take a part in this amusement, and the sport sometimes consists in trying to bring each other's kites down by dividing the strings.

The taste of the Chinese court as to its amusements was observed by the several embassies to be nearly as puerile as that of most other Asiatics. Farces, tumbling, and fireworks were the usual diversions with which the emperor and his guests were regaled. Two of the sovereigns of this Tartar dynasty, Kâng-hy and Kien-loong, maintained the hardy and warlike habits of the Manchows by frequent hunting expeditions to the northward of the great wall. They proceeded at the head of a little army, by which the game was enclosed in rings, and thus exposed to the skill of the emperor and his grandees. We find, from Père Gerbillon's account of his hunting expedition with Kâng-hy, that a portion of the train consisted of falconers, each of whom had the charge of a single bird. The personal skill and prowess of Kâng-hy appear to have been considerable, and we have the following description from Gerbillon of the death of a large bear: "This animal being heavy and unable to run for any length of time, he stopped on the declivity of a hill, and the emperor, standing on the side of the opposite hill, shot him at leisure, and with the first arrow pierced his side with a deadly wound. When the animal found himself hurt, he gave a dreadful roar, and turned his head with fury towards the arrow that stuck in his belly. In the endeavour to pull it out he broke it short, and then, running a few paces farther, he stopped exhausted. The emperor, upon this, alighting from his horse, took a half-pike, used by the Manchows against tigers, and, accompanied by four of the ablest hunters armed in the same way, he approached the bear and killed him outright with a stab of his half-pike."

The amusements of the emperor's court on the ice, during the severe winters of Peking, are thus given by Van Braam, who was one of the Dutch mission which proceeded from Canton soon after Lord Macartney's embassy:—"The emperor made his appearance on a sort of sledge, supported by the figures of four dragons. This machine was moved about by several mandarins, some dragging before, and others pushing behind. The four principal ministers of state were also drawn upon the ice in their sledges by inferior mandarins. Whole troops of civil and military officers soon appeared, some on sledges, some on skates, and others playing at football on the ice, and he that picked up the ball was rewarded by the emperor. The ball was then hung up in a kind of arch, and several mandarins shot at it, in passing on skates, with their bows and arrows. Their skates were cut off short under the heel, and the forepart was turned up at right angles." These diversions are quite in the spirit of the Tartars, whose original habits were strongly opposed to those of the quiet and effeminate Chinese. However robust and athletic the labouring classes in the southern provinces of the empire, those who are not supported by bodily exertion are in general extremely feeble and inactive. Unlike the European gentry, they seldom mount on a horse, if not of the military profession; and as nobody who can afford a chair ever moves in any other way, the benefits of walking are also lost to them. Nothing surprises one of these Chinese gentlemen more than the voluntary exertion which Europeans impose on themselves for the sake of health as well as amusement. Much of this inactivity of habit must of course be attributed to the great heat of the climate during a considerable portion of the year; and they would be greater sufferers from their sedentary lives, were it not for the beneficial custom of living entirely in the *open air*, with warm clothing, during even the winter months—that is, in the south; for, to the northward, the extreme cold compels them to resort to their stoves and flues, with closed windows and doors. The apartments of houses at Canton are always built quite open to the south, though defended from the bleak northerly winds by windows of oyster-shells or glass.

CHAPTER IX.

MANNERS AND CUSTOMS.

Costume of better Classes.—Absence of Arms or Weapons from Dress.—Summer and Winter Costume.—Paucity of Linen.—General use of Furs and Skins.—Sudden changes of Fashion not known.—All modes prescribed by a particular Tribunal.—Singular Honours to just Magistrates.—Shaving and Shampooing.—Female Dress.—Chinese Dwellings.—Description of a large Mansion.—Tiling of Roofs.—Gardens.—Furniture—Taste for Antiques.—Travelling by Land.—Government Post not available to Individuals.—Printed Itineraries.—Travelling by Water.—Public Passage-boats.—Passing a Sluice on the Canal.—Same practice six hundred years ago.

"When dressed, every Chinese of any station wears by his side a variety of accoutrements, which would strike a stranger as being of a warlike character, but which prove, on examination, to be very peaceful appendages. A worked silk sheath encloses a fan. A small leather bag, not unlike a cartouch box, suspended to the belt, supplies flint and steel for lighting the pipe; and the tobacco is carried in an embroidered purse or pouch." Dr. Abel thus describes the appearance of the first well-dressed Chinese whom he saw on reaching the shores of the Yellow Sea. Arms are, in fact, never worn on the person except by soldiers on parade; and even the military mandarins do not wear swords on ordinary occasions of ceremony. The common people are not allowed to be seen with arms except for specific purposes of self-protection, as when carrying off their property from a fire, or as a defence against river pirates, and the like.

The possession of *firearms* is altogether forbidden by the jealous government, as may be seen from the following extract from a Peking gazette:—"For the people to have firearms in their possession is contrary to law, and orders have already been issued to each provincial government to fix a period, within which all matchlocks belonging to individuals should be bought up at a valuation. . . . . With regard to those firearms which are in immediate use for the safeguard of the country, the said governor has already directed the proper officers to carve on every matchlock the name of the person to whom it is delivered, and to preserve a general register of the whole. Let the governor also give strict charge to make diligent search, and prevent the illicit storing up of firearms for the futuie; and let the workers in iron be rigidly looked after, lest they clandestinely manufacture and sell them; the evil may thus be cut off in its commencement. Those officers who have made full and complete musters within the limited period, the governor is directed to notice properly as an encouragement to others." Those Chinese near Canton who employ themselves in shooting wild fowl for sale, are said to belong mostly to the militia of the province.

The extremes of heat and cold which prevail throughout the country at opposite seasons of the year, joined to the general custom of living very much in the open air, are the causes which have probably given rise to the broad and marked distinctions that exist between the summer and the winter dress of the better classes. The difference is principally marked by the cap. The summer cap is a cone of finely woven filaments of bamboo, or a substance resembling chip, and surmounted, in persons of any rank, by a red, blue, white, or gilded ball at the apex or point of the cone. From the insertion of this ornamental ball descends all around, over the cap, a fringe, or rather bunch of crimson silk or of red horse hair; in front of the cap is sometimes worn a single large pearl.

The winter cap, instead of being a cone, fits closer to the shape of the head, and has a brim, turned sharply up all round, of black velvet, or fur, and rising a little higher in front and behind than at the sides. The dome-shaped top is surmounted by the same ball as in the other case, denoting the rank of the wearer; and from the point of insertion descends a bunch of fine crimson silk, just covering the dome. On the commencement of the cold or hot weather, the first person in each province, as the tsoong-to, or viceroy, assumes his winter or summer cap; the circumstance is noticed in the official gazette, or court circular, and this is the signal for every man under his government to make the same change. In the embassy of 1816, the imperial legate, who conducted the mission down to Canton, being for the time superior in rank to the viceroy, in this manner put on his winter cap, and gave the example to the province through which he was passing. Within doors they usually wear in cold weather a small scullcap, either plain or ornamented.

The summer garment of the better classes is a long loose gown of light silk, gauze, or linen, hanging free at ordinary times, but on occasions of dress gathered in round the middle by a girdle of strong wrought silk, which is fastened in front by a clasp of agate, or of the *jade*, which the Chinese call *yu*. In an oppressive climate, when the thermometer is at 80° or 90°, there is much ease and comfort in the loose sleeves, and the freedom from restraint about the neck, by which this dress is distinguished; and the tight sleeves and huge collars of Europeans very naturally make them objects of compassion, if not ridicule. To the girdle are fastened the various articles noticed by Dr. Abel, as the fan case, tobacco pouch, flint and steel, and sometimes a sheath with a small knife and pair of chopsticks. They are very proud of displaying a watch, which is inserted in an embroidered silk case or pouch.

Summer and Winter Caps.

The winter dress, being nearly as loose as that of summer, is less calculated to promote warmth and comfort than the European costume, and at the same time more unfavourable to bodily activity and exertion. Over a longer dress of silk or crape, which reaches to the ankles, they wear a large-sleeved spencer, called *ma-kwa*, (or riding coat,) which does not descend below the hips. This is often entirely of fur, but sometimes of silk or broadcloth, lined with skins. The neck, which in summer is left quite bare, is protected in winter with a narrow collar of silk or fur; their loose dresses always fold over to the right breast, where they are fastened from top to bottom, at intervals of a few inches, by gilt or crystal buttons (the latter in mourning) with loops.

In summer the nether garment is loose, and not unlike ancient Dutch breeches; but in winter an indescribable pair of tight leggins are drawn on separately over all, and fastened up to the sides of the person, leaving the voluminous article of dress above mentioned to hang out behind in a manner that is anything but pleasant. Stockings of cotton or silk, woven and not knit, are worn by all who can afford them; and in winter, persons of a certain rank wear boots of cloth, satin, or velvet, with the usual thick white sole, which is kept clean by *whiting* instead of *blacking*, in the usual style of contrariety to our customs. The thick soles of their boots and shoes in all probability arose from the circumstance of their not possessing such a substance as *well-tanned* leather, a thinner layer of which is sufficient to exclude the wet. The shoes made for Europeans at Canton are perfectly useless in rainy weather, and spoiled on the very first wetting.

The Chinese dresses of ceremony are exceedingly rich and handsome, and contrast to great advantage with the queer, unmeaning capings and skirtings of our coats. The colour of the spencer is usually dark blue, or purple, and the long dress beneath is commonly of some lighter and gayer hue. On state occasions this last is very splendidly embroidered with dragons or other devices, in silk and gold, and the cost amounts frequently to large sums. At the imperial feast of which the last embassy partook at Tein-tsin, the crowd of mandarins in full dress, surmounted by their crimson caps and various-coloured balls, certainly produced a striking effect.

The great sin of the Chinese costume is the paucity of white linen, and consequently of washing. Even their body garment is sometimes a species of light silk, but capable of purification. All the rest of their dress being of silks or furs, there is less demand for white calico or linen, in proportion to the numbers, than in any other country. They spread neither sheets upon their beds nor cloths on their tables, and the want of personal cleanliness has of course a tendency to promote cutaneous and leprous complaints. Their substitute for soap is an alkaline lye, derived from a mineral substance, and rather corrosive in its nature.

The skins of all animals are converted into apparel for the winter. The lower orders use those of sheep, cats, dogs, goats, and squirrels. Even rat and mouse skins are sown together for garments. The expensive fur dresses of the higher orders descend from father to son, and form sometimes no inconsiderable portion of the family inheritance. At an entertainment in Canton, where the party, according to the custom of the country, were seated in an open room without fires, the European guests began to complain of cold; upon which the host immediately accommodated the whole number of ten or twelve with handsome wide-sleeved spencers, all of the most costly furs, telling them at the same time that he had plenty more in reserve. They have one singular species of refinement on the score of skins. The young lamb *in utero*, after a certain period of gestation, is taken out, and its skin prepared with the fine silky wool upon it for dresses, which of course require, on account of their small size, a great number of lambs to be thus "untimely ripped," and the luxury is therefore an expensive one.

The Chinese, perhaps, may be said to possess an advantage in the absence of those perpetual and frequently absurd mutations of fashion in Europe, which at one period blow out the same individual like a balloon whom at another they contract to a mummy: and which are frequently ridiculed and followed in excess at one and the same time. They are not at the mercy and disposal, in matters of taste, of those who make their clothes, and their modes generally last as long as their garments. The human shape and dress are not varied with the infinite mutations of a kaleidoscope; and that peculiar, though indisputable species of merit, "being in the height of the fashion," the honours of which must be chiefly shared with the tailor and the milliner, is nearly unknown to them.

The only setter of fashions is the board of rites and ceremonies at Peking, and to depart materially from their ordinances would be considered as something worse than mere *mauvais ton*. It is their business not only to prescribe the forms on all occasions of worship, or of ceremony, but the costumes which are to be worn must be in strict conformity to rule. The dresses of all ranks and orders, and of both sexes, about the imperial palace, are specified, as regards cut, colour, and material, with as much precision as in any court of Europe. From the Tartar religion of the Lamas, the rosary of 108 beads has become a part of the ceremonial dress attached to the nine grades of official rank. It consists of a necklace of stones and coral nearly as large as a pigeon's egg, descending to the waist, and distinguished by various beads according to the quality of the wearer. There is a small rosary of only eighteen beads of inferior size, with which the bonzes count their prayers and ejaculations, exactly as in the Roman Catholic ritual. The laity in China sometimes wear this at the waist, perfumed with musk, and give it the name of *Heang-choo*, "fragrant beads."

The various appendages worn at the girdle, as the purse or pouch, the steel and flint case for lighting the pipe, the watch case, &c., are generally of the finest silk embroidery, which forms one of the principal accomplishments of the Chinese ladies. Indeed all the handsome crape shawls taken to England, some of which cost from sixty to eighty dollars, are entirely the work of women, many of whom earn more than twenty dollars a month by their labour. A Chinese is seldom seen without his snuff bottle, which is of oval construction, and less than two inches in length, the stopper having a small spoon attached similar to that for Cayenne pepper, with which a portion of snuff is laid on the left hand, at the lower joint of the thumb, and thus lifted to the nose. The material of these bottles is sometimes porcelain, or variegated glass, carved with considerable skill in the style of cameos; or rock crystal, with small figures or writing on the *inside*, performed in a manner which it is not easy to account for.

Among the presents sent to, or, in the language of Peking diplomacy, *conferred upon* foreign sovereigns, is the embroidered silk purse, one of which the old emperor Kien-loong took from his side, and gave to the youth who officiated as page to Lord Macartney. This, however, was of the imperial yellow colour, with the five-clawed dragon, and could hardly be worn by Chinese subjects, who always displayed the most profound reverence and admiration when they saw it, and knew it was from the great emperor's own person. The ornament which has sometimes, for want of a better name, been called a *sceptre*, is, in fact, an emblem of amity and good will, of a shape less bent than the letter S, about eighteen inches in length, and cut from the *jade* or *yu* stone. It is called *joo-ee*, "as you wish," and is simply exchanged as a costly mark of friendship; but that it had a religious origin seems indicated by the sacred flower of the lotus (*Nymphæa nelumbo*) being generally carved on the superior end.

The Chinese have some singular modes of demonstrating their respect and regard on the departure of any public magistrate, whose government has been marked by moderation and justice. A deputation sometimes waits upon him with a habit composed of every variety of colour, "a coat of many colours," as if made by a general contribution from the people. With this he is solemnly invested, and, though of course the garment is not intended to be worn, it is preserved as an honourable relic in the family. On quitting the district, he is accompanied by the crowds that follow his chair, or kneel by the wayside, while at intervals on the road are placed tables of provisions and sticks of incense burning. These honours were shown to a late Fooyuen of Canton, a man of a most eccentric but upright character, who, unlike so many others in his situation, would never take anything from the Hong merchants or others under his authority. He seemed to have a supreme indifference for human grandeur, and at length retired by his own choice and the emperor's permission into private life, from whence it is said he became a devotee of Budh. On his quitting Canton, a very singular custom was observed, in conformity with ancient Chinese usage on such rare occasions; when he had accepted the various demonstrations of homage and respect from those who had been deputed by the people to wait on him, he proceeded from his residence to the city gates, and, being there arrived, his *boots* were taken off, to be preserved as a valued relic, while their place was supplied by a new pair. This was repeated more than once as he proceeded on his way, the boots which he had only once drawn on being regarded as precious memorials. The conduct of the higher magistrates cannot fail to be influenced sometimes by the ambition of earning such popular honours, and there can be little doubt that, in places less exposed to the contagion of vice and temptation than Canton, there are good magistrates in China as well as elsewhere.

But to return to costumes. The head of the men, as we have before noticed, is invariably shaven, except at the top, whence the tail depends in conformity to the Tartar custom; the only change being in mourning, when the hair is allowed to grow. The Chinese having so little beard, the principal work for the razor is on the head, and consequently no person ever shaves himself. The great number of barbers is a striking feature in all towns, and sufficiently explained by the prevailing custom. They exercise the additional function of shampooing, which, with the antecedent shave, occupies altogether a considerable time. Every barber carries about with him, slung from a stick across his shoulder, all the instruments of his vocation in a compendious form. On one side hangs a stool, under which are drawers containing his instruments; and this is counterpoised at the other end by a small charcoal-furnace under a vessel of water which it serves to heat. Their razors are extremely clumsy in appearance, but very keen and efficient in use. It is not the custom for the men to wear mustaches before forty years of age, nor beards before sixty. These generally grow in thin tufts, and it is only in a few individuals that they assume the bushy appearance observable in other Asiatics.

The women would frequently be very pretty, were it not for the shocking custom of daubing their faces with white and red paint, to which may be added the deformity of cramped feet. In point of health, however, this is in a great degree made up by the total absence of tight lacing, and of all ligatures and confinements whatever about the vital parts. The consequence is that their children are all born very straight limbed, and births are scarcely ever attended with disaster. Their dress is extremely modest and becoming, and, in the higher classes, as splendid as the most exquisite silks and embroidery can make it; for the Chinese certainly reserve the best of their silk manufactures for themselves. What we often choose to call *dress* they would regard as absolute nudity, and all close fitting to the shape as only displaying what it affects to conceal.

Unmarried women wear their hair hanging down in long tresses, and the putting up of the hair is one of the ceremonies preparatory to marriage. It is twisted up towards the back of the head, ornamented with flowers or jewels, and fastened with two bodkins stuck in crosswise. They sometimes wear an ornament representing the foong hoâng, or Chinese phœnix, composed of gold and jewels, the wings hovering, and the beak of the bird hanging over the forehead, on an elastic spring. After a certain time of life, the women wear a silk wrapper round the head, in lieu of any other dress. The eyebrows of the young women are fashioned until they represent a fine curved line, which is compared to the new moon when only a day or two old, or to the young leaflet of the willow.

Pink and green, two colours often worn by women, are confined exclusively to them, and never seen on men. The ordinary dress is a large-sleeved robe of silk, or of cotton among the poorer sort, over a longer garment, sometimes of a pink colour, under which are loose trousers which are fastened round the ankle, just above the small foot and tight shoe. A proverbial expression among the Chinese, for the concealment of defects, is, "Long robes to hide large feet." Notwithstanding this, the Tartar women or their lords, have had the good sense to preserve the ladies' feet of the natural size. In other respects, however, they dress nearly as the Chinese, and paint their faces white and red in the same style.

Husbandman.

The ordinary dress of men among the labouring classes is extremely well suited to give full play to the body: it consists in summer of only a pair of loose cotton trousers tied round the middle, and a shirt or smock, equally loose, hanging over it. In very hot weather the smock is thrown off altogether, and only the trousers retained. They defend the head from the sun by a very broad umbrella-shaped hat of bamboo slips interwoven, which in winter is exchanged for a felt cap; and in rainy weather they have cloaks of a species of flags or reeds, from which the water runs as from a penthouse. A large portion of the peasantry wear no shoes, but some are furnished, particularly those who carry heavy burdens, with sandals of straw to protect the feet.

In describing the dwellings of the Chinese, we may observe that, in their ordinary plan, they bear a curious resemblance to the remains of the Roman habitations disinterred from the scoriæ and ashes of Pompeii. They consist usually of a ground floor, divided into several apartments within the dead wall that fronts the street, and lighted only by windows looking into the internal courtyard. The principal room next to the entrance serves to receive visiters as well as for eating; and within are the more private apartments, the doorways of which are screened by pendent curtains of silk or cotton. Near Peking, the embassies found most of the apartments furnished with a couch or bedplace of brickwork, having a furnace below to warm it during the winter. This was usually covered with a felt rug or mat, which, with the assistance of the warmth, gave perpetual lodging to swarms of vermin, and rendered the bedplaces quite unavailable to the English travellers. These flues, however, are very necessary during the severe winters, when the fires in the better houses are lighted on the outside; but in poorer ones the furnace is within, and serves the double purpose of cooking and warmth, the whole family huddling round it.

All houses of consequence are entered by a triple gateway, consisting of one large folding-door in the centre, and of a smaller one on either side. These last serve for ordinary occasions, while the first is thrown open for the reception of distinguished guests. Large lanterns of a cylindrical shape are hung at the sides, on which are inscribed the name and titles of the inhabitant of the mansion, so as to be read either by day, or at night when the lanterns are lighted. Just within the gates is the covered court, where the sedan chairs stand, surrounded by red varnished label boards, having inscribed in gilt characters the full titles of any person of rank and consequence. We cannot better describe one of their larger mansions than in the words of Sir George Staunton:* "This palace was built on the general

* Embassy, vol. ii., p. 139.

model of the dwellings of great mandarins. The whole enclosure was in the form of a parallelogram, and surrounded by a high brick wall, the outside of which exhibited a plain blank surface, except near one of its angles, where the gateway opened into a narrow street, little promising the handsome structures withinside. The wall in its whole length supported the upper ridge of roof, whose lower edges, resting upon an interior wall parallel to the other, formed a long range of buildings divided into apartments for servants and officers. The rest of the enclosure was subdivided into several quadrangular courts of different sizes. In each quadrangle were buildings upon platforms of granite, and surrounded by a colonnade. The columns were of wood, nearly sixteen feet in height, and as many inches in diameter at the lower end, decreasing to the upper extremity about one sixth. They had neither capital nor base, according to the strict meaning of those terms in the orders of Grecian architecture, nor any divisions of the space called the entablature, being plain to the very top, which supports the cornice; and were without any swell at the lower end, where they were let into hollows cut into stones for their reception, which formed a circular ring round each, somewhat in the Tuscan manner. Between the columns, for about one fourth of the length of the shaft from the cornice downward, was carved and ornamented woodwork, which might be termed the entablature, and was of a different colour from the columns, which were universally red. This colonnade served to support tha part of the roof which projected beyond the wall plate in a curve, turning up at the angles. By means of such roofed colonnades every part of those extensive buildings might be visited under cover. The number of pillars throughout the whole was not fewer than six hundred.

"Annexed to the principal apartment, now destined for the ambassador, was an elevated building, intended for the purposes of a private theatre and concertroom, with retiring apartments behind and a gallery for spectators round it. None of the buildings were above one story, except that which comprised the ladies' apartment during the residence of the owner: it was situated in the inmost quadrangle. The front consisted of one long and lofty hall, with windows of Corea paper, through which no object could be distinguished on the other side. On the back of this hall was carried a gallery, at the height of about ten feet, which led to several small rooms, lighted only from the hall. Those inner windows were of silk gauze, stretched on frames of wood, and worked with the needle in flowers, fruit, birds, and insects, and others painted in water colours. This apartment was fitted in a neater style, though upon a smaller scale, than most of the others. To this part of the building was attached a small back court with offices; the whole calculated for privacy.

"In one of the outer quadrangles was a piece of water, in the midst of which a stone room was built, exactly in the shape of one of the covered barges of the country. In others of the quadrangles were planted trees, and, in the largest, a huge heap of rocks rudely piled, but firmly fixed upon each other, and at one end was a spot laid out for a garden in miniature; but it did not appear to have been finished."

In the best Chinese mansions there are seldom any stairs beyond the few stone steps by which they are raised above the general level of the ground. The stonework of the foundation is extremely solid and handsome, and in the neighbourhood of Canton it is always of granite. The walls are of blue brick, frequently with an artificial facing or pointing, by which strangers are apt to be deceived as to the fineness of their brickwork. They work in stucco with great skill, representing animals, flowers, and fruits, which are sometimes coloured to imitate nature, and the cheapness of this ornament makes it very common. The partition walls of the inner courts are frequently broken into compartments, which are filled with an openwork of green varnished tile, or coarse porcelain. The mode in which they tile their roofs is evidently derived from the use of split bamboos for the same purpose, as it is practised to this day by the Malays, and described by Marsden. The transverse section of these titles being something of a semicircle, they are laid down the roof with their concave sides uppermost to serve as gutters, the upturned edges of every range being contiguous. But, as these would admit the rain at the lines of contact, other tiles are laid in a contrary position over them, and the whole secured in their places by mortar.

In towns, where space is of consequence, the houses and shops of the greater number of the inhabitants have a story above the ground floor, and on the roof is often erected a wooden stage or platform for drying goods, or for taking the air in hot evenings. This custom contributes to make their houses very liable to catch and to spread fires during a conflagration. Nothing surprises the Chinese more than the representations of descriptions of the five and six-storied houses of European cities; and the emperor is said to have inquired if it was the smallness of the territory that compelled the inhabitants to build their dwellings so near the clouds. They have the most absurd superstition in regard to the ill luck that attends the elevation of dwellings above a certain height; and the erection of a gable end (which they denominate by their character for *metal*, approaching to the same shape) will fill a whole family with consternation, until certain ceremonies have been performed to dispel the "evil influence." These remedies are about as well founded in common sense as the evils which they are employed to remove, and resemble exactly the charms and exorcisms used in our olden time against witches, ghosts, and devils. In the same way that a horseshoe, with us, nailed against the door was an infallible protection from a witch, the figure of a dragon, with its mouth wide open, opposite to the unlucky roof, swallows up all the *ngo-ky*, "the bad air, or influence." The Chinese, however, never seem to have reached that height of judicial acumen by which, in former times with us, many a helpless old woman was thrown into the water, to be drowned if she sank, or be burned if she floated.

The magnificence of Chinese mansions is estimated in some measure by the ground which they cover, and by the number and size of the courts and buildings. The real space is often eked out by winding and complicated passages or galleries, decorated with carving and trelliswork in very good taste. The walls are often paved with figured tiles. Large tanks or ponds, with the nelumbium, or sacred lotus, are essential to every country house, and these pools are generally filled with quantities of the golden carp, and other fish. Masses of artificial rock either rise out of the water, or are strewn about the ground in an affected imitation of nature, and on these are often planted their stunted trees. Sir William Chambers's description of Chinese gardening is a mere prose work of imagination, without a shadow of foundation in reality. Their taste is indeed extremely defective and vicious on this particular point, and, as an improvement of nature, ranks much on a par with the cramping of their women's feet. The only exception exists in the gardens, or rather parks, of the emperor at Yuen-ming-yuen, which Mr. Barrow describes as grand both in plan and extent; but for a subject to imitate these would be almost criminal, even if it were possible.

The apartments of the Chinese are by no means

so full of furniture as ours in England, and in this respect they have arrived at a point in luxury far short of our own. Perhaps, however, they are the only people of Asia who use chairs: these resemble the solid and lumbering pieces of furniture which were in fashion more than a century ago, as described by Cowper:—

> "But restless was the chair; the back erect
> Distress'd the weary loins, that felt no ease;
> The slippery seat betray'd the sliding part
> That press'd it, and the feet hung dangling down."

Cushions, with hangings for the back, are sometimes used of silks, or English woollens, generally of a scarlet colour embroidered in silk patterns by the Chinese women. Near the chairs are commonly placed those articles of furniture which the Portuguese call *cuspadores*, or spitting pots, rendered necessary by the universal habit of smoking. The disagreeable noise that attends the clearing the throat and fauces of the poison inhaled by this bestial practise, is perpetual among the Chinese, and makes one enter feelingly into the complaints which have proceeded from several visiters of the United States, in regard to similar habits among our transatlantic brethren.

Among the principal ornaments are the varied lanterns of silk, horn, and other materials, which are suspended from the roofs, adorned with crimson tassels, but which for purposes of illumination are so greatly behind our lamps, and produce more smoke than light. At a Chinese feast, one is always reminded of the lighting of a Roman entertainment:—

> "Sordidum flammæ trepidant rotantes
> Vertice fumum."

The great variety, and, in the eyes of a Chinese, the beauty of the written character, occasions its being adopted as an *ornament* on almost all occasions. Calligraphy (or fine handwriting) is much studied among them, and the autographs of a friend or patron, consisting of moral sentences, poetical couplets, or quotations from the sacred books, are kept as memorials, or displayed as ornaments in their apartments. They are generally inscribed largely upon labels of white satin, or fine coloured paper, and almost always *in pairs*, constituting those *parallelisms* which we shall have to notice under the head of literature and poetry.

In the forms of their furniture they often affect a departure from straight and uniform lines, and adopt what might be called a regular confusion, as in the divisions and shelves of a bookcase, or the compartments of a screen. Even in their doorways, instead of a regular right-angled aperture, one often sees a complete circle, or the shape of a leaf, or of a jar. This, however, is only when there are no doors required to be shut, their absence being often supplied by hanging-screens of silk and cloth, or bamboo blinds like those used in India. Their beds are generally very simple, with curtains of silk or cotton in the winter, and a fine moscheto net during the hot months, when they lie on a mat spread upon the hard bottom of the bed. Two or three boards, with a couple of narrow benches or forms on which to lay them, together with a mat, and three or four bamboo sticks, to stretch the moscheto curtains of coarse hempen cloth, constitute the bed of an ordinary Chinese.

It may be readily supposed that in the original country of porcelain, a very usual ornament of dwellings consists in vases and jars of that material, of which the antiquity is valued above every other quality. This taste has led to the manufacture of factitious antiques, not only in porcelain, but in bronze, and other substances—points on which strangers are often very egregiously taken in at Canton. The shapes of their tripods and other ancient vessels, real or imitated, are often fantastical, and not unlike similar vestiges in Europe. In these they place their sticks of incense, composed principally of sandalwood dust, which serve to perfume their chambers, as well as to regale the gods in their temples. The Chinese are great collectors of curiosities of all kinds, and the cabinets of some individuals at Canton are worth examining.

Having considered the accommodations of the Chinese when at rest, we may view them in locomotion, or when travelling. The manner in which the greater part of the empire is intersected by rivers and canals, makes water carriage the most common as well as commodious method of transit from place to place: but where that is impossible, they travel (towards the South) in chairs; and in the great flat about Peking in a one-horse tilted wagon, or *cart*—for it deserves no better name. The multiform inconveniences of these primitive machines were experienced by the members of the last embassy, and have been feelingly described by some of them. The wheels, frequently solid and without spokes, are low and fixed to very short axletrees. The bodies, covered with tilts of coarse cotton, open only in front, and are just wide enough to admit two persons closely wedged. They have no raised seats, and the only posture is to be stretched at length, or with the legs drawn up, the sufferer being always in close contact with the axle, without the intervention of springs. A servant of the ambassador, who was an invalid at the time, and had not strength to avoid the violence of the shocks, actually suffered a concussion of the brain.

The Chinese occasionally travel on horseback, but their best land conveyance by far is the sedan, a vehicle which certainly exists among them in perfection. Whether viewed in regard to lightness, comfort, or any other quality associated with such a mode of carriage, there is nothing so convenient elsewhere. Two bearers place upon their shoulders the poles, which are thin and elastic, and in shape something like the shafts of a gig connected near the ends; and in this manner they proceed forward with a measured step, an almost imperceptible motion, and sometimes with considerable speed. Instead of pannels, the sides and back of the chair consist of woollen cloth for the sake of lightness, with a covering of oilcloth against rain. The front is closed by a hanging-blind of the same materials, in lieu of a door, with a circular aperture of gauze to see through. The Europeans at Macao furnish theirs with Venetian blinds, and never make use of any other carriage. Private persons among the Chinese are restricted to two bearers, ordinary magistrates to four, and the viceroys to eight, while the emperor alone is great enough to require sixteen. They divide the weight by multiplying the number of shoulder sticks applied to the poles, as represented in a vignette to Staunton's embassy, in an instance where the number of bearers would be sixteen; and this rule is made applicable to the conveyance of the heaviest burdens by coolies or porters. The Chinese constantly remind one of ants, by the manner in which they conquer difficulties through dint of mere numbers; and they resemble those minute animals not less in their persevering and unconquerable industry.

There is no country of the same extent in which horses are so little used for the purposes of either carriage or draft, and this seems to arise, in some measure, from their grudging to animals that food which the earth otherwise provides for man. Their horses are in general miserable stunted creatures, of the smallest order of ponies, and almost always in the worst condition; nor is the caparison in most cases much better than the beast. The rider is wedged into a high saddle of the usual oriental character, of which every part, stirrups included, is extremely heavy and cumbrous. The bridles ought to be of stiched silk, but they are often of rope; and tufts of red horse hair are sometimes suspended from the chest of the animal. Where no rivers or canals afford the conveniences of water carriage, the roads, or rather broad pathways, are paved in the south for horses, chairs, and foot passengers; but no wheel carriages were met by the embassies, except in the flat country towards Peking.

Official persons are accommodated with lodging on their journeys in buildings called *Koong-kuan*, or government hotels, and where one of these does not exist, the priests of the Budh sect are called upon to provide for them in their temples. The gods appear sometimes to be treated with little ceremony on these occasions. In 1816, a portion of the great temple on the side of the river opposite to Canton was appropriated to the British embassy, and fitted up for them, at the requisition of the factory, in a very handsome style, altogether different from the mode in which they had been commonly lodged in the interior. Nothing surprised the Chinese more than the number of comforts and conveniences which the English seemed to require, and the quantity of their baggage. One of their own nation travels with little more than a hard pillow rolled up in a thin mattress, or a mat; and, as for his wardrobe, he carries it all on his back; that is, when not travelling by water. In the latter mode of carriage, the great officers of government sometimes convey no small quantity of goods, and, as their baggage is exempted from search, it is said that the privilege is often abused to smuggle opium.

There is no post regulated by the government for facilitating the general intercourse of its subjects; though one would imagine that a system of the kind might be made very serviceable by this jealous autocracy (as it has by some others) in promoting the special objects of its police. The government expresses are forwarded by land along a line of posts, at each of which a horse is always kept ready; and it is said that, when the haste is urgent, a feather is tied to the packet, and the express is called a *fei-ma*, "flying horse," on which occasions the courier is expected to go at the rate of about a hundred miles a day, until relieved. In this manner a despatch from Peking reaches Canton, or *vice versa*, a distance of 1,200 miles, in a fortnight or twelve days. A letter from the emperor himself is carried by an officer of some rank in a hollow tube, attached to his back. They have no telegraphs, but the embassies frequently observed that three conical, or rather sugar-loaf beacons were erected on the most conspicuous points, to serve as signals by day or night, with the assistance of lighted wood or straw in the hollow, chimneylike interior.

There is printed for general use a very accurate itinerary of the empire, containing the distances in Chinese *ly* from town to town; and one of these, on being compared with the actual distances on the map, as travelled by the last embassy, was found to correspond with sufficient exactness. But the greatest public accommodation consists in the arrangements for the conveyance of goods, which are regulated in the best manner. The public porters are under the management of a head man, who is responsible for them. The wages for the number agreed for are paid to him in advance, upon which he furnishes a corresponding number of tickets, and, when the work is done, these are delivered as vouchers to the several porters to carry back and receive their money. The ordinary pay is one mace, or under 8d. per diem; and so trustworthy are these poor people, that not a single article was known to be lost by the embassies in all the distance between the northern and southern extremes of the empire.

But, putting speed out of the question, there certainly is no country in the world in which travelling by water is so commodious as in China; and it seems reasonable to attribute this circumstance to the universal prevalence of that mode of locomotion. Indeed, all the river craft of this people may be said to be unrivalled. The small draft of water, and, at the same time, great burden and stiffness of their vessels, the perfect ease with which they are worked through the most intricate passages, and most crowded rivers, and the surprising accommodation which they afford, have always attracted attention. The Arab Ibn Batuta, whose travels we have before noticed, in describing the inland trading vessels of the Chinese, states that they were moved by "large oars, which might be compared to great masts, (in respect of size,) over which five-and-twenty men were sometimes placed, who worked standing." He evidently alludes to the enormous and very powerful sculls, which are worked at the stern of their vessels, exactly as he describes, at the present day.

From its situation in the line of the vessel's course, this machine takes up no room in the passage of their crowded rivers and canals, an advantage of no small consequence, if considered by itself. It is a moving power, precisely on the principle of a fish's tail, from which it is well known that the watery tribes derive nearly all their propelling force, as the fins do little more than serve to balance them. The composition of the two lateral forces, as the tail or the scull is worked to the right and left, of course drives the fish, or the vessel, forward in the diagonal of the forces, according to a well-known principle in mechanics. Although, in the Chinese river craft, there is always a rudder to steer with in sailing, the scull will at any time serve in its stead, by merely shifting the balance of impulse to either side as required. These sculls are sometimes thirty feet in length, and the friction is reduced to the least possible amount, by the fulcrum being a tenon and mortice of iron, working comparatively on a point.

The track ropes, made of narrow strips of the strong silicious surface of the bamboo, combining the greatest lightness with strength, are very exactly described by Marco Polo: "They have canes of the length of fifteen paces, such as have been already described, which they split in their whole length, into very thin pieces, and these, by twisting them together, they form into ropes 300 paces long: so skilfully are they manufactured that they are equal in strength to cordage made of hemp. With these ropes the vessels are tracked along the river by means of ten or twelve horses to each, as well upward against the current, as in the opposite direction." It is remarkable that the very instance, where the practice of the present day differs from this faithful traveller's narrative, may be considered as an additional proof of his general correctness. Horses are not now used to track the Chinese boats, although it may have been the practice under the first Mongol conquerors; but the emperor's warrant to each officer specifies a certain number of *horses*, according to his rank, and *men* are supplied as trackers, in lieu of horses, at the rate of three for each horse. Du Halde gives a very correct account of this in his second volume. The oars which they occasionally use towards the head of their boats, besides the scull abaft, are rather short, with broad blades. These are suspended with a loop on a strong peg at the side of the boat, and there is an advantage in its not being always necessary to unship them, as, when useless, they are drawn by the water close to the vessel's side, without any retarding effect. There is besides no friction, nor any noise in a rullock, and no encumbrance of oars within the boat.

The travelling barges, used by mandarins and opulent persons, afford a degree of comfort and accommodation quite unknown in boats of the same description elsewhere; but it must be repeated, that *speed* is a quality which they do not possess. The roof is not less than seven or eight feet in height, and the principal accommodations consist of an anteroom at the head for servants, a sittingroom about the centre of the boat, and a sleeping apartment and closet abaft. All the cooking goes on

Accommodation Barge.

upon the high overhanging stern, where the crew also are accommodated. There are gangways of boards on each side of the vessel, which serve for poling it along the shallows, by means of very long and light bamboos, and which also allow of the servants and crew passing from head to stern without incommoding the inmates. The better boats are very well lighted by glass windows at the sides, or by the thin interior laminæ of oyster shells. Others have transparent paper or gauze, on which are painted flowers, birds, and other devices, while the partitions, or bulkheads, of the apartments are varnished and gilded. The decks or floors of the cabins remove in square compartments, and admit of all the baggage being stowed away in the hold. Everything in their river boats is kept remarkably clean, and this habit presents a strong contrast to their general neglect of cleanliness in their houses on shore, which have not the same ready access to water, and are besides often very ill drained. In short, their travelling barges are as much superior to the crank and rickety budgerows of India, as our European ships are to the sea junks of the Chinese, who seem to have reserved all their ingenuity for their river craft, and to have afforded as little encouragement as possible to maritime or foreign adventure.

Where the expense is not regarded, Europeans often travel between Macao and Canton in the large Chinese boats, of some eighty tons' burden, which are commonly used in unloading the ships, but fitted up when required, with partitions, glass windows, and other conveniences for travelling. The charges of the mandarins, under the denomination of duties and fees, at length grew to be so oppressive, that the thing was brought to the notice of the viceroy, in 1825, and a considerable abatement made in the expense. Still, however, this is so considerable, and the delays interposed midway in the passage, for the purposes of scrutiny and examination, are so tedious and harassing, that most *barbarians* prefer going up and down by the ship's passage in European boats. In this, as well as many other instances, the cupidity of the mandarins has defeated its own purpose.

Nothing could more strongly characterize the busy trading character of the Chinese among themselves, and the activity of their internal traffic, than the vast numbers of passage boats which are constantly sailing along the rivers and canals, crowded both inside and out with a host of passengers. The *fare* in these vessels is, quaintly enough, termed *shuey-keo*, "water legs," as it serves in lieu of those limbs to transport the body. None, however, above the poorer classes avail themselves of these conveyances, as a small private boat can always be engaged, by natives, at a sufficiently cheap rate. That the company on board the public transports is not of the most select order, is plain from a caution generally pasted against the mast, "*Kin shin ho paou*," "Mind your purses." There is a species of tavern, or public house, a short way above the European factories in Canton, at the point whence all these passage boats are obliged to start by the regulation of the police, and where the crowd and concourse is sometimes really surprising. Regular passports are always required, and the whole system appears admirably arranged to promote the objects of a very cautious and vigilant government, in the maintenance of order, without impeding the general circulation of industry.

There is, in short, a businesslike character about the Chinese which assimilates them in a striking manner to the most intelligent nations of the West, and certainly marks them out, in very prominent relief, from the rest of the Asiatics. However oddly it may sound, it does not seem too much to say, that, in everything which enters into the composition of actively industrious and well-organized communities, there is vastly less difference between them and the English, French, and Americans, than between these and the inhabitants of Spain and Portugal, whose proneness to stolid bigotry and oriental laziness was perhaps in part imbibed from the Arabs. Through the influence of climate and other causes, these seem still retained in a surprising degree, though they must be expected to give way to the example of more enlightened nations.

Whenever the effects of our scientific machinery in abridging labour are explained to an intelligent Chinese, the first idea that strikes him is the disastrous effect that such a system would work upon his overpeopled country, if suddenly introduced into it, and he never fails to deprecate such an innovation as the most calamitous of visitations. We shall see hereafter that they have some ingenious contrivances by which to avail themselves of the natural moving powers presented by wind, water, and the force of gravity, and that they have managed to appropriate in practice most of the mechanical powers with surprising simplicity and effect; but of the strength that slumbers in the giant arm of steam they are at once theoretically and practically ignorant, although they both understand and apply, in their commonest cookery, the *heat* of steam under confinement to dress vegetables.

The canal and the Yellow river are a perpetual source of anxiety and expense to the government, to keep their banks in repair, and prevent those inundations to which the country in their neighbourhood is constantly liable. The use of steam vessels is therefore utterly precluded by the peculiar character and circumstance of *one* of the principal streams of China, as well as of the grand canal. But it was impossible to travel, with the embassy in 1816, along that noble river the Yang-tse-kiang, which divides as nearly as possible the empire into two equal parts, and flows through its finest climates, without wishing for steamboats; more especially while suffering under the delay that arose from sailing up against that mighty stream, which runs with a prevailing ebb towards the sea. It is indeed for such rivers as the Mississippi and the Keang that steamers are most peculiarly fitted, and nothing can be less like steamers than the progress of the Chinese travelling boats. Those very points of shape and construction, from which they derive their commodiousness and safety, render them extremely slow under the most favourable circumstances, and, with the exception of their smuggling boats, the Chinese may be said to be anything but economists of *time* on the water.

The following extract from an unpublished journal of the last embassy* exactly describes the singular process of passing the sluices which are substituted on the grand canal for *locks*. The advantage of the latter mode (which seems unknown to the Chinese) is, the vessel being raised or lowered to a different level by the gradual rise or fall of the water in which it floats, by which means the dangers of a sluice are completely obviated. "It was announced that some of our boats were come up for the purpose of passing through the sluice, upon which the ambassador proposed to the legate that we should walk up to the pier head, to see the manner in which this was effected. The legate said he would accompany us with pleasure, being himself curious to see the boats pass; and we all accordingly stood upon the pier head, while the four headmost boats (of sixty or seventy tons' burden) were shot through the sluice. By means of the precautions adopted, which consisted partly in hanging against the sides of the pier large fenders, or cushions, of rope to deaden an accidental concussion, the boats passed through with perfect safety. The fall was somewhat greater than that of the Thames under the arches of old London bridge, but still the hazard and difficulty seem to have been a good deal magnified. The stone abutments were constructed chiefly of large blocks of grey marble or limestone, with a few blocks of granite intermixed. After the boats had passed, we returned with the legate to the pavilion for a few minutes, and then rose to rejoin our sedans, and return in them to our boats.

* Journal of Sir George Staunton.

" At half past twelve we passed through a second sluice similar to the first, without taking the trouble to quit our boats. We then brought to for some time, and did not pass through the third sluice until about four. The fall here was fully as great, and the torrent as rapid, as in the first sluice; but we all declined the legate's second invitation to land while the boats were passing through. The passage was effected by the whole of our squadron without loss or accident. The boats of smaller dimensions steered directly for the sluice, and shot through the opening at once; but our common dinner boat, and those of the ambassador and commissioners, were obliged to be warped along the bank up to the pier head gradually. In both modes any failure or mistake from bad steerage or ropes giving way might have been attended with serious consequences; for if any of the smaller boats had struck on the pier head, or if any of the larger ones had swung round and presented their broadsides to the sluice, they would in both cases have run considerable hazard of being stove in and wrecked and some of the persons in them might have been drowned in the confusion. The large boat in which I was had been warped up to a proper position, and was on the point of being loosened from the ropes in order to shoot through the aperture, when a succession of small boats unexpectedly came up, and possessed themselves of the passage, compelling us to hold on against the stream for about a quarter of an hour, in a situation that was awkward, if not hazardous."

It is curious to find this description of the passage on the canal so exactly agreeing with that of an Arabian traveller not much less than six hundred years ago, soon after that artificial route by water was constructed under the Mongol conquerors of China. The difference of level is commonly from five to six feet at the sluices, but in passing by the town of Hoay-gan, near the embouchure of the Yellow river, the boats sailed at an elevation of between fifteen and twenty feet above the level of the city, and the travellers looked down upon the roofs of the houses, which any accident to the bank of the canal must inevitably have consigned to destruction. The existence of such a work in China, at a time when Europe was involved in comparative barbarism, affords curious subject for reflection.

CHAPTER X.

CITIES—PEKING.

External Walls of Peking.—Interior Aspect of Tartarian City.—Circuit of the Imperial Wall.—Southern or Chinese City.—Difficulty of Feeding the Population.—Dangers of the Emperor.—Gardens of Yuen-ming-yuen.—Occurrence there in the last Embassy.—Expenses of the Court.—Tartars and Chinese.—Police of Peking.—Efficiency of Chinese Police.—Case of a French Crew murdered.—Punishment of the Pirates.

The most striking feature of all the principal cities of China consists in the high castellated walls of blue brick by which they are surrounded, and of which the wall of Peking may be considered as a specimen, with some considerable difference, of course, in respect to its superior height and thickness. Like the ancient rampart of the empire, this consists of a mound of earth or rubbish incased with brick. The height is about thirty feet, the thin parapet being deeply embattled, with intermediate loopholes, but bearing no resemblance to regular embrasures for artillery. Indeed cannon are not often seen mounted on the walls, although there are generally some lying about near the gates. The thickness of the wall at the base is nearly twenty feet, diminishing, by the inclination of the inner surface, to twelve or more at the summit. The height and weight of this wall, with its perpendicular external face, would only serve to facilitate the operations of battering cannon, which, of course, would begin to breach from the base; but the principal weapon, in the wars of the Chinese and Tartars, has always been the bow and arrow. At each gate the wall is *doubled* by an outer enclosure in a semicircular shape, the entrance to which is not opposite to the principal gate, but lateral, with a view to security and defence. Over both gates are erected towers of several stories, which serve to lodge the soldiers who guard them. At intervals of about sixty yards along the length of the wall, are flanking towers or bastions of the same height, projecting about thirty feet from the curtain. Most of the plans of Peking represent a wet ditch entirely compassing the sides of the city, and it no doubt extends round a certain portion; but when the embassy passed, in 1816, it is quite certain that the northeast portion had not even a dry ditch, and that some of the gentlemen quitted their vehicles to take out specimens of the brick from numerous holes which time and neglect had produced in the face of the wall. The same thing was observed at Nanking, the ancient enclosure of which was nearly as lofty as the present bulwark of Peking, but no remains of a ditch could be perceived at that part which the travellers visited.

The area on which Nanking stood was more extensive than the space enclosed by the walls of Peking, but the greater portion of the surface surrounded by the ancient defence is now devoid of even the traces of buildings; and the city of Keang-ning-foo, as it is at present called, occupies only a corner of the original enclosure. Peking likewise contains so many void spaces of great extent, that it is very difficult, considering the lowness of the one-storied buildings, to imagine how it can hold such a monstrous population as some have attributed to it. A very large portion of the northern or Tartarian city is occupied by the enclosure which contains the palaces and pleasure grounds of the emperor; the remainder is studded over with official or religious buildings, all of them surrounded by large open courts; and the Chinese city to the south has some very extensive spaces occupied by immensely spreading buildings, and grounds attached, where the emperor sacrifices to Heaven, and performs the annual ceremony of ploughing; with various other rites. There are, besides, large sheets of water, and gardens devoted to the growth of vegetables for the city. With every allowance, therefore, for the extent of area enclosed by the walls, the population of Peking can hardly exceed that which is comprised within the London bills of mortality; though it has been stated at *double* that amount.

Father Hyacinth, long resident in the capital of China as a member of the Russian mission, has given a very circumstantial account of it, much of which is founded on personal observation, and the rest derived from inquiry or books. The short time which the mission of Earl Macartney passed there admitted of fewer opportunities of investigation; but Mr. Barrow, who was left at Peking and Yuen-ming-yuen, while the ambassador attended the emperor beyond the wall, made very good use of his time, and has given us a graphic description of what he saw. The streets of Canton and of most other cities are extremely narrow, admitting of only three or four foot passengers abreast; but the principal thoroughfares of Peking, which connect its different gates, are fully one hundred feet in width. These are unpaved, no doubt in consequence of the difficulty and expense of procuring stone in the immense alluvial flat on which the city stands; and every inhabitant is compelled by the police to clean and sprinkle with water, during the dry months, that portion of the street which fronts his abode, with a view to allay the dust. In rainy weather, however, the principal ways are said to be in a dreadful state, from the want of proper drains, and in consequence of the perfect level of the ground not allowing the water to flow off.

Sir George Staunton thus describes the appearance of the capital, when it was traversed by the embassy on the way to Yuen-ming-yuen: "The first street extended on a line directly to the westward, until it was interrupted by the eastern wall of the imperial palace, called the Yellow Wall,* from the colour of the small roof of varnished tiles with which the top of it is covered. Various public buildings, seen at the same time, and, considered as belonging to the emperor, were covered in the same manner. Those roofs, uninterrupted by chimneys, and indented in the sides and ridges into gentle curves, with an effect more pleasing than would be produced by long straight lines, were adorned with a variety of figures, either in imitation of real objects, or more commonly as mere works of fancy; the whole shining like gold under a brilliant sun, immediately caught the eye with an appearance of grandeur in that part of the buildings where it was not accustomed to be sought for. Immense magazines of rice were seen near the gate; and, looking from it to the left along the city wall, was perceived an elevated edifice, described as an observatory erected in the former dynasty, by the Emperor Yoong-lo, to whom the chief embellishments of Peking are said to be owing.

"Several circumstances, independently of the arrival of strangers, contributed to throng so wide a street. A procession was moving towards the gate,

* The Chinese name is "The Imperial Wall."

in which the white or bridal colour (according to European ideas) of the persons who formed it, seemed at first to announce a marriage ceremony; but the appearance of young men overwhelmed with grief showed it to be a funeral,* much more indeed than the corse itself, which was contained in a handsome square case, shaded with a canopy painted with gay and lively colours, and preceded by standards of variegated silks. Behind it were sedan chairs covered with white cloth containing the female relations of the deceased. The white colour, denoting in China the affliction of those who wear it, is sedulously avoided by such as wish to manifest sentiments of a contrary kind;† it is therefore never seen in the ceremony of nuptials, (met soon afterward,) where the lady, as yet unseen by the bridegroom, is carried in a gilded and gaudy chair, hung round with festoons of artificial flowers, and followed by relations, attendants, and servants bearing the paraphernalia, being the only portion given with a daughter in marriage by her parents. The crowd was not a little increased by the mandarins of rank appearing always with numerous attendants; and still more by circles of the populace round auctioneers, venders of medicines, fortunetellers, singers, jugglers, and storytellers, beguiling their hearers of a few of their *tchen*, or copper money, intended probably for other purposes. Among the stories that caught, at this moment, the imagination of the people, the arrival of the embassy was said to furnish no inconsiderable share. The presents brought by it to the emperor were asserted to include whatever was rare in other countries, or not known before to the Chinese. Of the animals that were brought, it was gravely mentioned that there was an elephant of the size of a

* The Chinese, who are not fond of using ill-omened words, call a funeral " a white affair."

† It is avoided as being unlucky, or ill omened. The colour of compliment or congratulation is red.

monkey, and as fierce as a lion, and a cock that fed on charcoal. * * * * * * *

"As soon as the persons belonging to the embassy had arrived at the eastern side of the Yellow Wall, they turned along it to the right, and found on its northern side much less bustle than in the former street. Instead of shops, all were private houses, not conspicuous in the front. Before each house was a wall or curtain, to prevent passengers from seeing the court into which the street door opened. This wall is called the wall of *respect*. A halt was made opposite the treble gates, which are nearly in the centre of this northern side of the palace wall. It appeared to enclose a large quantity of ground: it was not level like all the lands without the wall: some of it was raised into hills of steep ascent; the earth taken to form them left broad and deep hollows, now filled with water. Out of these artificial lakes, of which the margins were diversified and irregular, small islands rose, with a variety of fanciful edifices, interspersed with trees. On the hills of different heights the principal palaces for the emperor were erected. The whole had somewhat the appearance of enchantment. * * * * * * From the spot whence an opportunity thus offered to take a glance, through the gates of the palace wall, at part of what was enclosed within it, the eye, turning to the north, observed, through a street extending to the city wall, the great fabric, of considerable height, which includes a bell of prodigious size and cylindrical form, that, struck on the outside with a wooden mallet, emits a sound distinctly heard throughout the capital. Beyond it, but more to the westward, was one of the northern gates, the watch tower over which rendered it visible above the intermediate buildings. Proceeding on beyond the palace gates, directly to the westward, between the Yellow Wall and the northern buildings of the city, is a lake of some acres in extent, now, in autumn, almost entirely overspread with the peltated leaf of the *nymphæa nelumbo*, or *lien-wha* of the Chinese. * * * * * * * The route was continued westerly through the city. The dwellinghouse of some Russians was pointed out; and, what was more singular, a library of foreign manuscripts, one of which was said to be an Arabic copy of the Koran. Some Mohammedans were seen, distinguished by red caps. Among the spectators of the novel sight some women were observed; the greatest number were said to be natives of Tartary or of a Tartar race. Their feet were not cramped like those of the Chinese; and their shoes, with broad toes, and soles above an inch in thickness, were as clumsy as those of the original Chinese ladies were diminutive. A few of the former were well dressed, with delicate features, and their complexions heightened with the aid of art. A thick patch of vermilion on the middle of the lower lip seemed to be a favourite mode of using paint. Some of them were sitting in covered carriages, of which, as well as of horses, there are several to be found for hire in various parts of the town.* A few of the Tartar ladies were on horseback, and rode astride like men. Tradesmen, with their tools, searching for employment, and pedlars offering their wares for sale, were everywhere to be seen. Several of the streets were narrow, and at the entrance of them gates were erected, near which guards were stationed, it was said, to quell any occasional disturbance in the neighbourhood. Those gates are shut at night, and opened only in cases of exigence. The train of the embassy crossed a street which extended north and south the whole length of the Tartar city, almost four miles, and is interrupted only by several pai-loos, or triumphal fabrics; and passing by many temples and other capacious buildings and magazines, they reached, in little more than two

* None but privileged persons can use a chair so near to the emperor: but, in other parts, these are common conveyances.

hours from their entrance on the eastern side, to one of the western city gates."

From this they issued towards the imperial park of Yuen-ming-yuen, and the route, thus accurately described, can readily be traced on the plan of Peking. The Tartar city, through which they passed, is about three miles in breadth from east to west, and four in length from north to south. The portion traversed by the embassy was rather more than five miles, which was as much as they could accomplish, with all interruptions, in the space of time mentioned above. The observatory seen by them to the left on entering the city, was that of the *Kin-sing*, (or planet Venus,) near the southeast corner of the wall. A new set of instruments was made for it by order of Kâng-hy, under the direction of the Catholic missionaries; and the astronomical instruments brought out by Lord Macartney were subsequently deposited there. The high fabric, with its large cylindrical bell, which the travellers observed between the north gate of the imperial wall, and the extremity of the Tartar city on that side, is the *Choong-low*, or "Bell tower," near to which is the office of the "General of the Nine Gates," to whose charge is intrusted the police of the city. A wooden mallet, being struck upon the huge bell, makes known the five watches of the night, and the sound is heard through the greater part of the city.

Within the precincts of the Tartarian city, near the southern gate of the imperial wall, are the principal boards or tribunals of the supreme government; and not far from them is the college of the Russian mission, consisting of ten persons, who are periodically relieved from St. Petersburgh. Near the westernmost of the three southern gates, the Portuguese Jesuits had their college; but the last of this fraternity was sent away in the year 1827, in the person of Padre Serra, who then furnished us with some curious notes. The most favoured of the

Catholics, who were the French Jesuits employed by Kâng-hy, had their dwelling allotted within the circuit of the imperial wall, near the lake and gardens on the north and west of the enclosure. This great space, occupying an area of about two square miles, is just in the centre of the Tartarian city, and can be entered by none but authorized persons. It corresponds in shape to the outer limits of the city, being an oblong square, built on a very regular plan; and contains within itself a third and still more sacred enclosure, devoted exclusively to the emperor's abode, called "The Prohibited Wall." This contains the private palaces of the sovereign and his empress, communicating by a gate on the north with a square two thirds of a mile in length, in which are situated the artificial hills and woods mentioned by Sir George Staunton, as seen at a distance in his progress through Peking. The architecture and arrangements of the palaces and courts within the "prohibited wall" are described as far exceeding any other specimens of the kind in China.

In regard to population, the vast areas included within the imperial wall, and the central or prohibited wall, may be considered comparatively as empty spaces. Father Hyacinth describes the lakes and gardens which he saw as occupying nearly the whole western side of the larger parallelogram, the lake alone being upward of a mile in length. From his account it may be inferred that the palaces and gardens of the Chinese emperor are worthy of the master of so many millions of subjects, who have been estimated at a third of the whole human race. So much of the capital, however, being devoted to the emperor, it is not easy to find lodging within the remainder for the three millions of people which some have stated that its walls, and those of the southern or Chinese city, contain together. This number nearly equals the *whole population* of the kingdom of Portugal by the latest census. If we admit that the number of subjects who own the emperor of China for their master really exceeds the amount of three hundred millions, he may well speak with contempt of those states whose entire population goes not beyond the *hundredth part* of his own "black-haired race," as he calls them.

On the east side of the Tartarian city is the Altar of the Sun, because the luminary rises in that quarter; and for a similar, though not the same reason, the Altar of the Moon is on the western side, because at the opposition, or at full moon, she sets in the west, while the sun rises on the other side. This regard to the place of the sun's rising serves to explain several points in Chinese customs. Their climate makes it necessary to build all considerable houses fronting the south, but closed to the north; for the sake of admitting the southerly monsoon in summer, and excluding the northerly in winter. The eastern side of the house is the most honourable, for the reason above given, and the master of a family is therefore called *Tong-kea*, "East of the Household." But the *left hand* is likewise to the east of the principal seat in the hall of reception, which serves to explain the circumstance of their making the left side the place of honour, so contrary to the custom which generally prevails in other countries.

The Chinese town, which lies to the south of the Tartarian, or "City of Nine Gates," is not subject to the same rigid system of military police as that which contains the abode of the emperor; and its walls and defences are inferior to those of the other, being, in fact, like the ordinary Chinese towns. The included area is about equal to that of the Tartarian city, but of this a very considerable portion is occupied by the immense courts of the temples dedicated to "Heaven," and to the deified inventor of agriculture, (sometimes styled the Temple of "Earth,") where the emperor sacrifices annually, and performs the ceremony of ploughing the sacred field. The Altar to Heaven stands in a square enclosure, measuring about three miles in circuit, near the southern wall of the Chinese city. The terrace consists of three stages, diminishing from one hundred and twenty to sixty feet in diameter, each stage being surrounded by a marble balustrade, and ascended by steps of the same material. Towards the northwest of the enclosure is the Palace of Abstinence, where the emperor fasts for three days preparatory to offering sacrifices to the heavens at the winter solstice. On the other side of the great central street leading to the Tartarian city, and just over against the Temple of the Heavens, stands the Altar of the Earth. The square enclosure is about two miles in circuit, and contains the field which is once a year ploughed by the emperor and his great officers, and the produce reserved for sacrifices.

In the vicinity of the southeast angle of the Chinese city are extensive sheets of water, and large open spaces cultivated with grain and vegetables for the use of Peking. Towards the southwest angle, also, beyond the Temple of the Heavens and the Earth, is a huge pool or lake, dedicated to the genius of the watery element, under the designation of *He-loong*, the "Black Dragon," where the emperor either deprecates or prays for rain, according as the country may be afflicted by deluge or drought. These great chasms in the population of the capital, with the vast spaces occupied by the imperial palaces and gardens, make it very improbable that the population of Peking is more than twice that of London, especially as the houses are only of one story. The less strict police of the Chinese city makes it a place of retirement to many from the other, where the precautions for the emperor's personal safety and quiet produce a system of discipline not unlike that of a garrison town. The "General of the Nine Gates," under whose charge it is placed, was sent, in 1816, to urge the departure of the embassy from Yuen-ming-yuen, and he did his best to excite their alarm, by telling them that he commanded "a million of men."

There seems to be some reason for the care with which the Tartarian city is guarded, if we take into consideration the dangers arising from occasional scarcities in an immensely populous city, which is fed, in a great measure, with grain brought from the southern provinces. In the year 1824, the court was seriously alarmed by the consequences of a severe drought, which produced, first, want, and afterward pestilence at Peking. The present emperor, then reigning, issued a proclamation in these words: "The numerous resort of a hungry populace from the surrounding country has led to the occasional plundering of articles of food, and we have already issued our commands for restraining and controlling them. One of the censors has reported that sundry vagrants, with the excuse of want and starvation, have been committing depredations in the markets and other places of public resort, in contravention of the laws. The proper authorities are hereby commanded to issue proclamations on the subject, and to exercise a rigid control, that the neighbourhood of the imperial residence may be well governed and orderly. The erection of additional playhouses (according to the same report) being highly prejudicial to the morals of the people, the police of the city must also restrain and keep them within bounds."

Soon after was issued the subjoined: "The different stations at Peking have distributed grain during a long continued period; but on the 20th day of the 5th moon let them all be shut, and the distribution cease, as the stores will not admit of further donations. The harvest is now approaching, and the people may return to their several districts to seek a livelihood by their own labour. Let the governor of the province enjoin the district officers to exercise a strict vigilance, at the same time soothing the distressed populace, and preventing their wandering about in a dispersed and vagabond manner; thus seconding our paternal solicitude to cherish them in our bosom." To avert the drought which had created this distress, the emperor ordained certain religious observances, and we give an extract from his edict: "On account of the drought in the neighbourhood of the capital, and the destitution of the husbandman's fields, which have looked in vain for fertilizing showers, we sent down our will that altars should be erected at *He-loong Tan** and elsewhere. Although, during the last ten days, there has been a slight appearance of rain, it was quite inadequate to moisten the earth. Let our eldest son Ye-heng, on the 7th day of the present moon, proceed reverentially to the Temple of the Heavens to worship. Let our imperial relative, Mien-kae, proceed with reverence to the Temple of the Earth to sacrifice; and Mien-hia to the Temple of the Year. Let our son, Ye-chaou, likewise sacrifice at the Temple of the Winds. * * * * * * Having sent down our will regarding the sacrifices to be performed by the princes and great ministers on the 7th of the moon, we now intimate our intention to burn incense in person, on the same day, at the Altar of the Black Dragon."* This may serve as a specimen of the state worship of China.

But other dangers beset the emperor in his capital, either from the machinations of relatives, who may plot against the throne, or from the treason of secret societies or brotherhoods, of which we shall have to speak. "Though the succession to the throne," observed Padre Serra, "depends on the arbitrary nomination of the reigning prince, this does

* *He-loong* is the Saghalien, or *Black Dragon*, which represents the principal river of Manchow Tartary, worshipped by the reigning family. The dragon always signifies the watery element, or rivers.

not always prevent usurpations. An instance of this was seen in the succession of Yoong-ching to his father, the great Kâng-hy. The prince nominated was the *fourth;* but this latter being in Tartary at the period of the emperor's somewhat sudden demise, Yoong-ching, who was a privileged wâng, (or *regulus*,) entered the palace and seized the billet of nomination. Before the number four, which he there found, he boldly set the sign of ten, and thus made it appear that he, the *fourteenth* prince, was the one nominated. He possessed himself of the sceptre, and ordered his brother to be arrested and imprisoned in a place which is standing to this day, four leagues to the north of Peking, in which it is said that he died." On the 18th October, 1813, as the last emperor, Keaking, was about to enter Peking, on his return from the summer excursion to Je-ho, (the Hot Springs, about one hundred miles northeast of the capital,) a party of conspirators entered the imperial palace, and kept possession of a part of it for some time. The present emperor, who was only his second son, is said to have owed his elevation to the good conduct he displayed on this occasion. He shot two of the rebels, and assisted to intimidate the remainder of those who had penetrated within the precincts of the palace.

The first intimation of the preceding occurrence was conveyed in a proclamation from the emperor, of which the following is an extract: "Eighteen years have elapsed since, possessed of only inferior virtue, I looked up, and received with profound veneration the throne of my imperial father; since which I dared not resign myself to ease, or neglect the affairs of government. I had but just ascended the throne, when the sect of the *White Lily* seduced into a state of confusion four provinces, and the people suffered more than I can bear to express. I ordered my generals to proceed against them, and, after a protracted conflict, reduced them to submission. I then hoped that with my children (the people) I should have enjoyed increasing happiness and repose. On the 6th of the 8th moon, the sect of Tien-ly, (celestial reason,) a band of vagabonds, suddenly created disorder, and caused much injury, extending from the district of Chang-yuen in Pechele to that of Tsaou in Shantong. I hastened to direct Wun, the viceroy, to lead forth an army to exterminate them, and restore peace. This affair, however, still existed at the distance of one hundred leagues from Peking; but, suddenly, on the 15th of the 9th moon, rebellion arose under my own arm—the calamity sprung up in my own house. A banditti of upward of seventy men, of the sect Tien-ly, violated the prohibited gate, and entered withinside; they wounded the guard, and rushed into the inner palace. Four rebels were seized and bound; three others ascended the wall with a flag. My imperial second son seized a matchlock and shot two of them; my nephew killed the third. For this deliverance I am indebted to the energies of my second son."

About eight miles to the northwest of Peking are the gardens, or rather the park, of Yuen-ming-yuen, which Mr. Barrow (who spent his time between that place and Peking) estimates at an extent of twelve square miles. As the face of the country on this side of Peking begins to rise towards the Great Wall, the diversity of hill and dale has afforded some natural facilities for embellishment, which have been improved by art. According to the description of the forementioned writer, the landscape is diversified with woodlands and lawns, among which are numerous canals, rivulets, and sheets of water, the banks of which have been thrown up in an apparently fortuitous manner in imitation of the free hand of nature. Some parts are cultivated, and others purposely left wild: and wherever pleasure-houses are erected, the views appears to have been studied. It is said that within the enclosure of these gardens there exist no less than thirty distinct places of residence for the emperor and his numerous suite of ministers, eunuchs, and servants, each constituting a considerable village. The principal hall of audience, seen by Mr. Barrow, stood upon a platform of granite four feet high, and was surrounded by a sort of peristyle of large wooden columns, which supported the roof. The length of the hall within was one hundred and ten feet, the breadth forty-two, and the height twenty. The floor was paved with slabs of gray marble laid checkerwise, and the throne, made entirely of carved wood, placed in a recess. The only furniture of the hall were "a pair of brass kettle drums, two large paintings, two pairs of ancient blue porcelain vases, a few volumes of manuscripts, and a table placed at one end of the hall, on which stood an old English chimney clock, made in the seventeenth century."

It was at a place called Hae-tien, in the immediate vicinity of these gardens, that the strange scene occurred which terminated in the dismissal of the embassy of 1816. On his arrival there, about daylight in the morning, with the commissioners and a few other gentlemen, the ambassador was drawn to one of the emperor's temporary residences by an invitation from the Duke Ho, as he was called, the imperial relative charged with the conduct of the negotiations. After passing through an open court, where were assembled a vast number of mandarins in their dresses of ceremony, they were shown into a wretched room, and soon encompassed by a well-dressed crowd, among whom were princes of the blood by dozens, wearing yellow girdles. With a childish and unmannerly curiosity, consistent enough with the idle and disorderly life which many of them are said to lead, they examined the persons and dress of the gentlemen without ceremony; while these, tired with their sleepless journey, and disgusted at the behaviour of the celestials, turned their backs upon them, and laid themselves down to rest. Duke Ho soon appeared, and surprised the ambassador by urging him to proceed directly to an audience of the emperor, who was waiting for him. His lordship in vain remonstrated that to-morrow had been fixed for the first audience and that tired and dusty as they all were at present, it would be worthy neither of the emperor nor himself to wait on his majesty in a manner so unprepared. He urged, too, that he was unwell, and required immediate rest. Duke Ho became more and more pressing, and at length forgot himself so far as to grasp the ambassador's arm violently, and one of the others stepped up at the same time. His lordship immediately shook them off, and the gentlemen crowded about him; while the highest indignation was expressed at such treatment, and a determined resolution to proceed to no audience this morning. The ambassador at length retired, with the appearance of satisfaction, on the part of Duke Ho, that the audience should take place to-morrow. There is every reason, however, to suppose that this person had been largely bribed by the heads of the Canton local government to frustrate the views of the embassy, and prevent an audience of the emperor. The mission, at least, was on its way back in the afternoon of the same day.

The previous embassy of Lord Macartney, in 1793, attended the emperor's court at Je-ho, (sometimes written Zhehol,) or "the Hot Springs," at some distance north of the Great Wall, in Manchow Tartary. The elevation of this place, at some thousand feet above the plain in which Peking is situated, renders it a cool summer retreat during the excessive heats which prevail at the capital. The gardens and residences of the emperor, though considerable, are described as inferior in extent to those of Yuen-ming-yuen. Still, however, the accommodation of such a suite as the sovereign carries with him requires a town in itself. Peking, in fact, is chiefly supported throughout its vast bounds by the residence of the court and the supreme government. Being neither a seaport, nor a place naturally suited to inland trade and manufactures, it derives nearly its whole importance from being the dwelling-place of the "Son of Heaven."

His vast establishments are chiefly supported by the surplus revenue, both in money and stores, remitted by way of the grand canal from the provinces. An imperial relative of the first rank receives, according to P. Serra,* 10,000 taëls annually from the exchequer, with a large allowance of rice, and as many as three hundred and more servants. As the multiplication of these expensive idlers would soon ruin the government, their rank descends by one degree in each generation, until after five descents their heirs retain the simple privilege of wearing the yellow girdle, with a bare subsistence. From this degradation a few have been excepted by especial favour, as it happened to a grandson of Kien-loong, to whom that emperor granted the first grade for ten lives. The expense to the state of a wâng of the first rank is about 60,000 taëls, or 20,000*l.* annually, and this diminishes through the several grades down to the simple inheritors of the yellow girdle, who receive only three taëls a month, and two sacks of rice. But they are allowed 100 taëls when they marry, and 120 for a funeral; from which (says Serra) they take occasion to maltreat their wives, because, when they have killed one, they receive the allowance for her interment, as well as the dowry of the new wife, whom they take immediately! In 1825, appeared the following order from the emperor: "The Wâng (or *regulus*)

* Royal Asiat. Trans., vol. iii.

Chunshan has presented to us a petition, entreating our imperial favour in the advance of some years' salaries, wherewithal he may be enabled to repair the tombs of his family. We permit to be advanced to him the amount of his money allowances for ten years ensuing, and direct that his pay be annually deducted until the whole shall be repaid." This title of *wang* is the one by which the Chinese emperor styles the King of England, whose representative (consistently enough with such a broad assumption) is expected to beat his head nine times against the ground, on being admitted to the presence of the universal sovereign.

It is at Peking chiefly, and in its neighbourhood, that the privileges of Tartars, in contradistinction to Chinese, are most broadly marked, and most openly asserted. It must be sufficiently clear to a sagacious government, as that of the Manchows has always proved itself, that, being so enormously outnumbered by the original inhabitants of China, the wisest policy must be to display a tolerable partiality in the administration of the provinces, and especially the distant ones. An examination of the Chinese red book gave the following results. Of the *eight* viceroys, having each two provinces, or one of the largest, under his sway, there are no less than *six* Chinese; and of the *fifteen* lieutenant governors, *ten* are Chinese. On the other hand, the highest and most responsible military commands are always intrusted to Manchows. The probability is, that the genius of the Chinese is better adapted to fitting themselves for civil offices, the qualification for which is an adequate proficiency in that learning, which is entirely founded on the ancient literature of the country; while, for military commands, the Manchows are not only more likely to prove faithful to the present dynasty, but at the same time are better suited by nature and education. In the neighbourhood of the capital, very distinct ideas of local claims and jurisdictions appear to be entertained by the Tartars. When Lord Macartney had passed just to the north of the Great Wall, on his way to *Je-ho*, one of the attendants, who was a Tartar, having been ordered for punishment by a Chinese mandarin, immediately resisted with great vehemence, exclaiming against the authority of the latter on that side of the national barrier.

The strict system of police, by which such an immense population is kept in due order, is essentially the same through the different cities and towns of the empire. Its efficiency arises in a great measure from the principle of *responsibility*, which forms so marked a feature of Chinese rule, and is carried among them to an extent quite beyond our notions of equity. Every town is divided into tithings of ten houses, and these are combined into wards of one hundred; or, as the Chinese term it, "ten houses make a *kea*, ten *kea* make a *paou*," or hundred. The magistrate is responsible for his whole district, the hundreder and tithingman each for his respective charge, and the householder for the conduct of his family. From this gradation of authority all strangers and foreigners are rigidly excluded. So summary is the mode in which the objects of the police are effected, that it is no light matter to be once in their hands. The Chinese emphatically express their sense of this unfortunate condition, by the popular phrase, "The meat is on the chopping-block."

The gates of all Chinese towns are shut soon after it is dark, when the first watch is sounded by a huge bell, or drum, in some commanding station. At the end of every principal street is a strong barrier of timber, which is closed at the same time with the principal gates. These are only opened to such as can give a satisfactory reason for their being allowed to pass, or for being out at night; as, for instance, to call a midwife on a sudden emergency.

Every one is expected to carry a lantern, and is punished for being found without it. When the particular watch of the night has been indicated by a certain number of strokes on the drum or bell at the principal station, this is answered by all the rest; and a police soldier walks from one *corps de garde* to another, repeating the number of the watch (and thereby marking the time of night) by striking two hollow bamboos together.

The great jealousy with which the personal safety of the emperor is provided for, at Peking, renders the police very strict in regard to all access to the imperial palace and its neighbourhood. It has been well observed, that the subjects of a despot are well revenged by the fears in which such regulations originate. According to the penal code, "In all cases of persons, who have lived within the jurisdiction of the imperial city, being condemned to die by the sentence of the law, their families, and all persons whatsoever who resided under the same roof with them, shall remove forthwith." The principal duty of the military of China is to perform the office of a police; and it must be admitted that, by the aid of the unrelenting system of responsibility, there is no country in the world in which a more efficient police exists than there. Not being very scrupulous as to the means, the government generally contrives in some way or other to accomplish its ends; and it occasionally makes up for its own weakness by the policy of it measures. When the pirates at the commencement of the present Tartar dynasty ravaged the coasts of the maritime provinces, the want of a force to oppose them on the water rendered active measures impossible. The government, therefore, offered no active resistance; but merely obliged the inhabitants of the coast to move thirty *ly*, or about three leagues, inland—a plan which proved perfectly successful.

European residents in China have generally found

that their property has been as secure from violent invasion as it could be in any other country of the world; and in one or two instances, where flagrant acts of robbery combined with murder have occurred, the efficiency of the police has proved, in a very signal and remarkable manner, that the government was not only willing, but able to do them summary justice. In 1816, the American ship *Wabash*, having opium on board, came to anchor off Macao, and being manned by a very small number of hands, was suddenly carried by a boatful of desperate Chinese, who, coming on board under pretence of offering their services as pilots, stabbed those who were on deck, or forced them into the water; and then, confining the remainder of the crew to the forepart of the vessel, plundered her of all the opium. When the fact was represented to the local government, whose horror of piratical violence is extreme, such prompt and effective measures were taken for the discovery of the ruffians, that they were most of them caught and condemned to death, and their heads exposed in cages on the rocks near Macao, as a warning to others.

But the case of the French ship *Navigateur*, in 1828, was still more remarkable, and may be given nearly from the relation of M. Laplace, captain of the eighteen gun corvette *La Favourite*, whose observations on the Chinese we have had occasion to quote in another place. The *Navigateur*, a merchantman, was compelled by stress of weather to put into Touron Bay on the coast of Cochin China. The disabled state of the ship, the difficulty of effecting the necessary repairs, and the well-known unfriendliness of the local authorities, forced the captain and crew to the necessity of selling her to the King of Cochin China, and embarking themselves with their most valuable effects on board a Chinese junk, which was engaged to carry them to Macao. The voyage was short, but still long enough to enable the crew of the junk to conceive and execute a dreadful conspiracy against the Frenchmen. It was in vain that one of the oldest of the Chinese endeavoured by signs to draw the attention of the French captain to the danger that threatened him; the latter had contented himself with making one or two of his sailors keep watch by day, as well as during the night; but this charge was the more negligently executed, inasmuch as most of the people, in consequence of their previous sufferings, had to contend with fever or dysentery.

The junk was already within sight of the great Ladrone island, the mark by which Macao is made in the southerly monsoon, and the Chinese passengers disembarked at once into boats, with an eagerness which ought to have roused the suspicions of the Europeans, had they not been blinded by the most imprudent confidence. The night passed quietly, and the dawning light seemed to promise a happy landing to the Frenchmen; but it was destined to witness their massacre. These unfortunate men, the greater number still asleep, were despatched with hatchets and knives by the crew of the junk; and their captain, assailed by the assassins in the narrow cabin which he occupied with his mates, after killing several of the Chinese, fell himself the last. One seaman, however still remained, who, armed with an iron bar, continued to make a desperate resistance, although badly wounded in the head. Having reached the deck of the vessel, almost overcome as he was in this unequal conflict, he leaped into the sea, and appeared in this manner to ensure, by his certain death, impunity to the murderers.

He contrived, notwithstanding, to swim to the nearest fishing boat, but he was denied succour, with the usual selfish prudence of the Chinese; another boat, however, afterward received him on board, and landed him by night on the shore at Macao. Sick and wounded as he was, the poor man wandered unknown for some time about the streets, but at length discovered the abode of the French missionaries, who with their ready humanity relieved him at once from his immediate wants. In the mean while, the French consul had arrived from Canton, and the affair being brought by him to the notice of the Portuguese authorities at Macao, was placed by them in the hands of the Chinese mandarins. By means of the information obtained from the French sailor, the Chinese passengers who had quitted the junk previous to the massacre, and repaired in all haste to their respective homes, were summoned to Canton. From them was obtained a full evidence as to the criminals, and their design; and a strict embargo was at once laid on all the vessels within the ports of Canton and the neighbouring province of Fokien.

The assassins being soon arrested in their junk, were put into iron cages and conveyed to Canton for trial and judgment. On their arrival there, it was ordained by the emperor's strict order, that the trial and punishment should take place in the presence of the Europeans at that place. Among the English spectators was the interpreter of the East India Company, Dr. Morrison, the author of the Chinese dictionary, whose labours have been so useful towards illustrating the literature of the country, and who was destined on this occasion to experience a very gratifying reward for his pains in acquiring the language. His attention having been attracted by the loud complaints of an old man, who, like the others, was shut up in a cage with iron bars, and who, in protesting his innocence, called for the French sailor whose life he had contributed to save, Dr. Morrison approached the old man's prison, heard what he had to say, and promised him his assistance with the judges. In a word, accompanied by the Frenchman, he presented himself before the mandarins, pleaded the cause of his client, and called to their recollection that maxim of Chinese law, and of humanity in general, that "it is better to let even the guilty escape, than to punish the innocent." He obtained the consent of the court that the sailor should be confronted with the accused, and these, on the first sight of each other, immediately embraced and shed tears, to the great interest and sympathy of the audience. The judges themselves yielded to the general sentiment, and at once absolved the old man. Out of twenty-four prisoners, seventeen were condemned and decapitated at once, and their chief put to a lingering death in the presence of the Europeans.

Captain Laplace has made a great mistake in supposing that, when Dr. Morrison enunciated to the mandarins that merciful and wise maxim which contributed to save the man's life, he told them anything that they had never before heard. We could prove to him, by chapter and verse, that the precept is perfectly well known to the Chinese, however grossly it may have been violated by them in several cases where Europeans have *unintentionally* caused the death of natives. It is, in fact, this knowledge of what is right in criminal practice, that makes the conduct of the local government towards foreign homicides so perfectly unjustifiable, and renders it not only excusable, but imperative in Europeans to resist the execution, not of law, but of illegality. Were they treated like *natives* on these occasions, and according to the distinct provisions of the Chinese Penal Code, it might be difficult to make out a right to oppose the laws of the country in which they sojourn. But, as a just and equal administration of those laws to natives and foreigners must always be the necessary condition of submission on the part of the latter, the absurd injustice and partiality of the local government have deprived it of the right to complain, if Europeans, in cases of *accidental* homicide, refuse to deliver up their countrymen to be strangled without a trial, or with only the mockery of one.*

* See note at the end of this volume.

NOTE ON HOMICIDES AT CANTON.

The following observations are prefaced by the extracts here subjoined :—

" With reference to the important question which you recommend to my consideration, the expediency of establishing a judicial tribunal of our own at Canton, for the punishment of offenders—the evils of the present system are, I confess, great and undeniable. In order to save the innocent, we are compelled to do little less than systematically to screen the guilty ; yet the establishment of a criminal court within the limits of a foreign state, and without the sanction of that state, (for the Chinese, though they would authorize you to *convict*, would never, I apprehend, sanction your right to *acquit*,) is such an anomaly in legislation, that a very strong case of expediency must be made out before it would be listened to."

* * * " In my last letter, I just touched upon the subject you proposed to me, of the invention of a remedy for the very unsatisfactory state of the law, as applicable to your situation in China, in cases of homicide. The English laws are silent on the point, and the Chinese laws (or rather practice) speak a language to which you cannot either in honour or in policy entirely submit. The consequence is, that in order to protect the innocent, you are often obliged to screen the guilty ; the trade is disturbed, and crimes escape unpunished. I have thus fully acknowledged the evil, yet I cannot, I confess, quite see my way to a remedy. If it were likely that the Chinese might be prevailed on to sanction the establishment of a judicial court of our own at Canton, I think it possible that such a measure, though a very new and singular case, might be brought about : but it would be obviously worse than useless if the Chinese government did not agree to

sanction its decisions, which, when their own subjects are concerned, I cannot help looking on as hopeless. I wish, however, you would digest this matter in your mind; and if you should be able to sketch any plan of a remedy for the existing abuse, I hope you will send it me, for the information of the President of the Board of Control. If ever private traders from England should be admitted to compete in the tea trade at Canton with the company, the evil would of course increase, and the remedy become more needful."

The above was the view taken of this question some years since, by a high authority, in reply to a written application. There are, perhaps, some reasons for attaching less weight to the apprehended opposition on the Chinese side. Not to mention the Dutch, of whom the same is recorded long since, the Portuguese very lately both tried and executed their man themselves; and, according to Chinese notions, (on which of course this part of the difficulty entirely hinges,) the Portuguese at Macao are not at all less dependant on Chinese law than we at Canton. The Chinese would therefore be as ready to allow our right to condemn real murderers, on board our ships, as they are to allow the Portuguese at Macao; and if they saw that we were willing and ready to bring real murderers to condign punishment, they would not be long in allowing our right to acquit the innocent. It is the feeling of jealousy and resentment, (which we can hardly wonder at,) arising from the almost certain escape, under the present system, of real criminals, that makes them so anxious to get hold of all persons indiscriminately, and in fact causes them to act more from a *motive of revenge* than with a view to promoting the ends of substantial justice. This is a very barbarous and shocking state of things, little better on our side than on theirs, and it seems the duty of a great and civilized state, like England, to provide a remedy.

["From what foreigners," said Dr. Morrison. "have witnessed in cases of manslaughter, they have inferred that the Chinese government acted rather from a spirit of revenge than according to law. That this is true, appears from a state paper, quoted in the 34th section of the Chinese Penal Code. During the 13th year of Kien-loong, A.D. 1749, the then governor of Canton reported to the emperor that he had tried some Macao foreigners who caused the death of two Chinese,* and having sentenced them (through their own authorities) to be bastinadoed and transported, had to request that, according to *foreign laws*, they might be sent to *Temwan*—Demaun. To this the emperor replied, that the governor had managed very erroneously; that he should have required life for life. 'If,' it was added, 'you quote only our native laws, and according to them, sentence to the bastinado and transportation, then the fierce and unruly dispositions of the foreigners will cease to be awed.' The emperor thus declared (and his imperial decision is reprinted with every new edition of the laws) that the native law alone is *not* to be the guide of the local government when foreigners cause the death of natives. 'It is incumbent to have life for life,' in order to frighten and repress the barbarians."]

The propriety, and indeed necessity, of non-submission to the Chinese law, as suspended or perverted, and not *administered* towards strangers, is easily made out. Though it be a principle obviously founded in natural justice, and has therefore been universally acknowledged as an established maxim of the law of nations, "that foreigners shall be amenable to the laws of the country in which they happen to reside," still this rule (not to mention that China subscribes to no international code whatever) must always have its conditions. Protection

* The European account is, that two soldiers murdered two Chinese, and were falsely represented as insane.

from, and submission to, local laws must, like every other right and obligation, be strictly reciprocal; and the state that denies to strangers an equal administration of its laws with natives, seems to forfeit its claim on their submission. This point has been singularly illustrated in practice (as appears from Mr. Macfarlane's work) in the relations of European states with Turkey. "For many years, no such thing as an execution of Franks by Turkish law has been seen in the Levant, where offenders are given over to their respective consuls," &c. It is stated that this established immunity had been the result of the barbarity and injustice practised by the Turks towards all Franks accused of crimes; and it may easily be proved from repeated experience, that reasons for the same exist (in an aggravated degree) in our relations with the Chinese.

We are fairly in possession of the fact, that they clearly understand the distinctions between *malicious*, *excusable*, and *justifiable* homicide; and that in the case of their *own* subjects, the law distinguishes between—

1. Killing with an intention;
2. Killing by pure accident; and,
3. Killing in lawful self-defence, or in the execution of one's duty.

Although, according to an antiquated error in legislation, homicide is sometimes treated by them as a private, rather than as a public wrong, (being made redeemable by a fine to the relations of the deceased,) yet in the administration of the law towards natives, the above three distinctions are clearly observed in aggravation or mitigation of the particular offence. Thus (Leu-lee, 6th Div. 2d B.)—

1. In a *conspiracy to kill*, all those who actually contribute to the perpetration of the offence are equally punished with death, though there is the difference between beheading and strangling for the principals and accessaries. Even where the wounds

inflicted do not prove mortal, the principal suffers death.

2. Killing *by pure accident*, that is, where there was not any previous knowledge of the probable consequences, is redeemable by a fine of about twelve taëls to the relations of the deceased.

3. A householder killing a burglarious intruder, and a policeman killing a thief in taking him, are not punished *at all.*

The Chinese principle, with regard to the punishment of crime, is precisely the same as ours: "Better let the guilty escape, than put the innocent to death." How strangely this contrasts with their conduct to foreigners! Their ancient books say of capital punishment, "Thrice be it deferred;" and such is the actual practice at the present day; for the local magistrate sends the case to the provincial judge, the provincial judge to the criminal board, and the criminal board to the emperor. The Chinese government would pretend that foreigners are tried and sentenced *according* to the law; but we know from experience that every legal safeguard, provided for the native, is dispensed with in the case of the stranger. The benefit of the delay arising from an appeal to the emperor was expressly taken away from *foreign* homicides in 1753, at the recommendation of the Canton government. On this plain and intelligible ground we may rest the necessity, 1st, of non-submission to Chinese punishment; and, 2d, (which arises out of the first,) of a competent English court, on shipboard if not on shore, for the trial of homicides.

["If it be true," observes Dr. Morrison, "that foreigners are not protected by the laws of the land, the necessity for obedience is cancelled. Still foreigners living under a despotic government must be without resource, were that government to *compel* the obedience which it demands. Were physical force resorted to, and innocent persons seized as hostages, foreigners, unsupported by their own governments, must be obliged to submit. Such an unjust and violent measure has formerly, on various occasions, been resorted to; but of late years the plan adopted, in cases of homicide, has been to demand of the fellow-countrymen of the alleged manslayer, that the guilty person be found out and handed over to the Chinese for punishment. This is in effect to constitute them a criminal court. Were a man to be delivered up by the persons thus called upon, he would be regarded by the government as already condemned. His punishment, painful experience tells us, would be certain. Since, then, the Chinese are thus ready to regard foreigners as the judges of their fellow-countrymen, why should foreign governments hesitate to establish criminal courts? Courts so established will, it is true, meet with difficulty when compelled to acquit a man declared guilty by the Chinese, or to punish lightly one whom, by the unjust decree of Kienloong, the local government would capitally condemn: when, however, it is found by the Chinese that the guilty manslayer can no longer pass unpunished, it is probable that they will themselves remove every difficulty, and the decree of Kienloong will meet the disregard that it merits."]

END OF VOL. I.